Emotional and
Behavioral
Problems

Emotional and Behavioral Problems

A Handbook for Understanding and Handling Students

Paul Zionts
Laura Zionts
Richard L. Simpson

CORWIN PRESS, INC.
A Sage Publications Company
Thousand Oaks, California

For information:

Corwin Press, Inc.
A Sage Publications Company
2455 Teller Road
Thousand Oaks, California 91320
E-mail: order@corwinpress.com

Sage Publications Ltd.
6 Bonhill Street
London EC2A 4PU
United Kingdom

Sage Publications India Pvt. Ltd.
M-32 Market
Greater Kailash I
New Delhi 110 048 India

Printed in the United States of America

Library of Congress Cataloging-in-Publication Data
Zionts, Paul.
   Emotional and behavioral problems: A handbook for understanding and handling students / Paul Zionts, Laura Zionts, Richard L. Simpson.
      p. cm.
Includes bibliographical references and index.
 ISBN 0-7619-7703-1 -- ISBN 0-7619-7704-X (pbk.)
 1. Mentally ill children--Education--United States--Handbooks, manuals, etc. 2. Problem children--Education--United States--Handbooks, manuals, etc. I. Zionts, Laura. II. Simpson, Richard L., 1945- III. Title.
 LC4181 .Z56 2002
 371.94--dc21

                          2001007404

This book is printed on acid-free paper.
02 03 04 05 06 07 7 6 5 4 3 2 1

Acquisitions Editor	Robb Clouse
Associate Editor	Kylee Liegl
Editorial Assistant	Erin Buchanan
Production Editor	Olivia Weber
Typesetter/Designer	Siva Math Setters, Chennai, India
Copy Editor	Marilyn Power Scott
Indexer	Molly Hall
Cover Designer	Michael Dubowe

Contents

Preface

Conservative estimates from both educators and mental health professionals indicate that approximately 10% of children and adolescents in this country will experience emotional and behavioral problems serious enough to require professional attention. In addition, a sizeable percentage of children and youth can be expected to encounter periodic social and emotional adjustment difficulties. Based on these statistics, children and adolescents with emotional and behavioral conflicts are a reality for many families who must learn to cope with the day-to-day challenges of meeting the special needs of their children. Furthermore, many professionals—community agency personnel, nurses, and speech pathologists, to name a few—also work with these individuals with little or no direct training in the specific needs or characteristics of these children.

This book is designed for educators who teach children and adolescents who have emotional or behavioral disabilities or both. We also hope that parents and ancillary caregivers will find this book helpful in understanding and interacting with these individuals. In spite of the great number of young people who experience these problems, limited information is available on the topic; professionals report a paucity of basic information about childhood emotional problems. As a result, professionals and laypersons (including parents and family members) are often left groping for answers to questions about children's and adolescents' behavioral and emotional problems, including definitions, causes, treatment methods, and support services. This book will prove to be helpful to both of these reader groups. Parents and families will find it useful as they attempt to understand their children and the services available to meet their needs. And professionals having contact with children and youth who have emotional disturbances and behavior problems will gain a better understanding of these youngsters. Thus, this book is of particular value to myriad professionals, including:

- Physicians
- Nurses
- Social workers
- Judges
- Juvenile workers
- Occupational therapists
- Physical therapists
- Speech pathologists
- Teachers
- Counselors

It is our intention to provide straightforward, basic information about childhood and adolescent emotional and behavioral problems; issues that represent diversity will be integrated in the text. Interspersed throughout each chapter is content designed to highlight the most commonly perceived issues in a functional manner. The following is an outline of topics that will be discussed:

Chapter 1. Introduction to Emotional Disturbance and Behavioral Disorders

- An overview of issues related to understanding children and youth with emotional and behavioral problems
- Understanding that disturbing behavior may be a disability (such as visual impairment)
- Behavior problems that can be linked to a disability (e.g., serious emotional disturbance and related psychiatric problems, behavior disorders, attention deficit hyperactivity disorder, learning disabilities)
- Behavior problems that are primarily related to environmental and other non-(bio)physical factors

Chapter 2. Major Types of Emotional and Behavioral Disorders

- Various forms and subtypes of emotional and behavioral disorders of children and youth discussed in practical terms, including those primarily by school professionals and community mental health practitioners (e.g., hyperactivity, anxiety, phobias, depression, substance abuse, withdrawn behaviors, anorexia nervosa, conduct disorders)
- Characteristics and other salient information, such as prevalence, presented for the major forms of disorders

Chapter 3. Causes of Emotional and Behavioral Disorders

- The causes of emotional and behavioral problems and related disorders
- Family and community influences on behavior
- Setting-specific influences (school or home, etc.)
- Situation-specific influences (death, divorce)
- Biological (or possible genetic) influences
- Possibility of cure

Chapter 4. Evaluating and Assessing Students Who Have Emotional and Behavioral Disorders

- The purpose of evaluation
- Defining the troubling behavior or emotions (or both)
- Questions related to screening, diagnosing, and evaluating the progress of students identified as having emotional and behavioral problems
- The professionals involved in conducting evaluations
- Diagnostic and assessment methods, such as rating scales, interviews, and observations; examples of these methods provided

Chapter 5. Violence and Aggression in Schools

- The difference between aggressive and violent behaviors
- Responses to school violence and aggression
- Reducing and preventing violence and aggression in schools
- Juvenile delinquency

Chapter 6. Adolescents Who Have Emotional and Behavioral Disorders and the Juvenile Justice System

- Relationship between EBD and adjudication
- Ethnicity, mental health, and juvenile justice in the United States
- Educational options for adjudicated youth
- Special education in correctional settings

Chapter 7. Treatment of Emotional and Behavioral Disorders

- The nature and characteristics of different forms of treatment and intervention for children and youth with emotional and behavioral disorders
- Psychoanalytic, behavioral, cognitive, and other major treatment forms
- Different program options available in school and community settings

- Detailed management programs (rules, positive and negative consequences) for the home, classroom, and clinic settings
- Specific management techniques

Chapter 8. School-Based Placements

- How professionals and parents may identify and access appropriate resources for children and youth with emotional and behavioral disorders, including educational service options and the roles of various mental health services, such as community mental health, residential treatment, and so forth.
- Early childhood concerns (preschool, Head Start)

Chapter 9. Supporting Students With Emotional and Behavioral Disorders Outside the Public School Setting

- Medical interventions used to treat children and youth with emotional and behavioral disorders
- Major forms of medications prescribed for children with psychiatric problems, including how they work and how they are started, maintained, and discontinued
- Possible short-term and long-term effects
- Nontraditional interventions

Chapter 10. The Role of Families in Supporting Children With Emotional and Behavioral Concerns

- The role of effective parent and professional communication and partnership
- Effective planning and problem solving for children and youth with emotional and behavioral disorders: professionals and families participating in identifying, planning, and implementing educational strategies, support services, and problem-solving programs
- The role of school and community professionals in assisting parents and family members to plan for and use appropriate strategies to respond to various short-term and long-term issues and challenges of children and youth with emotional and behavioral disorders
- Facilitating social support and peer relations, including person-centered planning

Chapter 11. What Lies Ahead: Postschool Transition

- Information and recommendations for assisting professionals and families to successfully respond to transition challenges, such as work and adult living options
- EBD resources
- Resources in print
- Internet resources (organizations, parent sites, behavior sites)

ACKNOWLEDGMENTS

The following reviewers are gratefully acknowledged:

Krista Kutash
Associate Professor and Deputy Director
Research and Training Center for Children's Mental Health
University of South Florida
Tampa, FL

Melissa Campbell
Teacher
Mabry Junior High School
Inman, SC

Jean Cheng Gorman
Psychology Fellow
Brotman Medical Center
Santa Monica, CA

Mary F. Sinclair
University of Minnesota
Institute on Community Integration
College of Education and Human Development
Minneapolis, MN

Ann P. Daunic
Department of Special Education
University of Florida
Gainesville, FL

Maureen Keyes
Assistant Professor
University of Wisconsin–Milwaukee
Department of Exceptional Education
Milwaukee, WI

James Kauffman
University of Virginia
Department of Special Education
Charlottesville, VA

About the Authors

 **Paul Zionts** is a professor of special education and Chairperson of the Department of Educational Foundations and Special Services at Kent State University. He has been a teacher in a reform school and an inner-city high school, a program director, consultant, and teacher trainer. He has lectured and provided training in local, state, and national events and has conducted hundreds of workshops that have included teachers, counselors, psychologists, social workers, administrators, parents, secretaries, and bus drivers. He has authored *Teaching Disturbed and Disturbing Students* (2nd edition) and *Inclusion Strategies for Students with Learning and Behavior Problems*, and he has coauthored with Richard Simpson both *Autism* (2nd edition) and *Understanding Children and Youth with Emotional and Behavioral Problems*.

Laura Zionts, PhD, is an assistant professor at Texas A&M University in the Department of Educational Psychology's Special Education, At-Risk and Bilingual Education program. She has worked with students who have emotional and behavioral disorders as a classroom teacher and a transition specialist. She has enjoyed teaching in both early elementary and secondary classrooms in mostly urban settings. Her primary area of research is the disproportionate  representation of minority youth in programs for children and youth with behavioral disorders.

 **Richard L. Simpson** is Professor of Special Education and School Psychology at the University of Kansas and Acting Director of Special Education Programs at the University of Kansas Medical Center. He has worked as a special education teacher, school psychologist, and clinical psychologist. He is Senior Editor of the professional journal, *Focus on Autism and Other Developmental Disabilities*. With Paul Zionts, he has coauthored *Autism* (2nd edition) and *Understanding Children and Youth with Emotional and Behavioral Problems.*

Part One

Understanding Emotional and Behavioral Disorders

Introduction to Emotional Disturbance and Behavioral Disorders

1

Phone calls from school . . . disapproving looks from relatives and friends . . . difficulty finding someone for him or her to play with . . . always seems to be in "trouble" . . . or perhaps, is frequently alone, both on the playground and at home . . . rarely talks or plays with brothers and sisters. People are concerned about a child. Yet what can be done? What do we know? What do we need to know? The reason you are reading this book is that you either suspect or have already been told that your child or one that you know or are working with may have emotional disturbance or behavior disorder (throughout this book, we will refer to this condition using the letters EBD). Many questions and issues have likely crossed your mind. Does this mean that the child is "crazy"? Will the child have to undergo therapy for hours? Days? Years? Will the child have to be hospitalized? Does this mean medication? What does "EBD" mean? This book is designed to respond to these issues.

One of the most confusing and potentially explosive labels that can be attached to a child (and, perhaps, family) is EBD. Its exact impact on the family can only be speculated. A variety of reactions may occur. Compounding the potential family impact is the possible feeling of shame at having a child with emotional or behavioral problems. It is interesting that everyone seems to be an expert on this subject. The purpose of this chapter is to answer some of the initial questions that can cross the minds of those who live or work with children and youth who have EBD. Topics in this chapter will be discussed in more depth throughout the book.

BY ANY OTHER NAME: EMOTIONAL
AND BEHAVIORAL DISORDERS

Children and youth who exhibit significant emotional or behavioral problems have been described in many ways. As discussed later in this chapter, there are formal and informal labels for these students. It is critical to understand that many of these individuals exhibit disturbing behaviors because they have a disability. Some individuals may have EBD because of environmental factors, and when the factors change, they may learn to behave in appropriate ways. For example, a child exposed to a traumatic family event, such as a death, may show a reaction that causes others to be concerned. However, when children and youth behave or feel the way they do because it is part of an internal condition that they cannot control, their EBD is a disability.

To better understand this point, it may be helpful to think of other disabilities, such as visual impairment, hearing impairment, or mental retardation. Very few parents or professionals would expect a child who is blind to have vision, or a child who is deaf to hear, or a child who has significant mental retardation to be able to think as normally developing children do. We understand that their disabilities are conditions that these children possess. We do our best to teach them to manage their environments and as much information as we can. We are also tolerant when they have difficulties because of their disabilities. We certainly would not punish a child who possesses one of these disabilities for not being able to do a task that is physically or mentally beyond their capabilities. Can you imagine punishing a child who has a visual impairment because he could not read street signs, or a child with a hearing impairment because she could not sing along with the choir, or a child who has mental retardation because his disability does not allow him to read?

Nevertheless, we do not apply the same rationale to children who have EBD. When they exhibit behaviors that are indicative of their disability, they are often punished! In fact, we seem to spend more time punishing these children and youth than we do teaching them new ways to better navigate their world. Granted, the behaviors exhibited by children with EBD are more troublesome to the people around them, and we normally expect children to behave appropriately, or we punish them. But it must be understood that many of these children will never be "normal," similar to children with other disabilities. Consequently, they will not learn to behave by being punished. Furthermore, they will learn (very quickly) that their disability, no matter that they cannot control it, makes people (even those who love them) disapprove of them. Given these aspects of their disability, it is not surprising that the outlook for many of these children is not promising. We hope you will acquire information and learn many approaches from this book that will allow you and children who have EBD to better meet the challenges related to their disability.

POSSIBLE CAUSES OF EMOTIONAL DISTURBANCE AND BEHAVIORAL DISORDERS

EBD may be explained by (a) biological factors, such as genetics, brain damage or dysfunction, malnutrition and allergies, temperament, or physical illness; (b) family factors, such as the family definition and structure, family interaction, family influences on school success and failure, and external pressures affecting families; and (c) school factors, such as deficiencies in the ability of school personnel to accommodate students' variable intelligence, academic achievement, and social skills (Kauffman, 2001). Feelings and questions regarding causation are normal and are experienced by many parents and caregivers. Exploring and understanding these reactions is extremely important and may help both you and the child avoid secondary problems.

There is rarely a simple cause of EBD. In fact, it may be best to understand the significant difference between diagnosing physical problems and mental health problems. With regard to physical problems, it is believed that a "cause" needs to be discovered, which will then be followed by the best treatment, which will hopefully result in a "cure." However, for schools, cause is not as important as the behaviors that are currently being exhibited. Within schools, what is stressed is the intensity, duration, and level of impairment associated with the behaviors. Furthermore, although some behaviors can be cured, many other disorders that have longer durations must be managed and the people habilitated to their conditions.

Diagnosis may occur at any time in an individual's life, as emotional problems can surface at any age. In fact, it is common for all of us to be emotionally disturbed occasionally, as evidenced in bouts of severe anger, depression, or extreme frustration. Complex factors, such as a student's environment, a deeply rooted psychological problem, or a biophysical imbalance, may each contribute to different feelings or behavioral problems. Furthermore, there may be several factors interacting with one another, such as a biophysical imbalance that coincides with a family crisis.

Briefly, when the *environment* is considered to be a major contributor to students' problems, many questions are explored: What is happening at home? Is the home culturally different from the school, resulting in behaviors being accepted at home and not at school? Are the economic conditions at home significantly less favorable than those of others, preventing equal participation in school activities (play sports having fees, etc.)? And do the significant people (teachers, community, relatives) in children's lives create problems of differing expectations? In other words, identification of disturbing behaviors may be a result of the degree of flexibility and tolerance the concerned members of the child's environment demonstrate as well as myriad other factors.

Deeply rooted psychological problems involve uneven or deficient personality development, as reflected in pathological (repeated, long-term) behavioral difficulties. Traditionally, most behavioral problems have been perceived as the result of a disturbed psyche. One form of these behavioral problems is *phobias*. Phobias are extreme fears and anxieties that prevent people from behaving more or less normally or appropriately in everyday situations. Like other types of disturbances, phobias may be temporary or long term.

In the 1950s, '60s, and '70s, much of the thought and practice in school psychology was heavily influenced by psychological theory. In recent years, the psychological theory of disturbance has become less popular, especially when school-based disturbances (problems that only surface in the schools) were considered. This is primarily due to the rather inefficient process normally associated with the psychological approach—it takes a long time before results are apparent. Most teachers believe that they don't have the time and, perhaps, expertise to effectively use the counseling techniques associated with these approaches. Nevertheless, community-based mental health agencies are often able to effectively use this approach.

A *biophysical imbalance* or medical problem implies that the students' problems are internally based. That is, the students cannot change their behaviors at will because of a biophysical problem. Many theories suggest that prenatal (before birth) or perinatal (around the time of birth) illnesses, unusually long childbirth, heredity, or inappropriate levels of certain body chemicals may contribute to or cause emotional disorders. As with other areas of disturbance, much controversy and debate surround these theories of direct links to specific emotional or behavioral disturbance.

Whatever the cause or label, it is important that both professionals and families understand the exact nature of the problem. What is meant by a given label in a particular case? What is the child doing to be labeled, and, more important, what can the child do, and what are some realistic behavioral expectations? When unclear about the manner in which the term *emotional disturbance* is being used, families are encouraged to ask for clarification, especially if causation is implied. Remember that it is sometimes difficult to discern between a psychological and a biophysical cause. This may have a considerable impact on the intervention chosen (e.g., counseling therapy or medication). Concerned individuals have the right to know as much as possible. A more detailed discussion of causation or etiology will follow in Chapter 3.

A focus on blame will rarely help anybody and, in many cases, may hinder a child's progress. It is critical not to blame a child in relation to his or her EBD. For example, a teacher once commented about a child, "He's smart enough to behave better." This raises a very important point. Intelligence may have little to do with the occurrence of emotional problems. Although it is natural to feel frustration when a smart child seemingly should know better, being smart doesn't necessarily mean health. Many very intelligent people have emotional problems.

INCIDENCE

Incidence, or the number of children and adolescents identified as having EBD, is a subject of major controversy among professionals. As there is confusion regarding the definition of the problem, it follows that the percentage of students who are labeled EBD will vary according to the group or individual doing the labeling. This is not surprising in view of the range of behaviors, ages, circumstances, duration, and intensity of many problem behaviors.

Except in the most severe cases, it is extremely difficult to arrive at an exact number of individuals who have EBD. The U.S. Department of Education (1996) reported that 1% of the kindergarten-through-12th-grade student population have EBD. Yet many states are hard-pressed to officially identify 1% of their population this way. Professionals in this field believe that these numbers are very low (Center & Obringer, 1987; Forness, 1991; Kauffman, 2001; Paul & Epanchin, 1991). It was estimated in a report by the Surgeon General (U.S. Department of Health and Human Services, 1999) that about 20% of all children have mental disorders, with at least mild functional impairment. Friedman, Katz-Levey, Manderschied, and Sondheimer (1996) suggested that 5% to 9% of those students would qualify for special education, a number far greater than is currently being served. As will be discussed later, many people have differing ideas about the definition of EBD. Consequently, the number of children so identified varies. Also, there may be other factors that enable or hinder identification of these children and youth.

Various groups have estimated percentages of behaviorally disordered and emotionally disturbed children ranging from 1% to 40% of the school-age population (see Zionts, 1996). In comparison, public school administrators believe that the number of children and youth so classified is approximately 3% to 6%, whereas teachers have contended that between 10% and 40% of their students have problems severe enough to warrant professional attention. These discrepancies are compounded by the fact that some students who exhibit maladaptive behaviors at school do not exhibit them at home. Furthermore, it is often difficult to determine if a child's problems are going to be short-lived (growing pains) or if they will drastically affect the long-term emotional growth of the child.

To determine if a child's problems are, in fact, growing pains, one must understand how other children of a similar age behave and express their emotions. By definition, a child is an individual who is not fully developed: cognitively, physically, socially, and emotionally. Therefore, it is important to be aware of behaviors that are common to particular age groups. One study suggested that one third to one half of 8-year-olds may be identified as overactive and restless. Again, it is when a child is significantly different from peers that concern should arise.

Henley, Ramsey, and Algozzine (1999) perhaps said it best when they contended that students who are "seriously emotionally disturbed are identified by their severe deficits in perception, communication and behavior. Such behaviors as delusions and lack of affect are marked examples of the extreme behavioral disturbances in seriously emotionally disturbed students" (p. 115). Complicating matters is the identification of more males, African Americans, and those who are economically disadvantaged than one would find statistically in the population (U.S. Department of Education, 1998).

SERIOUS EMOTIONAL DISTURBANCE OR BEHAVIORAL DISORDERS OR EBD: WHAT'S THE DIFFERENCE?

Much of the time, there's no difference in behaviors; the only difference is in the labels. In this regard, it might be helpful to distinguish between two types of labels: official labels, which are used on official documents and heard in such formal environments as school and clinics, and informal labels, which may occur in private or maybe only in one's thoughts! Prior to discussing these labels, one must remember that there is also a controversy regarding the diagnosis (how one is identified and labeled) as EBD. As mentioned earlier, at least three different views exist regarding cause. Diagnostic test results are frequently less valid than usual due to the child's behaviors during the testing situation.

The first official label is often given to a disturbing child by school personnel. Labels for a child's behavior may vary vastly depending on the state of residence. Frequently used labels include *serious emotionally disturbed, emotionally impaired, behaviorally disordered, conduct disordered, socially maladjusted,* or the more general *educationally handicapped.* The official label applied by the federal government is *emotionally disturbed.* This label is used when identifying and providing special educational services for children and youth who have EBD.

The foregoing labels usually have the same meaning for both educators and parents. That is, they are used to identify and describe students who have significant social, behavioral, or emotional differences when compared to their normally developing peers. Much time and energy are spent on determining the most appropriate label. We believe that it is the manner in which the labels are used (e.g., socially excluding certain groups of children), not the labels themselves, that causes problems. As of this writing, labels are required for children to receive special education services and, hopefully, appropriate treatments.

For children and youth who exhibit extremely different (or deviant) behaviors, the word *severely* may be attached to their labels, such as *severely emotionally disturbed*. Severely emotionally disturbed students often cannot handle the rigors of a regular classroom setting, requiring instead a specialized classroom in a public school or another alternative setting. Regardless of the label, it is important to remember that the focus should be on the child. These children are probably more similar to other children than dissimilar. They have good days and bad days, as is the case with their peers—and the rest of us.

What Are Informal Labels?

Informal labels are oftentimes more of a problem for children and youth than formal labels. Informal labels are automatically attached to a person's behavior when it is very different from what is expected. People may label either the behavior or the person as "weird," and so forth. That is, some individuals may label a person's essence rather than a particular behavior, especially when the behavior is unusual in a negative way. In other words, if someone does something that is not normally accepted, he or she might be thought of as being crazy, hyper, or bad.

HOW PROFESSIONALS VIEW LABELS

Although the preceding information holds true for the way most practitioners view EBD, some practitioners and researchers believe that a label gives some very specific information about the cause of an individual's problems. Generally speaking, they believe that when students are labeled as emotionally disturbed, they may have deeply rooted psychological problems that call for an intervention program of psychotherapy. Or they may have a biophysical cause, and collaboration with medical personnel may be necessary, possibly resulting in the prescription of medications.

In contrast, if students are labeled *behaviorally disordered*, their problems may be observable and thought of as more easily identified, and an effective intervention program is thought to be more readily designed and implemented by teachers and parents. According to the Individuals with Disabilities Education Act ([IDEA], 1997), both approaches may be implemented, depending on the needs of the student.

IDENTIFICATION OF EBD

Three factors are often considered when determining if a child is disturbed: intensity, pattern, and duration of behavior.

- *Intensity* refers to the severity of the child's problem. How does it get in the way of the child's (or society's) goals? How much does it draw attention from others? For obvious reasons, this factor is the easiest to identify.
- *Pattern* refers to the times when the problems occur. Do problems only occur during the school day? Only during math class? At bedtime? Answers to these questions may yield very helpful diagnostic and remediation information.
- *Duration* refers to the length of time the child's problem has been present. For example, some school districts require a 3-month duration before they suggest that a child has an emotional or behavioral problem.

Bower (1969) proposed a developmental continuum for identifying emotional disturbance in children and youth, and his work has served as the foundation for the definition of EBD. Although this definition is problematic for teachers and psychologists, it nonetheless serves as a useful reference point because it speaks to the kinds of support these students may require in school or at home or both:

Stage 1: Children who experience and demonstrate the normal problems of everyday living, growing, exploration, and reality testing

Stage 2: Children who develop a greater number and degree of symptoms of emotional problems as a result of crises or traumatic experiences

Stage 3: Children in whom symptoms persist to some extent beyond normal expectation but who can adjust adequately to school

Stage 4: Children with fixed and recurring symptoms of emotional disturbance who can, with help, maintain some positive relationships in a school setting

Stage 5: Children with fixed and recurring symptoms of emotional difficulties who are best educated in a residential school setting or temporarily in a home setting

Clearly, by referring to these five stages, almost any child who is different from what is considered normal may be labeled EBD. A closer look at these stages suggests that according to Stage 1, most children exhibit disturbing behaviors sometime in their childhood. Thus parents, educators, and other professionals should be careful not to overreact to an isolated disturbing event in a child's life. Furthermore, it is currently less likely that students in Stage 5 will be placed in a residential school setting than it was in Bower's day—1969!

BEHAVIORS THAT FIT INTO EDUCATIONAL STAGES

As an alternative to the Bower model, Forness and Knitzer (1992) proposed the following definition, which has been adopted by many organizations (but not the federal law), such as the Council for Children with Behavior Disorders and Head Start:

I. The term emotional or behavior disorder means a disability characterized by behavioral or emotional responses in school programs so different from appropriate age, cultural, or ethnic norms that they adversely affect educational performance, including academic, social, vocational or personal skills, and which:

(a) is more than a temporary, expected response to stressful events in the environment;

(b) is consistently exhibited in two different settings, at one of which is school related; and

(c) persists despite individualized interventions within the education program, unless in the judgments of the team, the child's or youth's history indicates that such interventions would not be effective.

Emotional or behavioral disorders can co-exist with other disabilities.

II. This category may include children or youth that are with schizophrenic disorders, affective disorders, anxiety disorders, or other sustained disturbances of conduct or adjustment when they adversely affect educational performance in accordance with section I. (p. 13)

One important message associated with these definitions is that the term *emotional disturbance* (or *behavioral disorder, social maladjustment, emotional handicap,* etc.) may be extremely general and ambiguous. It can mean a variety of things to different people. Many research studies have found that the term has different meanings for parents, teachers, counselors, principals, doctors, and even the child's friends. In this context, the following two vignettes illustrate how difficult it is to identify and understand emotional disturbance and behavioral disorders:

Sally has been a very pleasant student in her 5th-grade classroom all year. She is attractive, well-mannered, and does well in school. She sits in the front row and smiles appropriately, answers questions, and participates in group discussions. She is an only child, and her parents have traditionally taken an active interest in her school progress. She is extremely close to her mother.

Tragically, her mother is in a car accident and subsequently dies. Sally becomes sullen and withdrawn, refusing to go to school. Her father leaves her alone, believing she is undergoing a normal grieving period. However, 10 days pass, and Sally's withdrawn behavior continues. Her father decides that it would be best for her to return to school to help her come out of the depression.

On Sally's return, she quietly moves her seat to the back of the classroom. The teacher tries gently to persuade Sally to participate in class but also understands what Sally must be going through and decides to leave her alone. When the teacher has time, she attempts to counsel Sally. However, no matter what is done to help her, Sally's withdrawn behavior continues. After a meeting with other school professionals, it was decided to let Sally stay in class in the hope that, with time, she will return to her normal self.

Joe has been a pain in the neck to almost everybody he has been in contact with this year. He is unkempt, ill mannered, and a C–D (below average) student. Joe's teacher always seemed to be calling out his name for classroom infractions. His mother was initially responsive to contacts from the school, but she stopped her attempts to cooperate. She admitted to the principal that she was at the end of her rope with Joe at home. Joe's father, although professing concern, worked long hours in his new business and was generally uninvolved with his son.

Suddenly, one day, Joe's mother died. During the next week, Joe, who had been extremely close to his mother, engaged in many tantrums. His father left him alone, believing that this was normal grieving. While taking the week off from work, his father found it very difficult to communicate with Joe. Finally, he decided that Joe should return to school.

On Joe's return to school, he stormed into the classroom, kicking chairs and throwing papers all over the room. He ran to his desk screaming, "I hate her! I hate her! She left me, the bitch! I hate her, I hate her, I hate her!" The teacher tried to quiet Joe, with no success. After a meeting with other school professionals, it was decided that Joe might need special help.

Joe and Sally represent students who may be equally disturbed, yet their behaviors demonstrate that the natures of their disturbances are different. Although undergoing the same type of catastrophic experience, Joe was disturbing and Sally was withdrawn. Consequently, society's reactions to Joe and Sally are different. Although both examples focus on the death of a mother and its effects on children, rarely will the children's reactions be as strong as those portrayed. Nevertheless, in most instances, somebody like Sally will be allowed to continue to act disturbed in her quiet, withdrawn manner. Students like Joe, on the other hand, will most likely be removed from the regular classroom, and treatment may be deemed necessary.

Some people believe that it is only those children who are *disturbing*, such as Joe, who are regularly identified as having EBD. Withdrawn students, such as Sally, are often more difficult to identify and, ultimately, help. As we've mentioned, children are diagnosed as having EBD when their behavior is very different from that of their peers or what is expected of them. The problem behaviors may be recent and short-lived or they may be long-term. The disturbances may be demonstrated in the classroom, where such abstract assignments as reading and writing are required, or only in the home, where tasks are frequently more concrete, such as taking out the garbage, washing dishes, or mowing the lawn.

Refer again to the three factors that generally determine assignment of a label. Both Sally and Joe seem to belong in Bower's (1969) Stage 2. That is, their feelings and behaviors seem to be a result of a one-time traumatic experience. Yet the action that parents and concerned professionals take may influence either child's future emotional growth. It the responsibility of all parties to be careful observers of the behavior of children after a traumatic event occurs.

CHARACTERISTICS OF EMOTIONALLY DISTURBED OR BEHAVIORALLY DISORDERED CHILDREN AND YOUTH

Characteristics of a disturbed child are best described in behavioral terms. Rather than talking about a child as crazy or acting out, a more detailed explanation of specific behaviors and emotions allows all concerned parties to approach the problem with an equal understanding. General categories, such as hyperactive and withdrawn, may be good starting points but give little useful information for diagnosis or treatment options.

The following behavioral characteristics are intended to explain some of the vague categories that are often used to describe EBD. You are cautioned not to make hasty generalizations based on familiar behaviors in the categories. If an acquaintance exhibits two or three of these behaviors, it probably does not mean that the person has a major (pathological) problem. As discussed earlier, factors such as the intensity of the emotion and the length of time it is exhibited must be considered when making an appropriate professional diagnosis.

Conduct Disorders

Fights, hits others
Destroys property
Commits crimes against society
Easily frustrated
Steals
Undependable
Boisterous
Truant
Runs away from home
Lies persistently
Abuses substances
Engages in inappropriate sexual activity
Blames others

Attention and Concentration

Can't sit still
Is highly distracted by everything
Has short attention span—may be as short as 20 seconds
Doesn't seem to listen
Is drowsy
Shows lack of interest

Hyperactivity; Attention Deficit

Can't sit still, fidgets
Rushes work
Seems to be talking all the time
May have nervous mannerisms such as twitches
Constantly seeks attention of others
Demonstrates poor organizational skills
Shows lack of goals, direction
Has short attention span
Can't ignore environmental influences
Is impulsive
Excessively climbs on things
Needs consistent supervision

Interrupts others
Has frequent temper tantrums

Withdrawal

Seems tired
Avoids interaction with others
Demonstrates lack of interest
Is depressed, sad
Is passive
Is easily embarrassed
Rarely expresses emotions
Doesn't have self-confidence
Feels inferior to others
Is shy, timid, fearful

Function Disorders

Eating disorders
Voluntary regurgitation
Obesity
Eating inedible objects (habitually)
Refusal to eat
Elimination disorders
Inability to control bladder (no physical reasons)
Inability to control bowels (no physical reasons)

Severe EBD

Illogical thinking
Delusions
Hallucinations
Disjunctive talking
Unusual perceptions
Self-injurious behavior

The purpose of listing these categories is to provide a glossary of behaviors that are often attached to these general and sometimes vague descriptions. Please resist the temptation to become an armchair psychologist. Instead, we encourage you to ask the professionals about the specific characteristics a child is exhibiting when he or she is described as hyperactive, for instance.

A rule of thumb is to decide if the observed behaviors are deviant enough to attract the attention of at least one other person. The behaviors must be significantly apparent and interfering with the student's goals or environment. Listing these behaviors may aid you in noticing potential signs of trouble. Generally, you should begin to be concerned if changes occur in the child's behavioral pattern. After observations and information have been shared with a concerned parent, two critical questions normally follow:

How much of this information should we share with our child?

A very important point to consider is the child's feelings and perspective. Does he perceive the behavior(s) that are so upsetting to others? By involving children in the various interactions and meetings that take place regarding their problems, some youth may be able to participate in remediation attempts.

Talking with children can sometimes shed light on matters that have been incorrectly perceived or interpreted by others. A knowledge of what a child can handle and consultation with school or counseling personnel can best answer this question.

How will my child be treated at school?

This depends on the type of emotional disturbance or behavioral disorder the child has. If children are demonstrating negative attention-getting behaviors, they are likely receiving negative feedback from their parents, their teachers, and, possibly, their friends.

It doesn't necessarily follow that others will view a child's problems as "new" once they have been identified. If the diagnosis leads to a new educational placement for the child, it may become necessary to help the child cope with the new setting.

SUMMARY

The purpose of this chapter has been to introduce you to a general overview of emotional disturbance and behavioral disorders. Each of the topics discussed will be explored in greater depth in other sections of this book. General issues and questions about the topics were raised so that you might critically examine the everyday problems of working and living with youth who have emotional disturbances and behavior disorders.

Various theories of causation may be useful when trying to understand a child, but it is important to remember that it is extremely difficult to pinpoint any one reason for a child's behavior. Furthermore, the central purpose of determining causation or, for that matter, any diagnosis, is to generate interventions. To merely know why something happens has little use.

Emotional disturbance and *behavioral disorders* mean different things to different people. Parents, friends of the family, neighbors, teachers, school administrators, shopkeepers, and doctors may each have their own "expert" opinions. Therefore, communication about the child's *individual* problem must occur. Most often, it will be your responsibility to insist on getting a clear, understandable message from those concerned. We hope to aid you in that regard.

REFERENCES

Bower, E. M. (1969). *Early identification of emotionally handicapped children* (2nd ed.). Springfield, IL: Charles C Thomas.

Center, D. B., & Obringer, J. (1987). A search for variables affecting underidentification of behaviorally disordered students. *Behavioral Disorders, 12,* 147–169.

Forness, S. R. (1991). Resolving the definitional and diagnostic issue of serious emotional disturbance in the schools. In S. Braaten & G. Wrobel (Eds.), *Perceptions on the diagnosis and treatment of students with emotional/behavioral disorders* (pp. 1–15). Minneapolis, MN: Minneapolis Educators of the Emotionally Disturbed–Minnesota Council for Children with Behavioral Disorders.

Forness, S. R., & Knitzer, J. (1992). A new proposed definition and terminology to replace "serious emotional disturbance" in Individuals with Disabilities Education Act. *School Psychology Review, 21,* 12–20.

Friedman, R. M., Katz-Levey, J. W., Manderschied, R. W., & Sondheimer, D. L. (1996). Prevalence of serious emotional disturbance in children and adolescents. In R. W. Manderschied & M. A. Sonnnenschein (Eds.), *Mental health, United States, 1996* (pp. 71–88). Rockville, MD: Center for Mental Health Services.

Henley, M., Ramsey, R. S., & Algozzine, R. F. (1999). *Teaching students with mild disabilities* (3rd ed.). Boston: Allyn & Bacon.

Individuals with Disabilities Education Act of 1997, Pub. L. No. 105–17, 20 U.S.C., Ch. 33, §§1400–1491.

Kauffman, J. M. (2001). *Characteristics of emotional and behavioral disorders of children and youth* (7th ed.). Upper Saddle River, NJ: Prentice Hall.

Paul, J. L., & Epanchin, B. C. (1991). *Educating emotionally disturbed children and youth.* New York: Merrill.

U.S. Department of Education. (1996). *Eighteenth annual report to Congress on implementation of the Individuals with Disabilities Education Act.* Washington, DC: Author.

U.S. Department of Education. (1998). *Twentieth annual report to Congress on implementation of the Individuals with Disabilities Education Act.* Washington, DC: Author.

U.S. Department of Health and Human Services. (1999). *Mental health: A report of the surgeon general.* Rockville, MD: Author.

Zionts, P. (1996). *Teaching disturbed and disturbing students* (2nd ed.). Austin, TX: PRO-ED.

Major Types of Emotional and Behavioral Disorders

2

T he purpose of this chapter is to describe the characteristics of the various labels attached to children and youth who have EBD. The disorders are described in general terms to acquaint the reader with the terminology and related characteristics. In this connection, we strongly contend that attention should be given to children and youth who are very different from what is considered normal. Indeed, the American Psychiatric Association (1994) suggested that three criteria must be met prior to suggesting that one has a psychological disorder: (a) The person experiences significant pain or distress, an inability to work or play, an increased risk of death, or a loss of freedom in important areas of life; (b) the source of the problem lies within the person, due to biological factors, learned habits, or mental processes, and is not simply a normal response to specific life events, such as the death of a loved one; and (c) the problem is not a deliberate reaction to conditions such as poverty, prejudice, government policy, or other conflicts with society. Although the APA was addressing psychological disorders, the points made are certainly applicable to other possible causes of EBD as well. Therefore, the reader should be cautioned not to make hasty generalizations about people who may possess *some* of these characteristics.

This chapter is intended to demystify some of the often confusing labels that are commonly used. Behaviors that will be discussed fall into two categories: *externalizing behaviors* that are annoying to observers and *internalizing behaviors* that may go unnoticed. In some cases, the distinctions are not easy to make. For example, some individuals who have depression may also be withdrawn or aggressive.

Another important point to consider is that each of the examples of EBD described are serious. Referring again to the Joe and Sally vignettes in Chapter 1, you may recall that behaviors of both children are clearly indicative of EBD, even though they expressed them in markedly different ways. It is unfortunate that all too often we only pay attention to those who externalize their feelings and behavior rather than also attending to those who internalize them.

EXTERNALIZING BEHAVIORS

Externalizing behaviors may be described as those that are disturbing to other people. Children and youth who exhibit these behaviors intrude on the rights of others (e.g., to learn in school or to teach a lesson) and often violate the norms of the environment (e.g., classroom, community).

Externalizing behaviors prevent the child, or other children, from learning and behaving appropriately. When this description is applied to students, it means that they demonstrate inappropriate behaviors that significantly disturb people in the student's environment (Kazdin, 1995). Examples of externalizing behaviors include when a student

- Is often "out of seat"
- Constantly talks to others or self
- Makes noises
- Doesn't pay attention to task(s)
- Ignores classroom rules
- Refuses to work
- Is disobedient to teachers
- Physically bothers students
- Is truant
- Fights with others
- Runs away
- Persistently lies
- Constantly blames others

Many things may call forth these behaviors. For example, a student with conduct disorders may be experiencing frustration with school work, boredom with assignments, insecurity among friends, a need for attention, or perhaps having problems outside the classroom, such as the bus, playground, or home. Chapter 3 explains more fully what can contribute to externalizing disorders.

An interesting component in identifying these students is the value system of the identifier! There is little doubt that individuals have different tolerances for certain behaviors. For example, there are most likely things you would accept as tolerable but that your best friend would not tolerate. Some teachers may not mind if students talk quietly among themselves, get up often to do minor tasks, tap quietly on their desks, or occasionally look out the window. Other teachers believe such behaviors are unacceptable. They might set up a very strict classroom rule system whereby the occurrence of such behaviors results in immediate negative consequences. Clearly, students who violate the rules, for whatever reason, will be punished.

It is important to remember that different teachers (and parents) have different levels of tolerance. Although it would obviously be preferable that teachers all carry similar tolerances, it would be unrealistic to have such an expectation. Consider the following questions:

> *The teacher says that Gary stares out the window much of the time. How is this a conduct disorder?*
>
> Gary's teacher believes that the constant staring is getting in the way of his learning. His conduct, therefore, is interfering with him getting the information that his teacher feels is necessary for him to achieve in the classroom.
>
> *Is it possible for my child to be conduct disordered at school and not at home?*
>
> Yes. Many tasks at school differ from those at home. Walker (1979) suggested that only about half of the students who frequently misbehave at school also misbehave at home. For example, at home and in the community, children and youth are not usually required to respond to such academic tasks as reading and mathematics. Because these activities are not a regular part of their home life, children may find it difficult to adjust in school. At home, on the other hand, where many activities involve behaviors that require them to actively do something, such as chores, children may be compliant and show little frustration.

Furthermore, some children may be accustomed to a great deal of attention at home. When teachers have class sizes of 25 to 35 students, children may receive considerably less attention than they do at home. This may lead to attention-getting behaviors on the part of some. If children are not able to gain enough attention through success at school-related activities, such as academics or sports, they may behave in a manner that draws negative attention.

Discipline may represent another area of different practices between home and school. For example, parents may use physical punishment as a means to ensure obedience, whereas the teacher may use other methods, such as sending students out of the room. For these students, being sent out of the room may not invoke the same fear as being punished at home does. Far from being a plea for use of corporal punishment in the schools, this observation points to the realization that differences in types of management between school and home may result in different levels of compliance to rules and consequences.

School requires children to interact and also function in groups. For the most part, these are behaviors that children bring to school from home. Many young students have not had many opportunities to interact with others for extended periods of time. Moreover, the inability of some to respect the rights and property of others might lead to classroom problems.

Attention Deficit Hyperactivity Disorder (ADHD)

One of the most frequently described externalizing behaviors is hyperactivity, also called *hyper* or *ADHD*. These terms are frequently used interchangeably and seem to have many definitions (Hallahan & Cortone, 1997). Simply put, these terms reflect disorders in activity and attention. Students exhibiting these behaviors may be categorized in the schools as having EBD, learning disabilities, or physical or other health impairments.

Students who have ADHD may not be eligible for special education services at all but instead would receive services under Section 504 of the Rehabilitation Act (1973). Only those students who have had a special education label applied may receive special education services, and ADHD is not an official special education category. However, ADHD *is* a recognized disability. Section 504 requires that schools make the necessary accommodation(s) to help these students (most often, in the general education setting). Consequently, the delivery of services to these students may be confusing to those involved; not all parents are aware of the services provided under Section 504.

Teachers and parents who have children that exhibit hyperactive behaviors have sentiments such as the following:

> My child cannot sit down for more than a minute! Even when he's sitting, his legs are swinging, his hands are moving, or he's rocking his whole body. He just won't sit still!

> Tim is so easily frustrated. Last week he was playing with his truck, and when the wheel fell off, he threw the truck at his sister. She had to get three stitches!

One way to describe hyperactivity is to look at the word itself. *Hyper* means excessive or too much. Hyperactivity is just that, too much of a particular activity (or behavior). In both of the preceding examples, the children reacted with too much activity. Hyperactivity refers to behaviors that occur too often or too quickly and are inappropriate for particular settings. In school, hyperactivity interferes with learning and causes academic and social problems. The term is often used to describe the behavior problems of learning disabled students because of their inability to complete their work successfully. It has been suggested that hyperactivity may have a bio-physical cause. Consequently, medications may form some aspect of the student's treatment (see Chapter 9). Some common behaviors and parent comments associated with hyperactivity are as follows:

- Stubbornness: "She absolutely refuses to do anything that I ask!"
- Negativity: "He never allows himself to have a good time." "She thinks that nobody likes her."
- Impulsivity: "He doesn't think before he acts. He just acts!"
- Temper outbursts: "Any time she has any difficulty, she screams and acts crazy!"
- Inattentive: "He doesn't concentrate . . . doesn't seem to listen."
- Bossy: "She always has to be in charge. She gets upset when she doesn't have her way."
- Low frustration tolerance: "The slightest problem becomes a major catastrophe to him."
- Lack of response: "It doesn't matter what I do. Nothing seems to get through!"
- Motor activity: "He can't be still. He is always moving around, even when he is in bed."

Hyperactivity is usually described as a chronic condition, something that occurs fairly consistently over time. The term may be used incorrectly to describe children's behavior during certain special events, such as parties, trips, or group gatherings.

It is important to understand that for many children, ADHD is a condition that does not just go away. Up to 50% of all children identified as having ADHD will continue to experience it into adulthood (Weiss & Hechtman, 1993).

Aggressive and Violent Behaviors

Aggression is another term that has different definitions to different people (this topic will be discussed in more depth in Chapter 5). We prefer to define aggression as behavior that severely interferes with others. In other words, aggression can be seen when a child becomes abusive to others or to objects in the environment. Aggression can take many forms. Some milder and sometimes accepted examples of aggression include teasing, clowning around, bullying, tattling, and displaying threats of aggression.

Once again, teachers may react differently to these behaviors. To some people, the examples given are not considered very serious and are tolerated. Other and more severe aggressive acts include threats of physical aggression, physical attacks on people, destruction of property, and cruelty to animals.

Again, it is critical to distinguish between different levels of these externalizing behaviors. For example, a child having a temper tantrum (screaming and stomping but not invading the physical space of others), although disturbing, usually poses no threat to self, others, or property and does not fit our definition of aggression in that it does not pose a threat to anyone or anything. With both aggression and temper tantrums, the child may be considered to be out of control. Both forms of behavior may be due to an inability to cope with frustration. In many cases, temper tantrums can be ignored, which might, in turn, lower their frequency. Obviously, however, aggression cannot be ignored because of its severity, not to mention the rights of potential victims.

Temper tantrums may be tolerated by some professionals. Nevertheless, such behavior clearly interferes with learning. Furthermore, temper tantrums may lead to aggression if left unchecked. For example, an otherwise passive student or sibling might be provoked enough by constant teasing to physically retaliate.

It is important, and often difficult, to remember that students with EBD who exhibit aggressive and violent behavior may do so because it is an integral part of their disability. These students should not be blamed for it (e.g., called "bad" kids).

Oppositional Defiant Disorder (ODD)

This is a problem that has been diagnosed in increasing numbers in recent years. It is one disorder that is clearly defined by its name. Indeed, individuals with this disorder consistently oppose, defy, and are hostile to all authority figures in their environment. Their behavior is normally aggressive (as opposed to quietly walking away when somebody asks or tells them to do something). According to *DSM-IV* (American Psychiatric Association, 1994), the symptoms of ODD are when a student

- Often loses his or her temper
- Often argues with adults
- Often actively defies or refuses to comply with adults' requests or rules

- Often deliberately annoys people
- Often blames others for his or her mistakes or misbehavior
- Is often touchy or easily annoyed by others
- Is often angry and resentful
- Is often spiteful and vindictive

Juvenile Delinquency

The term *juvenile delinquent* is a legal one; however, it has also been applied to youth who are troublesome. Twenty percent of students who have EBD have been arrested. This percentage increases to 35% after they leave school (Wagner et al., 1991). In most states, juvenile delinquents are those youth under the age of 18 who have been found guilty of an illegal act by a court. Crimes may include acts for which adults would not be arrested, such as truancy, running away from home, and incorrigibility. A *socialized delinquent* is a child or youth who, for all intents and purposes, is normal yet highly influenced by peers. A common trait of a socialized delinquent is membership in a youth gang or club. Other delinquents have few or no friends. They may seem irritable, aggressive, defiant, quarrelsome, and unmotivated by praise or punishment.

Some delinquents tend to be extremely unhappy. In contrast to the youth with ODD, these children and youth experience genuine remorse and anxiety over their behaviors. Many of them are withdrawn and seem shy. Although these delinquents generally do not repeat their acts, their disorders can be very serious. For these children and adolescents, the delinquency seems to be a secondary problem that has resulted from their emotional problems.

Some young people who have learning disabilities may exhibit delinquent behaviors if their frustrations with their disabilities are not dealt with at home or at school. There are many theories of delinquency, ranging from the sociological to the behavioral to the psychological. Again, causation should not be the major concern. Rather, both educators and parents should focus on remediation.

INTERNALIZING BEHAVIORS

Depression

Problems of depression and suicide have been increasingly evident among North American children and youth over the past several decades. Many of the factors related to such problems are evident in exceptional children, which sometimes go unnoticed by both parents and school professionals. (Guetzloe, 1991, p. 1)

Historically, it was believed that children couldn't be depressed because of the notion that there simply wasn't anything that could depress an 8-year-old. However, depression is evident in some children and youth in our schools. In children and adolescents, an episode of depression lasts on average from 7 to 9 months (Birmaher, Ryan, Williamson, Brent, & Kaufman, 1996) and may have many clinical features similar to those in adults. It is one of the most difficult forms of emotional disturbance or behavioral disorder to diagnose. Its cause may be biological or psychological.

In a large, general education classroom setting, depressed students can easily be overlooked. Teachers have difficulty enough teaching those students who are not attending to their schoolwork. These students are usually easy to identify because of behaviors that disturb the teacher or fellow students. Depressed children, in contrast, are rarely disturbing to others. They are sometimes categorized as being turned off by school rather than as being emotionally disturbed.

Identifying depressed children and youth usually requires understanding their histories. Is their current behavior markedly different from their previous behavior? Behavior changes can serve as warning signals of depression. Many times, such behavior changes are coupled with general feelings of sadness. Contrary to popular belief, an exhibition of sadness does not always accompany depression. Unexplained—and many times, significant—behavior changes that may signify depression include the following:

- Crying
- Withdrawing from friends
- Disinterest in school
- Physical complaints
- Change in sleeping habits (too much or too little sleep)
- Change in eating habits (too much or too little)
- Lack of bladder control
- Reduced physical activity
- Apathy
- Drug or alcohol abuse
- Delinquency
- Suicidal ideation (verbal or written statements)

Children and youth face problems that they perceive to be as catastrophic as any an adult may face. In fact, some people believe that depression may be learned. Children may be modeling the reactions, as they perceive them, that their parents exhibit as a result of unfortunate events. Others believe that depression is biological and is not a learned emotion. Traumatic events that may trigger depression in children include the following:

- Death of a significant other (parent, sibling)
- Divorce of parents
- Family stresses (money, relationship problems)

It would be incorrect to suggest that these events alone cause depression. People have their own way of perceiving events. The depressed child looks at events in a much more negative, helpless, and perhaps hopeless manner than others. It is incumbent on the educator to pay as careful attention to this "lack of behaviors" in a child as they would to a child who is disturbing others.

Anxiety Disorders

Anxiety is a "painful uneasiness of mind usually over an impending or anticipated ill, a fearful concern" (Mish et al., 1994). It is a very normal response to threatening events. Individuals suffering from an anxiety disorder may perceive events as very threatening, even though they might prove to be nonthreatening or at the most, unpleasant. In fact, individuals who have this disorder may be in a general anxious state not linked to a specific source (Barlow, 1988). It is among the most common EBD disorders (Costello et al., 1996). Anxious people tend to work themselves into such a state that they are unable to achieve at their level of competence. For example,

> Sue is a good student, yet she frets so much. She worries about everything. She worries about school, about having friends, about how she looks. You name it, she worries about it. Even when things work out for her, she goes on to worry about the next thing. She is impossible to be around during these times.

Sue has an anxiety disorder. She worries excessively over a wide range of areas, including academics and social acceptance. It is not unusual for people such as Sue to experience severe anxiety (or be anxious) about such things as

- Possible injuries or illnesses
- The ability to live up to the expectations of others
- Taking field trips with a school group
- Talking to others

Each of these examples may give rise to concern or mild anxiety in most people, but they usually are able to complete their tasks despite their concern. The anxious individual, in contrast, is overly concerned and may not be able to attempt or complete a task.

Young children may also experience anxiety. A parent reported that her child "becomes hysterical when I leave him in kindergarten, or even if I leave him at a friend's house when I do a short errand." This is a problem that is sometimes called *separation anxiety*. Separation anxiety refers to a specific type of fear, namely, the fear that a loved one or significant other will not return. Such anxiety is intense, sometimes approaching panic. Some children may develop problems going to sleep, and when they do, they might have nightmares. Young adolescents may also have separation anxiety, and in some cases, the condition can last through adulthood (U.S. Department of Heath and Human Services, 1996).

Once again, it is difficult to be sure of a particular diagnosis, especially because it is difficult to gather concrete information about the level of severity and psychology issues underlying such behavior. If parents or others are concerned about children who seem to experience the emotions and behaviors described in this chapter, a complete evaluation may be in order.

The term *phobia* is rarely used in educational circles and is more often discussed by psychologists or psychiatrists. Phobias are intense fears of specific objects or events that pose little or no threat to the individual. A school phobia (sometimes called *social anxiety disorder*) is a refusal to attend school because the child is unusually afraid of the school and the school environment. They may be very afraid of being embarrassed in social situations. They may avoid participating on any level when other people are present (Black, Leonard, & Rapoport, 1997). This differs from separation anxiety, where the child is afraid to go anywhere if it means being apart from the parents.

People, and especially children, are afraid of all sorts of things, for example, darkness and animals. It is only when this fear is so overwhelming that it becomes debilitating and significantly interferes with the child's functioning that it is considered a phobia. If Jenny was afraid to go to sleep, to leave the house, or participate in various activities because of fear of a neighbor's dog, she would have a phobia (or be phobic) about the dog.

Substance Abuse

If children or youth are experiencing such feelings as anxiety or depression and do not receive proper attention by those around them, other problems can arise. By definition, those who exhibit behaviors that are indicative of depression are rarely disturbing. If, however, a significant change in behavior occurs, even one that does not bother others, parents and teachers should try to determine the cause and help the individual. Alcohol and drug abuse often is the result of emotional problems such as depression. In fact, in a national study, it was found that the majority of individuals who experienced substance abuse also had EBD (Kessler et al., 1996). Other studies have shown that many depressed adolescents turn to drugs because of reported

- Low self-concept
- Need to escape boredom
- Peer pressure
- Enjoyment

Many children experiment with substances such as marijuana, alcohol, valium, Quaaludes, cocaine, glue, correction fluid, markers, and paint, to name a few. Drug users display a variety of symptoms related to each specific drug. However, common symptoms are

- Sleepiness
- Slurring of speech
- Incoherent, confused state
- Mood swings
- Bloodshot eyes

As with all the forms of emotional disturbance and behavioral disorders that have been discussed, substance intake is a problem when it calls attention to itself. Consider the following:

> I take a drink in the morning, just to . . . you know . . . get it going. Facing Mom and Dad is such a hassle. A little vodka just takes the edge off . . . you know? I keep my old Flintstones thermos in my locker at school. No one would ever look in there. I keep vodka or whiskey. Whichever is easier to get. Sometimes I steal it from my parents. They'd never guess . . . you know?
>
> School's such a drag. Although, sometimes I get really tired in school. When I go home, I go up to my room to drink. Who cares? At least I'm not popping pills like my friends. I use a little breath spray to cover up while I eat dinner. Then I really get blitzed until I can't feel anything anymore. What's the big deal? Everybody drinks . . . you know? I might stop when I'm 14, though. Who knows?

Alcoholics and other substance abusers usually need intake at least daily. The need for the substance often becomes physiological (the body becomes addicted) as well as psychological. Alcoholics may have regularly defined drinking periods, such as weekends, or they may binge. A binge is when the individual undergoes periods of sobriety interspersed with periods of heavy intake that may last days, weeks, or months.

Alcohol is a socially accepted substance and is easy to obtain. It is also the most commonly abused. Whatever the substance, it may not be long before the major goal of the child's day (and, perhaps life) is to obtain the substance.

Withdrawn Behaviors

Some children and youth exhibit withdrawn behaviors without being depressed. Withdrawal is one way students may escape unpleasant situations. It may result from lack of social skills required in certain situations. Children may not know how to behave in social groups or in classroom situations. Or they may have experienced rejection or humiliation in those groups and learned that it is better not to associate with others than risk failing again. Some typical withdrawn behaviors include the following:

- Avoidance of eye contact
- Avoidance of association with peers
- Seeming embarrassment
- Refusal to participate in group discussions
- Physical isolation
- Playing most often with inanimate objects

Withdrawn behaviors are the most difficult to identify. Most often, teachers will attend to those students who are problematic and leave withdrawn students alone. Consider the following vignette:

> Susan is in the fifth grade. She never causes trouble and is very quiet. She will answer questions but does not initiate conversations with anyone. She doesn't have any friends. The kids in class tease her, but she doesn't seem to mind. She just goes off to be by herself.

Clearly, Susan poses no immediate problems in the classroom. However, if she is not taught to understand her problem and deal with it, more severe mental health problems may develop, such as depression. Susan's type of social withdrawal may delay normal social development, and if it lasts into her high school years, where interrelationships take on added importance, it could also hamper her ability to achieve.

FUNCTION DISORDERS

Anorexia Nervosa

A student who has anorexia nervosa is usually an adolescent girl who has a distorted self-image. These students may be extremely underweight and yet believe they are overweight. The adolescent or young adult with anorexia nervosa experiences a severe weight loss that, in turn, can cause many other physical problems. Individuals with anorexia believe that their perceptions of being overweight are accurate. They may also experience an intense fear or concern about weight gain. To complicate matters, they are not disturbing to others (Mizes, 1995). Consider the following example:

> Our Cathy is such a good girl. She never causes us trouble. In fact, sometimes we think she pushes herself too hard. She gets all As, is active in cheerleading and our church. She studies hard and keeps her room as neat as a pin.
>
> We still feel that something is wrong. She is so skinny. She sits with us at dinner but seems to just play with her food. Last night, my husband forced her to eat. A little while later, I was on my way upstairs when I heard her vomiting. When I went into the bathroom, she had her fingers down her throat. I confronted her, and she told me that she was under control. She broke down and said that she was too fat. She looks like she is starving, and she says that she is too fat. Though emaciated, Sally stands in front of the mirror and her bones stick out. Yet she cries that she can still pull skin away from her body.

As with the many other problems discussed in this chapter, the following symptoms are meant to be warning signals that might indicate anorexia nervosa.

- A preoccupied fear of obesity
- An inability to logically view the body, a fear of being fat
- An inability to maintain body weight because of vomiting, strenuous exercise, intake of huge amounts of laxatives, a strict refusal to eat
- Excessive weight loss, at least 25% body weight
- No known physical illness that accounts for weight loss
- Obsessive, ritualistic behaviors: "Her clothes and shoes are in perfect order, she places silverware and dishes in a specific way, and I think she even chews her food a certain number of times and in a certain way!"

There is no known cause of anorexia nervosa. Although it is largely viewed as a psychological problem that can cause physical problems, some recent evidence suggests that it might be due to the individual's metabolism or psychological problems with perfection.

Bulimia Nervosa

Bulimia is exhibited by frequent episodes of uncontrollable eating. A person with bulimia consumes vast amounts of food within a short period of time. The person feels unable to stop eating; he or she will binge. Bulimics alternate bingeing with self-induced vomiting or extreme laxative use, called *purging*. Purging rids the body of the large amounts of food eaten. Bulimics are able to view what they are doing as being abnormal, but they cannot control or stop the behavior. Anorectics do not view their behavior as abnormal. Bulimia most frequently occurs in late adolescence (American Psychiatric Association [APA], 1994).

Enuresis

Enuresis is the involuntary voiding of urine that is *not* due to physical problems. Many professionals believe enuresis may be a symptom of underlying stress or a problem the child is experiencing. The condition may also be due to delayed or incomplete toilet training. Some recent research has centered around the intensity of sleep of children with enuresis to test the theory that some children sleep so deeply that they fail to respond to the sensation of a full bladder. Consultation with a pediatrician is highly recommended.

Encopresis

The voluntary or involuntary passage of feces in inappropriate places is called *encopresis.* Involuntary soiling applies to children who soil themselves when a problem such as severe constipation is present, whereas voluntary means that the soiling is deliberate. Like enuresis, the condition is usually diagnosed after all organic or physical causes have been ruled out. As for enuresis, the causes usually are due to stress or underlying problems. Again, organic or physical problems must be ruled out before enuresis or encopresis can be determined.

Other Physical Manifestations of EBD

Physical problems may result from emotional problems. Some of these are briefly discussed in the following paragraphs. If a child has one of these problems, it does not necessarily mean that it is accompanied by an emotional problem, however. Some physical problems that may have a relationship to emotional problems include

- Childhood asthma: severe difficulties breathing (coughing, shortness of breath) resulting from infections, allergies, or stress

- Ulcerative colitis: disorder of the gastrointestinal system resulting in severe diarrhea, abdominal pains, and damage to the intestinal lining
- Elective mutism: child virtually refuses to speak in certain situations or chooses only to speak to specific people. Most commonly, the child refuses to speak in school, to strangers, or in other stressful situations.
- Obesity: defined as body weight that is 20% or greater than the norm for the height of the child. An obese child is one who may use food as a substitute for affection and social attention or as a release from stress. Many obese children have few friends and find school traumatic. They may appear to be dependent and immature; yet in many cases, they are demanding with their parents.

Childhood Schizophrenia

Schizophrenia refers to a group of disorders that are characterized by disturbances in thinking, mood, and behavior. These disturbances are basically misinterpretations of reality. For example, children who have schizophrenia may have speech ability, yet their speech will have no meaning to others. It is a very low-incidence disability (it is very rare).

Disturbances in mood involve inappropriate emotional responses. Examples of this might include laughing when someone is seriously hurt or crying over cartoons. Disturbances in behavior might be total withdrawal or exhibiting bizarre and highly unusual behavior. Consider the descriptions of the following children:

> My son is fascinated with elevators. When we travel anywhere, he runs to find an elevator. Once he finds one, he will question for hours whether it has a gate or door and whether it's operated by hand or buttons. He never stops asking the same questions.

> Sam was such a good baby. However, he seems to be so preoccupied with things. At 5, we had to constantly watch him because he would collect everyone's doormats in the neighborhood. He loved doormats.

Other examples of the bizarre behaviors that children with schizophrenia may exhibit include the following:

- Delayed or incoherent speech: "I ask him if he's hungry, and he asks me if the elevator is running."
- Disordered thought process: "Although completely toilet trained, Jerry became anxious and confused if he had to urinate and have a

bowel movement at the same time. He would run to an adult and ask if he was a boy or a girl. His reasoning was that a boy urinates standing up, a girl sitting down. Therefore, if he sat down for a bowel movement and urinated at the same time, he might be a girl."

- Delusions: somebody or something is controlling their minds
- Hallucinations: hearing or seeing things that do not exist
- Preoccupation with objects, displaying compulsive rituals: "He has to circle the table exactly 22 times before sitting down to eat."
- Extreme hyperactivity

At this time, there is no single known cause of schizophrenia. Certainly, it is not necessarily caused by the actions of parents. Instead, there is a widespread belief that *genetic vulnerability* may be an underlying factor. Genetic vulnerability means that if a grandfather, for example, had adult schizophrena, the chances for a child or grandchild to have schizophrenia are greater than for somebody who has had no schizophrenia in the family. Having genetic vulnerability does not mean that it will definitely occur; it only means that the chances are greater. In fact, it is still very rare. It is also generally accepted that childhood schizophrenia is associated with chemical imbalances. Such factors as enzyme levels and metabolisms are being studied to determine their contribution to this illness.

SUMMARY

When parents are faced with a troubled child or adolescent, they may be overwhelmed with the labels or terms used to describe their child. This chapter has provided brief descriptions of a number of emotional and behavioral disorders. We hope the information will serve as a point from which you can begin to understand these otherwise often scary and confusing terms.

REFERENCES

American Psychiatric Association. (1994). *Diagnostic and statistical manual of mental disorders* (4th ed.). Washington, DC: Author.

Barlow, D. H. (1988). *Anxiety and its disorders.* New York: Guilford.

Birmaher, B., Ryan, N. D., Williamson, D. E., Brent, D. A., & Kaufman, J. (1996). Childhood and adolescent depression: A review of the past 10 years. Part II. *Journal of the American Academy of Child and Adolescent Psychiatry, 35,* 1575–1583.

Black, B., Leonard, H. L., & Rapoport, J. L. (1997). Specific phobia, panic disorder, social phobia, and selective mutism. In J. M. Weiner (Ed.), *Textbook of child and adolescent psychiatry* (2nd ed., pp. 491–506). Washington, DC: American Academy of Child and Adolescent Psychiatry, American Psychiatric Press.

Costello, E. J., Angold, A., Burns, B. J., Stangl, D. K., Tweed, D. L., Erkanli, A., & Worthman, C. M. (1996). The Great Smoky Mountains study of youth. Goals, design, methods, and the prevalence of *DSM-III-R* disorders. *Archives of General Psychiatry, 53,* 1129–1136.

Guetzloe, E. C. (1991). *Depression and suicide: Special education students at risk.* Reston, VA: Council for Exceptional Children.

Hallahan, D. P., & Cortone, E. A. (1997). Attention deficit hyperactivity disorder. In T. E. Scruggs & M. A. Mastropieri (Eds.), *Advances in learning and behavioral disabilities* (Vol. 11, pp. 27–67). Greenwich, CT: JAL.

Kazdin, A. E. (1995). *Conduct disorders in childhood and adolescence* (2nd ed.). Thousand Oaks, CA: Sage.

Kessler, R. C., Nelson, C. B., McKonagle, K. A., Edlund, M. J., Frank, R. G., & Leaf, P. J. (1996). The epidemiology of co-occurring addictive and mental disorders: Implications for prevention and service utilization. *American Journal of Orthopsychiatry, 66,* 17–31.

Mish, F. C., et al. (1994). *Merriam-Webster's collegiate dictionary* (10th ed.). Springfield, MA: Merriam-Webster.

Mizes, J. S. (1995). Eating disorders. In M. Hersen & R. T. Ammerman (Eds.), *Advanced abnormal child psychology* (pp. 375–391). Hillsdale, NJ: Erlbaum.

Rehabilitation Act of 1973, 29 U.S.C. §794, Sec. 504.

U.S. Department of Health and Human Services. (1996). *Mental health: A report of the surgeon general—Executive summary.* Rockville, MD: Author.

Wagner, M., Newman, L., D'Amico, R., Jay, E. D., Butler-Nalin, P., Marder, P., & Cox, R. (1991). *Youth with disabilities: How are they doing? The first comprehensive report for the National Longitudinal Transition Study of transition study.* Menlo Park, CA: SRI.

Walker, H. M. (1979). *The acting out child: Coping with classroom disruption.* Boston: Allyn & Bacon.

Weiss, G., & Hechtman, L. (1993). *Hyperactive children grow up.* New York: Guilford.

Causes of Emotional and Behavioral Disorders 3

An initial reaction of parents, teachers, relatives, and friends of children experiencing problems is to look for a cause. It is only natural to want to know why. Parents of a young hard-of-hearing boy indicated they were distressed to learn their son had a hearing problem but relieved to know why he failed to develop speech and respond to them. They also reported feeling a sense of relief when shown a diagram of the ear revealing the location of the hearing damage. Parents and teachers of children and adolescents experiencing emotional and behavioral disorders have the same need to know why their children behave as they do. They desperately want to know why these children act differently from others and often refuse to do the things they are expected to do.

Thus, parents and relatives may search their family tree for ancestors with similar problems, attempt to recall the circumstances surrounding accidents and injuries, or debate the impact of a traumatic event, such as the death of a family member or friend, or a divorce. Unlike the case involving hearing loss, no simple diagrams exist to explain emotional difficulties. This chapter will examine some reasons why children and youth develop emotional and behavioral disorders.

A number of scientific theories are used to explain emotional and behavioral disorders of children and adolescents. A multitude of not-so-scientific explanations can also be heard, including "bad genes," "bad blood," and "family problems." Yet in spite of all this speculation, the exact cause or causes of a child's problems and conflict is rarely known. This does not mean that nothing is known of cause; a good deal is known, and more is being learned. However, the exact cause of most EBD problems remains a mystery. There are several reasons for this lack of clarity: (a) disagreement over the definition of emotional and behavioral disorders; (b) the complexity of human behavior; and (c) the manner in which scientific studies of the causes of emotional and behavioral conditions are conducted (Zionts & Simpson, 1988).

There is considerable disagreement about what constitutes an emotional or behavioral problem. One parent's "active boy" or "creative individualist" may be another's "behavior-disordered" or "withdrawn" child. Similarly, teachers have a variety of expectations for classroom behavior. Some incorporate activity and discussion; others foster an environment of reflection and individual effort in one's seat. Clearly, these differential interpretations of and expectations for children's behaviors can create a lack of agreement over the meaning of a so-called behavior problem. Without agreeing on what constitutes appropriate behavior, it is difficult to agree on a cause.

UNDERSTANDING FACTORS
RELATED TO THE DEVELOPMENT OF EBD

Despite the lack of agreement about what constitutes a behavior problem, there is a body of information available to help us understand how emotional and behavioral disorders may be formed. The presently known causes of children's emotional and behavioral disorders are best understood by considering two major factors: tendencies to develop certain problems (known as *predisposing factors*) and contributing events (known as *precipitating agents*). Tendencies or predisposing factors are any conditions that increase a child's risk of developing an emotional problem. Tendencies or predisposing agents may include (but are not limited to) physical illness and disability, shyness, hyperactive behavior, heredity, and an emotionally unhealthy home. It is important to note that many children and adolescents who experience these conditions do not develop emotional problems. Thus, it is incorrect to assume that a child will develop an emotional problem because he has asthma, is shy, or lives in a violent environment. Many mentally healthy persons live constructive lives despite difficult situations. Yet we must also recognize that these conditions may increase a child's chance of experiencing emotional problems.

Contributing or precipitating factors refer to specific incidents that may trigger maladaptive behavior. Included are death, desertion, divorce, or other crisis situations. One 7-year-old who was overly dependent on his parents became at risk for emotional problems when his father deserted the family. Although this boy was emotionally able to survive his ordeal, largely as a result of professional counseling, he was susceptible to emotional problems for a period of time. Contributing factors may not be readily apparent—they don't always take such obvious forms as death and divorce. Furthermore, children and adolescents may not show immediate reactions to contributing events.

Even when tendencies and contributing factors exist, a child may or may not develop EBD. This is one of the confusing aspects of human behavior. Due to individual differences, situations produce different reactions. This helps explain why children from the same family act differently or why seemingly identical children react differently to the same situation.

UNDERSTANDING POTENTIAL CAUSES OF EBD

The known potential causes of emotional and behavioral disturbances are divided into two general categories: biological and environmental. *Biological* refers to physical, medical, and genetic factors. *Environmental* causes, on the other hand, involve those conditions and experiences that make up our day-to-day world. Family, school, and community conditions are the environmental influences of greatest importance.

Biological Causes of EBD

All of us are products of our biology. Our instincts, muscles, nerves, and genetic influences determine, at least to some extent, the manner in which we say, think, and do things. The nervous system, of which the brain is a part, consists of a massive collection of interconnected nerve cells that affect every aspect of life, including our senses and behavior. Thus, some behavior and emotional problems are thought to be the result of biological accidents or influences. Frequently discussed biological causes include

- Genetic influences
- Neurological impairment (brain damage)
- Nutrition
- Physical health

Genetics refers to heredity. Genetic influences have long been used to explain emotional and behavioral disorders. One may hear comments such as, "He gets so angry and irrational, just like his father did when he was that age" and "It's no wonder Joan is such a problem in school; she inherited the same bad genes as her older brothers." Such statements are usually inaccurate. When we assume that children and adolescents demonstrate the same behavioral patterns, either positive or negative, as other family members, we frequently overlook the powerful influence of environment and numerous other conditions that affect behavior. For example, if a child of shy parents demonstrates a lack of interest in people, it is difficult to know if this behavior pattern is a result of the parents' modeling shy behavior, heredity, or other conditions. Behavior may be influenced by genetic factors. According to recent studies of early development, a child's genetics only provides a structure or framework for future development. It is the child's early experiences in life that affect most strongly how a child develops (Dodge, 1996; Erickson, 1998).

However, there are indications that genetic influences are closely associated with certain types of mental illness. In particular, schizophrenia (a severe form of mental illness characterized by extreme withdrawal, reduced functioning capacity, hallucinations, and delusions) has been found to be more common among blood relatives (Gottesman & Molden, 1999). Although schizophrenia occurs in about 1% of the general population, the risk of the condition increases proportionately with the degree of blood relationship one has with a diagnosed schizophrenic. For example, the rate of schizophrenia among children who have one schizophrenic parent is about 13%, and having two schizophrenic parents increases the probability to about 46%. These percentages are increased when a person has more family members who have the disease in addition to the parent (Gottesman & Moldin, 1999).

A cause of some types of emotional and behavioral disorders is also found in neurological syndromes. For example, Tourette's syndrome (a syndrome that causes multiple vocal and muscular tics, as well as marked impairment in important areas of daily functioning) is believed to be caused by an abnormal metabolism of a neurotransmitter called *dopamine* (National Alliance for the Mentally Ill, 1996). It is believed that Tourette's syndrome is transmitted as a dominant gene; hence, a parent has a 50% chance of passing the gene to their child. However, girls are slightly less likely than boys to develop symptoms associated with Tourette's syndrome.

A male genetic variation consisting of an extra Y chromosome has been associated with overly aggressive behavior (Kumra et al., 1998). However, because the scientific study of genetic influences is only in its infancy, it is difficult to evaluate the impact of genetics on behavior. Thus, in spite of indications of genetic influence, especially in severe emotional disturbance, more evidence must be collected before final conclusions can be drawn. Furthermore, even when hereditary influences are associated with emotional problems, they are usually only a partial explanation of cause.

The term *neurological impairment,* or *brain damage,* is both threatening and confusing. Neurological injuries range from severe destruction of tissue, resulting in serious disability, to tiny injuries producing little or no behavior change. It has long been assumed that damage to the brain and its wrappings is associated with childhood emotional and behavioral disorders. However, neither the meaning of neurological impairment nor its influence as a cause of emotional problems has been agreed upon by researchers. Brain damage suggests dysfunction due to injury. The damage may be to brain cells (neurons), glia (non-brain-cell material), or blood vessels. If severe, such damage may lead to loss or deterioration of certain functions (e.g., vision, coordination). Damage may occur as a result of anoxia (lack of oxygen), physical injury, high fever, infection, or toxins such as poison or drugs. Although brain damage can result in serious and permanent disability, most instances of alleged neurological impairment do not entail severe or permanent consequences. Furthermore, there is limited evidence to suggest that such problems are associated with behavioral and emotional difficulties.

Hard and soft signs are commonly used to describe neurological conditions. A hard sign refers to specific neurological damage responsible for a particular problem or deficit. For example, a child with an identifiable injury (referred to as a *lesion*) may experience uncontrolled, jerky, and irregular motor movements. Soft damage, on the other hand, refers to an alleged minimal and unidentifiable injury. Although the actual damage cannot be identified, it is assumed to exist because of certain behaviors thought to develop in relation to the extent and location of the injury, a child's personality, and environmental influences. The most common terms associated with soft damage are *minimal brain dysfunction* and *attention deficit disorder*. These terms are used to describe children who demonstrate hyperactivity, learning problems, distractibility, perceptual difficulties, and clumsiness. However, physicians who conduct child evaluations based on such characteristics often express to parents and teachers that the diagnosis of minimal brain damage is questionable and speculative.

Although the influence of brain damage must not be overlooked, it is important to carefully consider its significance. First, the relationship between brain damage and emotional disturbance has not been clearly established. Brain damage can and does produce abnormal behavior. However, it cannot automatically be concluded that emotional and behavioral disorders result from neurological difficulties. This conclusion is based on the finding that the vast majority of emotionally and behaviorally disturbed children and adolescents do not show convincing signs of neurological impairment. Although brain damage may be a factor in the development of some emotional problems, it does not appear to be a major cause.

A number of biological causes of emotional disturbance have been suggested. Among those, physical health and malnutrition are two that are more easily substantiated by research. There is no doubt that malnutrition is associated with learning problems and, in some instances, emotional problems. Kids who are malnourished possess neither the strength nor the motivation to do well in school or to display acceptable behaviors. In extreme cases, malnutrition may cause brain damage and mental retardation. In addition, certain foods, particularly food additives and food dye, are thought by some to cause hyperactivity and other behavioral problems. Although definite conclusions have not been drawn regarding much of this area, certain children may indeed respond poorly to specific foods.

One myth, however, is that refined sugar is a cause of hyperactivity in children. A study published in the *New England Journal of Medicine* (Wolraich et al., 1994) examined the effects of high-, moderate-, and no-sugar diets on children who were reported by their families to be sugar sensitive. They concluded that even when the amount of sugar ingested exceeded the normal dietary recommendations, there was no effect on cognitive or behavioral performance. Furthermore, an analysis of many previous research studies conducted on sugar and hyperactivity in children was published in the *Journal of the American Medical Association* (Wolraich, Wilson, & White, 1995). The researchers concluded that across the previous studies, sugar intake did not affect the children's behavior. The results of the AMA study have been reported widely through news media (e.g., CNN, WebMD, and several special education resources, such as Dr. John Wills Lloyd's special education Web site hosted by the University of Virginia at http://curry.edschool.virginia.edu/curry/dept/cise/ose/information/hypersugar.html). Yet as the AMA researchers noted, some adults will persist in their belief that sugar has a negative impact on a child's behavior.

Because teachers and parents alike, however, have noted that children seem more hyperactive after ingesting sugar (e.g., think, day after Halloween), several researchers have attempted to provide alternate explanations for the observations. A study published in the *Journal of Abnormal Child Psychology* (Hoover & Milich, 1994) asked parents to rate their child's behavior after being told that their child had ingested sugar. They hypothesized that their observations might be explained by a simple case of self-fulfilling prophecy. In that study, parents were indeed more likely to rate their child as more active after being told the child had ingested large amounts of sugar. Incidentally, these same parents tended to then interact with their child using more criticism of the child and closer physical contact with the child, each of which can affect a child's behavior.

Children and adolescents with severe, long-term health problems and physical handicaps may suffer from emotional problems, including depression, anger, and suicidal tendencies. As with other possible causes, this does not mean that all such children will experience these problems or that such conditions cause emotional difficulties. However, health problems and physical handicaps do cause additional stress and, in some instances, are thought to result in emotional conflicts. Specifically, patients who have been treated for cancer have been shown to evidence emotional and behavioral problems likely due to the long-term emotional stress and pain caused by this illness (Grassi, Malacarne, Maestri, & Ramelli, 1997). Children who have epilepsy have also developed emotional and behavioral problems, perhaps due to side effects of the medications used to treat the condition (Harboard, 2000).

There is no question that biological conditions may contribute to behavioral and emotional problems. In particular, genetic accidents, brain damage, malnutrition, and physical illness and impairment may increase children's susceptibility to certain types of difficulties. However, most behaviorally disordered and emotionally disturbed children and adolescents do not have problems exclusively because of biological factors. It is most often thought to be a complex interaction between biological and environmental factors that causes such disorders in this population.

Environmental Causes

Environment is everything external to a child. Thus, *environmental cause* relates to the notion that a child's world, including home experiences, parent and family relationships, community, and school experiences, influences mental health. This view should come as no surprise because it is apparent that the values, attitudes, experiences, and expectations to which children are exposed affect their behavior. Thus, children who are exposed to unhealthy conditions are thought to be more susceptible to emotional problems.

The family has long been considered a primary determinant of a child's personality development and mental health. Parents have the potential to be with their school-age children about two thirds of every day during the school year and all day weekends and vacations. It is no wonder, then, that parents and other family members are important to children's development by helping them develop their views of the world and their self-concepts. Therefore, the question of whether less-than-favorable experiences contribute to emotional and behavioral disorders is logical.

It is important to recognize (and accept) that parents and families do not always cause children's problems. This is not to suggest that parents and families do not have a significant influence on children or that some cases of emotional disturbance and behavioral problems can be attributed to parents. In numerous cases, children and youth develop problems of which parents are not the cause. Yet society is quick to blame parents for their offspring's problems. Even professionals have been guilty of this offense. For example, several years ago, it was popular to assume that parents' interactions with and attitudes toward their children were the cause of autism (a severe developmental disability characterized by language delays, retardation, and social withdrawal). This allegation has absolutely no truth. Currently, it is hypothesized that some cases of autism may be caused by genetics, although no one gene has been identified as the causal agent (Potgieter & Fryns, 1999). The simple fact is that there is overwhelming evidence to suggest that children's problems are not always attributable to parents' actions and behaviors.

Family Stressors

Several conditions or experiences may influence the behavior and emotional status of children. In particular, conditions that increase parent, family, or children's stress is important, including economic problems, relocation to new cities, parent career changes, role changes (e.g., a mother who takes a full-time job out of the home or a father whose new job requires him to work in the evening), and similar situations. Readers should recognize that change is not necessarily negative, however. Just because a mother chooses to take a job or a career opportunity that necessitates a move does not mean that children will suffer. Yet such changes may increase stress, at least temporarily, and some children may react negatively.

An example involves a family, consisting of a mother, father, and three elementary-age children, who experienced severe economic problems and subsequent family changes. The family owned and operated a small farm in the Midwest. As many farmers have in this decade, the family fell behind in their bank payments and faced what appeared to be loss of their farm. The father experienced extreme depression over his plight and subsequently was forced to take a job he disliked and considered demeaning. His wife, who had never worked outside the home, took a job as an aide in a nursing home, a position she also disliked. The children, for the first time in their lives, were without adult supervision for periods of time in the afternoon. Furthermore, they were regularly exposed to their parents' anxieties and stresses. Subsequently, one of the children, an 8-year-old boy, developed academic and behavioral problems at school. He also demonstrated fear of abandonment and severe anxiety at home. The youngster's problems were dealt with in part through counseling provided by the school; however, significant improvement did not occur until his parents' financial situation improved.

The foregoing example illustrates the potential impact of family experiences on children. Not every child or adolescent will be affected; however, awareness of and sensitivity to the potential of such conditions are important.

It is no surprise that two-parent homes characterized by harmony and good will tend to have a positive influence on children. Such homes, however, do not protect children and adolescents from emotional and behavioral disorders. Even the best homes may have a child who has EBD. In a similar fashion, many children from single-parent families adjust well to their circumstances. Thus, although experts agree that separation and divorce are seldom good experiences, these events do not always lead to problems. In fact, one study (Dunn, Deater-Deckard, Pickering, O'Connor, & Golding, 1998) showed that when one accounted for factors such as negativity in family relationships, maternal education level, mother's social support networks, and the family's financial and housing circumstances, the actual family structure (stepfamily, single parent or dual parent) had little impact on children's prosocial behavior.

Divorce

The impact of divorce on children and adolescents has been widely debated. Although there continue to be more questions than answers, some patterns may be discerned. First, children seem to respond to the breakup of their families not only in accordance with their unique personalities but also their ages and genders. That is, young children respond differently from older children and boys often differently from girls. Furthermore, children usually experience distress over a divorce or separation regardless of the amount of discord and anxiety that existed prior to the separation. Contrary to the popular notion that children are relieved following the departure of one parent, the opposite often is true. In fact, relief is only common when an abusive parent leaves the home. Furthermore, the relationship that existed between the children and the parent who is leaving is frequently unrelated to the degree to which children are upset over the breakup of their family. In many cases, children's sadness over a separation or divorce is associated with their grief and anxiety over the breakup of their family rather than how close they were to the departing parent.

Children of all ages may show a number of emotional reactions to their parents' separation and divorce, including sadness, anger, depression, shame, guilt, fear, and rejection. It is also common for children to try to reunite their parents, thus restoring the family. Too, conflicts in loyalty may become an issue for a child whose parents are divorcing (American Academy of Pediatrics, 1995). However, such an event does not automatically lead to emotional and behavioral disorders. The notion that divorce and separation *directly cause* emotional and behavioral disorders in children and adolescents is unfounded.

Children and adolescents can be expected to respond in varying degrees to the emotional and personal problems of the adults in their lives during the difficult period of separation and divorce. Adults going through these stages often feel a sense of failure, anger, stress, anxiety, and loss of self-esteem. Thus, at times when children may most require the support of their parents, these individuals may be so involved in their own problems that they are of limited help to others. Furthermore, children may be drawn into disputes between feuding parents.

The question of whether divorce causes emotional and behavioral disorders in children is not easily answered. On the one hand, experts agree that divorce does have a significant effect, seldom of a positive nature. On the other hand, it is *not* safe to conclude that divorce causes emotional disturbance. Although separation and divorce may be potential contributors to emotional problems, these events have not been shown to cause emotional disturbance. Even though most children and adolescents whose parents divorce do not develop emotional disturbances, they will probably experience some distress.

Parent-Child Interactions

Parents' personal problems, especially in combination with an unhealthy home environment, may contribute to children's emotional disturbance. Thus, unstable and inconsistent parents more commonly have children with emotional and behavioral disorders. Not all children and adolescents develop emotional and behavioral disorders because of these conditions. However, certain parental and family patterns and events—both positive and negative—can make children more susceptible to emotional problems. For example, hostile and aggressive children are more common in hostile and aggressive families. This does not necessarily mean that hostile family interactions cause hostility in children. On the contrary, it is possible, for example, for children with emotional and behavioral disorders to cause families to behave in a more hostile and aggressive manner.

The way in which parents discipline their children has long been thought to relate to children's mental health. As one might guess, parents who are warm and loving and who consistently and fairly discipline their kids seem to get the best results. Hostile and inconsistent methods of discipline, in contrast, are thought to be the least effective and the most apt to produce problems in children. Most kids are able to adapt as long as rules and rule enforcement are relatively consistent and fair. Thus, many experts believe that children are most secure knowing that rules exist and that the adults in their lives are concerned enough to place limits on their behavior. In fact, Ramsey and Walker (1988) found differences among parents of fourth graders with and without emotional and behavioral disorders in four key areas: discipline, monitoring, positive reinforcement, and problem solving.

There is no doubt that parents and families do play a part in children's behavior and mental health. For example, a child's or adolescent's chances of becoming delinquent are increased by living in a disorganized home (*disorganized* refers to lax and inconsistent rule setting and enforcement; Green, 1992) and by families where parents have been in prison. In a similar fashion, children who have been physically and sexually abused can be expected to evidence more psychological problems than other children. Although we cannot automatically conclude that such homes will always produce children with problems, neither can we dismiss their potential negative influence. Green also describes the overorganized home (*overorganized* refers to rigid and controlling rule setting), resulting in the child's obsessive worry, performance anxiety, or oppositional behavior.

Variance Within Environmental Situations

There are numerous examples of children and adolescents who have behavioral disorders at school but who demonstrate acceptable behavior at home and in the community. Similarly, some children whose parents find extremely difficult to control at home seem to avoid problems at school. Thus, although many children with behavioral and emotional problems can be expected to encounter difficulty in a variety of settings, there are exceptions.

There are several possible explanations for such differences. One is related to expectation, where children are expected to do different things at school and at home. For example, a child may be motivated and good at doing chores at home but poor at completing academic assignments at school. For such a youngster, school-related conflict will be more common than home conflict.

Another explanation relates to structure. Some children are able to do well at school but not at home because of clearly stated school rules and consequences. One 11-year-old, for example, related that he did "pretty good in school" because his teacher clearly stated and enforced behavioral limits and consequences, conditions that did not exist when he went home.

A final explanation of variations in responses is related to definition. That is, school personnel and parents may not agree on what constitutes a problem. For example, regular use of profanity may be considered a problem at school, whereas at home, such language may be accepted.

The Community

When children or adolescents are not with their families, they are apt to be in school or elsewhere in the community. Thus, schools and communities have the potential to either further or hinder children's emotional development.

Although other aspects of a child's world may be chaotic and unhealthy, school is usually considered a positive influence. Yet even schools are sometimes potential contributors to children's problems. One way in which schools may contribute to children's problems is by failing to accommodate individual needs and personalities. Because they serve large groups of children, schools tend to aim learning experiences toward the average student. As a result, every fourth grader usually uses the same books, receives the same instruction, and is exposed to the same experiences. In essence, each student is treated like every other student in that grade. Obviously, students in the same grade are not the same. They vary in intelligence, maturity, skills, experiences, and ability. Thus, when children are treated the same with only limited accommodation for differences, those with even minor problems may be considered misfits. For example, even though all third-grade boys and girls are expected to read at the third-grade level, individual differences exist. Children who read below the designated level will probably be required to use the same text as pupils reading at or above grade level, leading to a lower self-image for students who are unable to reach some set standard. The resulting frustration and failure may help explain why some of these children misbehave or withdraw. Consequently, by failing to treat children as individuals, schools may promote problems. Teachers may rightfully contend that large class sizes and other restrictions make it unrealistic to carry out individual planning. Yet such conditions may contribute to students' emotional and behavioral disorders.

Schools may also contribute to emotional and behavioral disorders of children and youth by failing to provide the best teachers. Currently, one of the most important jobs in our society—educating young people—is often carried out by individuals who are not the most qualified, due to problems such as teacher shortages, high rates of turnover among teachers of students with EBD, and temporary (also called *emergency*) teaching certifications. There are many excellent educators whose dedication and hard work enable them to create the conditions required for educational growth and development. Yet the highest-quality teachers are not always available. Most children and adolescents adjust to quality differences among their teachers, but those students who are most vulnerable to problems may not. By failing to reward and retain the most capable individuals in the teaching profession, our educational system may place vulnerable students in jeopardy.

Schools may further contribute to students' problems by inconsistent rules and policies. Children and adolescents who are most susceptible to emotional and behavioral disorders are best served by clearly stated rules and conditions. Although children and adolescents are reluctant to agree, they generally benefit from consistent enforcement of rules and absence of the unpredictability that often characterizes other parts of their world. By failing to provide the necessary structure and consistency, schools may contribute to emotional and behavioral disorders. One parent whose adolescent son had been labeled EBD had begged teachers and school administrators to show consistent punishment of her son's inappropriate behaviors (such as arriving significantly late to class or failing to complete his homework or in-class assignments). Her son was an attractive young man who possessed a certain amount of charisma and was frequently able to talk his way out of punishments by appealing to the novelty of the situation that created his rule infraction. Teachers continued to call home to complain of the son's behaviors but failed to recognize that by cutting him slack, not only were they were enabling him to continue his inappropriate behavior, but his behaviors were causing him to fail to earn needed credits in his classes that would allow him to graduate with his peers.

Last, school personnel may contribute to children's emotional and behavioral problems by not striving to communicate and cooperate with parents. In spite of advances in this area, teacher-parent relationships are often less than adequate. Although not totally a school problem, this issue can affect children. In instances of mistrust and absence of parent-teacher communication, children and adolescents prone to problems become more vulnerable. In the schools today, a fear of legal compliance issues and due process regulations can stifle the willingness of parents and schools to cooperate, resulting in both sides becoming wary of the other. Often, however, the schools can take a leadership role in this issue by initiating frequent informational visits with parents to make sure they know what steps the school is taking to proactively address the child's situation (not necessarily punitively, but at times that may be the case) and by keeping clear and easily interpreted records of student work, social problems, and the like. Many times, teachers could more easily make a case to parents if they had more concrete examples of the student's work or ability in an area compared with that of his peers (e.g., show both the book report of the child and also one from another child that earned an average grade). At times, parents find it easier to comprehend the problem when provided concrete illustrations rather than percentile ranks from across the country.

A final area of community influence on the emotional and behavioral problems in children is that of recreational opportunities. Towns and cities that provide adequate recreational facilities and other opportunities for young people to spend time together are most apt to foster good behavioral and emotional development. Furthermore, communities that offer adequate mental health services and counseling are best able to deal with those problems that arise in the course of everyday living. Without suitable social agencies, psychological services, and counseling programs, even minor problems may become serious. Successful examples of integrated community services that provide support to families who have children with or at risk of developing emotional and behavioral disorders will be detailed in a subsequent chapter.

SUMMARY

Identification of exact causes of emotional and behavioral disorders is complex. A variety of possible reasons exist. Although each explanation may have some validity, no single reason can be pinpointed as *the cause*.

Several genetic or biological influences seem to increase the risk of a child developing an emotional or behavioral disorder (although it bears reinforcing again that such risks do not mean that a person *will* develop an EBD). Such risk factors include inherited genetic tendency, such as ADHD, Tourette's syndrome, or schizophrenia; neurological impairments; malnutrition; and physical disabilities or chronic illnesses.

In spite of strong indications that certain parent and family conditions may contribute, either positively or negatively, to children's personality and social development, there is no clear-cut evidence that such events are the *causes* of emotional and behavioral disorders. Families that tend to influence positive emotional and behavioral growth are those who have clear and consistent expectations, have frequent communication with children, use positive reinforcement, and assist their children in learning problem-solving skills. Factors that seem to increase *risk* for development of EBD in children are inconsistent rules and punishments, frequent or harsh criticism, abuse of alcohol or other drugs by parents, imprisonment of parents, and at times, problems resulting from postdivorce situations (i.e., lack of supervision, changes to parental stress levels or depression, changes to socioeconomic situation for the child).

It must be remembered that each child's behavior is the result of a complex interaction of personality, temperament, and the various experiences that make up the environment. Given these differences, it is easy to understand why each child responds in a unique way.

By looking at our own family members and friends, we recognize that our ways of adjusting to the world are based on both biological and environmental mechanisms. Because of each person's individuality and a multitude of biological and environmental influences, it is no wonder that the causes of emotional and behavioral disorders are so difficult to identify.

REFERENCES

American Academy of Pediatrics. (1995). Separation, divorce, and the school-aged child. In E. Schor (Ed.), *Caring for your school-age child*. New York: Bantam.

Dodge, K. A. (1996). The legacy of Hobbs and Gray: Research on the development and prevention of conduct problems. *Peabody Journal of Education, 71*(4), 86–98.

Dunn, J., Deater-Deckard, D. J., Pickering, K., O'Connor, T. G., & Golding, J. (1998). Children's adjustment and prosocial behavior in step-, single-parent, and non-stepfamily settings: Findings from a community study. ALSPAC Study Team. Avon Longitudinal Study of Pregnancy and Childhood. *Journal of Child Psychology and Psychiatry, 39*(8), 1083–1095.

Erickson, M. T. (1998). Etiological factors. In T. H. Ollendick & M. Hersen (Eds.), *Handbook of child psychopathology* (3rd ed., pp. 37–61). New York: Plenum.

Gottesman, I. I., & Moldin, S. O. (1999). *Schizophrenia and genetic risks: A guide to genetic counseling for consumers, their families, and mental health workers* (2nd ed.). Arlington, VA: National Alliance for the Mentally Ill.

Grassi, L., Malacarne, P., Maestri, A., & Ramelli, E. (1997). Depression, psychosocial variables and occurrence of life events among patients with cancer. *Journal of Affective Disorders, 44*, 21–30.

Green, R. (1992). Learning to learn and the family system: New perspectives on underachievement and learning disorders. In M. J. Fine & C. Carlson (Eds.), *The handbook of family-school interventions: A systems perspective* (pp. 157–174). Boston: Allyn & Bacon.

Harboard, M. G. (2000). Significant anticonvulsant side-effects in children and adolescents. *Journal of Clinical Neuroscience, 7*, 213–216.

Hoover, D. W., & Milich, R. (1994). Effects of sugar ingestion expectancies on mother-child interactions. *Journal of Abnormal Child Psychology, 22*(4), 501–515.

Kumra, S., Wiggs, E., Krasnewich, D., Meck, J., Smith, A. C., Bedwell, J., Fernandez, T., Jacobsen, L. K., Lenane, M., & Rapoport, J. L. (1998). Brief report: Association of sex chromosome anomalies with childhood-onset psychotic disorders. *Journal of the American Academy of Child and Adolescent Psychiatry, 37*(3), 292–296.

National Alliance for the Mentally Ill. (1996). *Facts about Tourette's syndrome.* Arlington, VA: Author.

Potgieter, S. T., & Fryns, J. P. (1999). The neurobiology of autism. *Genetic Counseling,10*(2), 117–122.

Ramsey, E., & Walker, H. M. (1988). Family management correlates of antisocial behavior among middle school boys. *Behavioral Disorders, 14*, 7–14.

Wolraich, M. L., Lindgreen, S. D., Stumbo, P. J., Stegink, L. D., Appelbaum, M. I., & Kiritsy, M. C. (1994). Effects of diets high in sucrose or asperatame on the behavior and cognitive performance of children, *New England Journal of Medicine, 330*, 301–307.

Wolraich, M. L., Wilson, D. B., & White, J. W. (1995). The effect of sugar on behavior or cognition in children. A meta analysis. *Journal of the American Medical Association, 274*, 1617–1621.

Zionts, P., & Simpson, R. L. (1988). *Understanding children and youth with emotional and behavioral disorders.* Austin, TX: PRO-ED.

Evaluating and Assessing Students Who Have Emotional and Behavioral Disorders

4

Laura Zionts and Katherine deGeorge

Psychologists, psychiatrists, and educators usually determine which children and adolescents are labeled emotionally disturbed. Using methods that are often poorly understood by the public and by many teachers, these professionals attempt to identify treatment and educational plans for children and youth who require special educational and mental health programs and services. Mental health professionals and educators experience little difficulty identifying as disturbed those persons who demonstrate highly irrational or other extremely deviant behavior over an extended period of time. However, because the problems of most children and youth with emotional and behavioral problems are more subtle, the identification process tends to be complex with this group of individuals. This chapter will focus on the methods used to identify and diagnose children and adolescents with emotional and behavioral problems.

THE PURPOSE OF EVALUATION

Evaluations are rarely carried out for the sole purpose of finding out whether or not a child is disturbed. Rather, the assessment process is designed to provide information about each child's psychological and educational strengths and weaknesses and unique ways of dealing with the world as well as possible problem-solving and treatment options. Child and adolescent behavioral assessment seeks to gather information from a variety of sources that allows others to understand the child's behavior (Ollendick & King, 1999). At the same time, one of the expected outcomes of an evaluation is that a professional judgment will be made regarding a child's or adolescent's emotional and behavioral health. Thus, in addition to providing an educational and psychological understanding of a child and recommending appropriate treatment methods, mental health and educational professionals must determine if a youngster is evidencing a true emotional or behavioral problem.

Not every child or adolescent who violates school, home, or community rules or who displays behavior that is of concern to an adult has an emotional problem. Such problems may be the result of short-term troubles, normal individual differences, or a host of other factors. For example, a child whose parents worry because he does not spend enough time playing with other children could be (a) passing through a phase, (b) demonstrating a unique yet normal personality trait, or (c) showing any one of a number of normal behavior patterns. As a result of the numerous explanations for children's behavior and the subtlety of most emotional problems, mental health and school personnel are often called on to make astute emotional-fitness discriminations.

To further complicate the process, such discriminations are frequently based on imprecise measurement methods. The diagnostic methods available to psychologists and psychiatrists are sometimes poorly understood; many believe they are as much an art as a science. Such conditions may explain why it is not unusual for persons, including professionals, to disagree on the exact nature and significance of children's problems.

As indicated, evaluation of a child's personality and emotional status is not easy and seldom leads to a clear-cut conclusion about the presence of an emotional problem. Furthermore, as publicized in the media, the accuracy of such diagnostic procedures has been subjected to much criticism. In the words of some of the world's most respected mental health professionals, the evaluation process is an imperfect science. Yet in spite of their limitations, evaluations are important as a necessary step toward appropriate services. Evaluations will provide a wide variety of information about individuals, including diagnostic information and information important for intervention and treatment (Kubiszyn et al., 2000). With all of the limitations, evaluation results still provide more information about an individual's strengths and limitations and the nature of emotional problems he or she is experiencing than if no evaluation is conducted.

One of the number of reasons for conducting evaluations is to ensure that children and adolescents receive appropriate treatment and intervention. Because treatment and education plans are individualized on the basis of each child's strengths and weaknesses, they must be developed through an evaluation. Simply stated, an appropriate educational or treatment plan requires as accurate and complete assessment information as is humanly possible to gather.

Another reason to conduct psychological and behavioral evaluation is to ensure that the limited mental health and educational resources available to children and adolescents are provided to those most needing them. Yet another reason for conducting evaluations relates to the existence of normal individual differences. Simply because a child responds uniquely or fails to do something in exactly the same way as another person does not mean that he or she is emotionally disturbed. One of the benefits of assessment is that it gives a more objective report of whether or not a particular difference is psychologically significant. In his book *Welcome to the Monkey House*, Kurt Vonnegut, Jr. (1961) skillfully pointed out the reality of human differences and the absurdity of expecting everyone to look and act the same. Vonnegut wrote,

> The year was 2081, and everybody was finally equal. They weren't only equal before God and the law. They were equal every which way. Nobody was smarter than anybody else. Nobody was better looking than anybody else. All this equality was due to the 211th, 212th and 213th Amendments to the Constitution, and to the unceasing vigilance of agents of the United States Handicapper General. (p. 7)

In this excerpt, Vonnegut (1961) reminds us that differences in human characteristics and behavior are to be expected. To expect or work to achieve complete "sameness" would be absurd. Still, certain deviations may be so significant as to require professional attention. Their presence must be identified by qualified persons.

AN OVERVIEW OF EBD EVALUATION

The process of EBD evaluation is intended to provide valuable information to parents and professionals about the student's strengths and support needs. Even when a child or adolescent has been determined to have emotional or behavioral problems, it does not necessarily follow that the child or adolescent will qualify as having emotional disturbance as defined in IDEA (1997); as already mentioned, IDEA is the federal law that provides special education services for children and youth who have disabilities. McLoughlin and Lewis (2001) offer a model of assessment to guide an EBD evaluation that is built around a set of questions:

Is there a school performance problem?

IDEA specifies that if there is no educational performance problem, regardless of the presence of a disability such as EBD, then the child does not qualify for special education services. That child may still be eligible to receive educational support through Section 504 of the Rehabilitation Act of 1973 or under the Americans with Disabilities Act (ADA). However, each of these additional laws are commonly used in education settings to provide students with opportunities to learn that are equal to their peers and not negatively affected by their disabilities.

Is the school performance problem related to a disability?

Students may only receive special education services when they meet the state and federally determined definitions of disability. For EBD, the federal definition is explained in Chapter 1 of this book. Your local school or state education agency can easily provide information regarding your state definition. State definitions must coincide with the federal definition but often contain caveats or other differences.

What are the child's educational needs?

Basic school skills are assessed once it is likely that a child will meet the criteria for special education services. In addition, the relationship of the student's learning problems to the classroom demands and considerations for classroom success are considered under this question.

What types of services are required to meet those needs?

This question addresses the need to determine an educational plan for the coming year to meet the needs of the student. Long-term and short-term goals for the student's progress are determined. Also considered at this time are special factors, such as a student's need for intensive behavioral support through specific interventions (examples of these will be explained in subsequent chapters of this book). Other special considerations might be issues of culture or language or communication or medication use that might affect the educational program or might require additional support or planning. Still other topics of discussion by the multidisciplinary planning team, which includes parents, would be the need for supplementary services modifications and supports. For students who have EBD, these might include alternate transportation to and from school, an aide in the classroom, counseling services, or breaks at predetermined intervals during formal testing to relieve stress or limited attention span. Last, transition services (also discussed in depth later in this book) are determined at this point in the assessment process. Beginning at the student's age of 14, the IEP (individual education plan) team must plan for transition needs as they relate to other service agency coordination after the student completes school or employment-related supports that will be needed.

How effective is the educational program?

In the final section of this assessment model, the team examines the effectiveness of the program plan made for the student. Typically, this process is ongoing through periodic reports to parents and through faculty communication, but it culminates a minimum of one time per year at the annual IEP meeting. This evaluation phase includes examination of educational progress through the curriculum, continued need for services and supports, and modifications that need to be made to the student's educational plan in order for it to remain effective. Every 3 years or so, the student must go through a thorough evaluation process, to document that a need still exists for the student to remain part of the special education system.

SPECIFIC ASPECTS OF THE EVALUATION PROCESS AS THEY RELATE TO EBD

Screening and Child Find

The federal IDEA legislation requires each state to conduct ongoing "child find" activities: The states must actively search for and evaluate children who may have disabilities. Although most state education agencies use a variety of techniques to meet this mandate, *screening* is one such approach (McLoughlin & Lewis, 2001). Screening is the process of selecting a subset of children and adolescents from a larger population for a thorough evaluation. Screening usually takes place through a brief instrument (such as asking teachers to recommend which of all of their students have certain characteristics that are known to be associated with emotional or behavioral problems). This broad method of evaluating students is intended to flag students who teachers or parents believe should be examined in more depth to determine whether there are any significant concerns.

Other types of school-related screening that all children experience are kindergarten readiness and vision and hearing screening. In the latter example, children are screened relative to an absolute standard (for example, with vision, the standard measure used is 20/20 vision). For example, if *most* kindergarteners (say, two thirds) can zip their jackets when they enter kindergarten, then that skill may be used to determine which kindergarten candidates may be at risk for failing in that environment. However, more information would be needed about a child's other skills and abilities before a determination about his or her potential to succeed in kindergarten could be made.

A difficulty in designing effective screening devices is accuracy level. Screening that fails to accurately identify children for further study may interfere with delivery of needed services and therefore with a child's ability to succeed in his or her education. Children who have needs but who are not accurately detected by a screening instrument are called *false negatives*. That is, they needed help, but the screening instrument didn't catch them. On the other hand, procedures that select too many children and adolescents for further evaluation when it was not necessary can cause overloads—in time and resources for those professionals responsible for conducting evaluations and emotional stress for the children and their families. Children identified by screening instruments for further assessment who do not have emotional or behavioral problems are referred to as *false positives*. That is, they were thought to need help, but they didn't. Every screening process will produce a certain number of false positive and false negative identifications. The important point is to insist on using screening instruments that are as accurate as possible, balancing accuracy with expense and time efficiency.

Mental health professionals often recommend a process called *multiple-gated screening*. This is a process that often results in more accurate screening and identification. In a multigated procedure, the initial level of screening produces a subset of students who are identified from the larger school body. Once nominated by teachers or other referring professionals, a second, more detailed screening instrument is administered (called a second *gate*), perhaps a rating scale filled out by the professional about each individual already identified. After reviewing the results of the second screen for those students about whom significant concerns still remain, a third layer or gate may or may not be administered before further evaluation is conducted with the students. The intent is that the accuracy of the screening process be enhanced by multiple opportunities to weed through which students show serious signs of concern due to their behavioral excesses or deficits.

Studies have shown that teachers are very effective at identifying children and adolescents with problems significant enough to warrant assessment. For example, teacher reports of school readiness in kindergarten were predictive of difficulties with peer and teacher interaction in first grade (Wehby, Dodge, Valente, & Conduct Disorders Prevention Research Group, 1993). These individuals may occasionally use formal educational procedures to aid in the identification; however, more commonly, they rely on their own experience, observation skills, and professional intuition.

Parents can also be effective at determining if their children require professional attention. Parent reports of behavior problems at home were predictive of difficulties with peer and teacher interaction in first grade (Wehby et al., 1993). Not only do parents have more contact, relevant history, and intimate knowledge about their offspring than anybody else, they are usually more committed to securing the best possible services and programs to support their children.

Complete evaluations of these children and youth should reveal the nature of the assumed difficulties and help identify the most suitable interventions. Unlike routine medical and dental checkups, mental health evaluations are often conducted only with children and adolescents whose behavior attracts attention—usually from parents and teachers—due to excesses or deficits (Salvia & Ysseldyke, 1998). Excesses usually involve aggressiveness, impulsiveness, antisocial behavior, acting out, disruptiveness, and similar acts. In contrast, behavioral deficits, too little of a desired behavior, include social withdrawal, shyness, and timidity.

Referral for Special Education Evaluation

In an educational sense, when students have been identified through a screening process or through a teacher's formal referral, they will undergo a formal evaluation within special education. However, it should be noted that some children and adolescents may be identified first as having a form of mental illness through medical or social agency channels apart from the educational system. This chapter will focus on educational evaluation for the special education label of EBD.

When a child's teachers have attempted and documented many pre-referral interventions (changes made within the general education environment, teaching techniques, or behavioral interventions), and the child continues to struggle in the classroom, a formal referral for special education evaluation is made to the school's multidisciplinary team. That team will assemble a committee of professionals to work collaboratively with the parent(s) to determine whether the child is eligible for special education services related to EBD.

During this phase of the evaluation process, a plan is created to specifically address the individual child's abilities and the nature of the problems he or she is experiencing in the general education classroom. There are several provisions regarding special education assessment written into IDEA: It must be made using nonbiased assessments administered in the child's native language, it must be completed by trained professionals, and parents must give their consent to the assessment process and understand what tests and other information will be used and for what purposes.

Decisions About Eligibility

Professionals representing a variety of disciplines are involved in an educational evaluation. These persons may be associated with schools or mental health agencies. The following is a listing of some of these professionals along with a descripion of their roles in the assessment process.

- Psychologists: School and clinical psychologists collect and interpret information about intellectual ability, personality characteristics, academic achievement level, and perceptual and neurological strengths and weaknesses. Psychologists use tests, parent and child interviews, rating scales, and direct observation methods.

- Psychiatrists: Psychiatrists are concerned with many of the same areas as psychologists. However, psychiatrists rely more on interviews and direct observations of behavior than on tests. Because they hold medical degrees (Medical Doctor or Doctor of Osteopathy), they may prescribe medications for children, if necessary.

- Educators: Educators test academic strengths and weaknesses and conditions under which learning is best achieved. They use tests as well as observation and interview techniques.

- Social workers: Both school and psychiatric social workers perform a variety of functions. However, their primary job is to serve as a link between evaluation personnel and families, schools, and community agencies. Social workers provide other diagnostic personnel with a complete history of a given child, and they also gather relevant information from such sources as legal authorities, welfare workers, and clergy.

- Speech pathologists: These professionals are involved in evaluations only under certain circumstances. Speech pathologists use a variety of tests and procedures to determine the manner in which children receive and process language, and how children and adolescents express themselves. For example, in instances where there are no apparent speech or language problems, they may serve a minor role. In other cases, communication impairments may exacerbate behavior problems. Therefore, by strengthening speech and language abilities, some behavior problems can be greatly reduced.

- Audiologists: These professionals participate in evaluations when a child's ability to hear is questioned. Where indicated, they use a number of methods and testing procedures to assess children's ability to hear.

- Physical therapists: These professionals use tests as well as observational skills to assess physical ability and muscle control. They are most likely to participate in evaluations involving neurological or perceptual problems.

- Occupational therapists: Although there is some overlap with the same areas that physical therapists deal with, they are more concerned with assessing self-help, daily-living, and similar skills. They use both observational and testing methods.

- Medical personnel: When necessary, medical professionals—including nurses, pediatricians, neurologists, family practitioners, and optometrists—are involved in evaluations. These individuals' specialty skills add to a more thorough understanding of children and youth. Medical and psychological personnel may also be particularly helpful when a child is using medications to control behavior.

A child's problems, abilities, and behaviors can only be analyzed through a complete and comprehensive evaluation. Here, *complete* means that a variety of individuals representing several professional disciplines (e.g., psychologists, educators, and audiologists) are involved; *comprehensive* refers to the use of an array of procedures and techniques to gain a thorough understanding of a child. Multiple methods and multiple informants (people who share their opinions and experiences with the child) should be used in an evaluation. Evaluations may be carried out by either school or community personnel. Even though school personnel tend to put more emphasis on educational matters than mental health professionals do, both groups provide effective evaluations. Because both school and community professionals provide diagnostic and assessment services, it is important for these groups to work together. Evaluations should include cross-disciplinary cooperation (Gordon, 1998), which usually results in more effective understanding and treatment of emotionally and behaviorally troubled children and youth. Furthermore, it is becoming increasingly necessary for professionals from these groups to work together during evaluations due to continued changes to IDEA. For example, in the most recent reauthorization, general educators are required members of the IEP team for a child who receives services in the general education environment. That was not always the case.

EVALUATION TECHNIQUES
USED TO DETERMINE ELIGIBILITY

Many techniques and procedures may be used to assess the behavior problems of children and adolescents. Such procedures give information in the following areas: intellectual-cognitive, environmental-ecological, physical-medical, emotional, and educational. Although a number of other areas are suitable for assessment, these are considered the most significant and relevant.

Intellectual-Cognitive Ability

There are subtle and technical differences between intellectual and cognitive abilities. However, for all practical purposes, the terms are used interchangeably to refer to the mental abilities by which children and adolescents gain knowledge and interact with their world.

A variety of tests are available for assessing intelligence and cognitive ability. These tests can be divided into two general categories: group and individual scales. For the most part, group tests are pencil-and-paper scales, administered by written or oral directions by a trained examiner to a group of children or adolescents. Typically, these measures are used for large-group assessment, as might be required for induction into the military or admission to a college or university. Although group tests may be used during screening, they are rarely suited for evaluation purposes.

Individualized tests, on the other hand, are designed for use with one person at a time. These tests, which must also be administered by a professionally trained examiner, are designed to evaluate cognitive and intellectual abilities and to allow comparison between individual results and those of a group of other persons of similar age and characteristics. The comparison group is referred to as a *norm group, standardization sample,* or *standardization group.* Through the use of such standardization groups, a child can be compared on intelligence and related abilities to other children of the same age.

When placed on a graph, intelligence test scores produce a bell-shaped curve (see Figure 4.1). Imagine, for example, that all students in a school system were given an intelligence test. If their scores were placed on a graph with a baseline ranging from the highest to the lowest IQ scores and another line representing the number of students with particular scores, a large hump would appear in the middle of the curve and taper off at the ends. This bell-shaped curve simply means that the largest number of intelligence test scores would fall in the middle (average range) of the curve, whereas high and low scores would be represented at the ends. Sixty-eight percent of students would be expected to demonstrate average intellectual ability (IQs between 85–115), whereas only about 2% of those tested would score in the superior range (130 and above) or in the intellectually deficient range (IQs of 70 and below).

Intellectual Performance and EBD

Because children and adolescents with behavioral and emotional problems often have difficulty acquiring information and skills, evaluation of their intellectual abilities is important. Furthermore, intellectual ability is considered one of the best predictors of a child's overall prognosis (a prediction of future outcome). A relationship exists between a person's intelligence and his or her ability to learn (Braden, 1997). Although there are exceptions, most emotionally and behaviorally disordered children and adolescents will score lower than their nonhandicapped peers, although both groups' scores fall within the near-average range (IQs of 85–115).

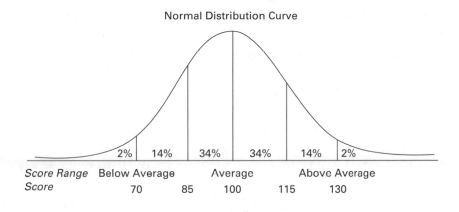

Figure 4.1   Percentage of Cases by Portion of Normal Distribution

The most widely used individualized intelligence tests are the Wechsler series. The Wechsler Preschool and Primary Scale of Intelligence-Revised (WPPSI-R; Wechsler, 1989) is designed for children between the ages of 3 years to 7 years 3 months; the Wechsler Intelligence Scale for Children-Third Edition (WISC-III; Wechsler, 1991) is aimed at children and adolescents 6 to 17; and the Wechsler Adult Intelligence Scale-Third Edition (WAIS-III; Wechsler, 1997) is aimed at individuals 17 and older. Each of these tests yields three separate IQ scores: a verbal IQ, a performance IQ, and a full-scale score (a combined verbal and performance IQ). As suggested by the name, the verbal scales focus on such areas as vocabulary, general information, and ability to understand social situations. In contrast, the performance areas do not require verbal answers but target such skills such as visual-motor coordination, nonverbal reasoning, and the ability to synthesize parts into a meaningful whole.

Professionals conducting intellectual evaluations are interested in far more than a child's mere intelligence. Type and quality of answers as well as behavioral observations, for example, are just as significant for the overall assessment. Thus, one psychologist noted that an adolescent became extremely upset whenever time demands were introduced. When asked about his behavior at a later time, the youth answered, "I don't like people telling me what to do and how much time I have to do it."

Environmental-Ecological Assessment

This assessment area covers environmental factors that influence behavior. That is, attention has shifted from influences on behavior that are a part of the child (e.g., personality and genetic history) to factors outside the child, such as parents, family, school, and other environmental conditions. An understanding of these influences provides a more thorough understanding of children and their problems.

The most frequently used means of obtaining environmental and ecological information is a parental (or legal custodian) interview. Because parents have more intimate contact with and possess relevant history about their children, they are the logical source of such information. Furthermore, parents tend to be more motivated and have more legal rights to be involved in the evaluation than anybody else. Evaluation personnel may also study community characteristics and conditions and other factors that may influence a child's behavior or attitude (e.g., presence of neighborhood youth gangs, recreational and leisure resources).

Although each parent interview will have its own emphasis and objectives, certain elements are universal. First, interviewers can be expected to begin by asking parents to share information about their child's alleged problem and the degree to which it is a concern. Parental impressions will be sought before parents are offered examples of other people's impressions of the alleged problem. This strategy is used to prevent parental responses from being tainted by others' impressions. In instances where parents make referrals, this approach rarely creates problems. That is, when parents seek assistance because of an alleged emotional or behavioral problem, they usually wish to share their perceptions. However, the situation may be different when parents are told that their child may have a problem and that an evaluation is consequently needed. Under such conditions, parents may be more interested in learning why someone considers their child to have a problem than in offering information about a condition of which they may not be aware. In situations when school personnel make the contact, for example, parents should be provided with the background of the alleged problem.

Parents should also expect to be asked about their child's developmental history during an interview. Questions will cover significant events, beginning with the mother's pregnancy and continuing to the present. In particular, emotional stress or unusual circumstances during pregnancy, delivery problems, illnesses, accidents and complications, and the age at which developmental milestones (e.g., walking, toilet training, and speech) were achieved are of primary concern. Much of this information may be obtained prior to the interview from records and from asking parents to complete a developmental history form (Sattler, 1998).

Medical and Physical Developmental History

The purpose for which developmental history is used may vary. In some instances, it may provide a useful clue to early problems or delays. In one case, information about a child's ear infections led to the diagnosis of chronic ear infection, a condition that, in turn, was related to the child's inattention, academic problems, and inability to get along with others. In other situations, developmental history allows the evaluator to rule out other types of problems. In all instances, accurate developmental information can lead to a better understanding of children.

The relationship between a person's emotional and behavioral problems and physical condition has been well documented. Problems such as malnutrition, poor health, drug or alcohol abuse or dependence, and hearing and visual disorders can contribute to emotional and behavioral problems in addition to being important considerations in the development of treatment programs. For example, one behaviorally disordered adolescent was found to have an educationally significant visual problem. The frustration of not being able to see clearly, particularly in class, caused the youngster to act out in the classroom. Once he understood the nature of his problem and started wearing glasses, the child's behavior improved dramatically.

Professionals involved in assessing physical and medical factors will be interested in a variety of things, including the following:

- Frequent school absence
- Reduced physical stamina
- Frequent headaches, pains, and other physical symptoms
- Restlessness, inattention, and evidence of boredom
- Motor control problems, including poor visual-motor coordination and body balance
- Evidence of visual problems, including rubbing of eyes, excessive blinking, inflammation, and reddened eyes
- Evidence of hearing problems, including frequent colds or upper-respiratory infection, frequent request for repetition of directions or questions, turning one ear toward the speaker, and faulty word pronunciation
- Frequent periods of crying, excessive laughter, and other strong emotional responses, especially when a situation does not warrant such behavior
- Patterns of extreme excitability or anxiety
- Depression
- Frequent unpredictable mood shifts
- Enuresis (involuntary urination) or encopresis (soiling)
- Unkempt physical appearance
- Signs of alcohol or drug abuse or dependence

Few educational and psychological scales are specifically designed to yield physical and medical information. Thus, much of the information obtained in the physical-medical area is based on observations (e.g., teacher or parent reports), interviews, clinical methods (e.g., examination by a physician or nurse), or tests designed to assess areas other than physical functioning (e.g., evidence of possible hearing impairment during intellectual testing).

Perceptual-Motor Abilities

Specific instruments are available to evaluators and evaluation teams for assessment of these skills. Some professionals consider the development of perceptual-motor abilities an essential prerequisite to school achievement and social success, so perceptual evaluation scales may be part of the evaluation. These tests are designed to determine problems in use of the senses to transmit information to the brain and to effectively use such information. The theory is that perceptual difficulties prevent children from seeing and hearing the same things as other children, thus creating social and academic problems. To test these skills, an array of scales may be used; most of them require the child to trace a maze, reproduce a geometric design or form with pencil and paper, match geometric forms, or identify partially hidden objects in a picture. In spite of the popularity of these tests, only limited validity (testing the construct that it claims to test) exists for a significant relationship between perceptual functioning and social and academic skills. Consequently, the results of these scales should be cautiously interpreted.

Physical and medical information is often of greatest value when interpreted along with other diagnostic information. This was found to be the case in the evaluation of a 14-year-old girl. During the assessment, her parents and teachers reported that she was frequently absent from school due to a variety of pains or illnesses. However, the importance of this pattern was unknown until it was learned that the teenager had recently been using alcohol to excess.

Emotional and Behavioral Functioning

The nature of emotional and behavioral evaluations varies depending on the person conducting the evaluation and the children and adolescents under study. In general, however, psychologists, educators, and other examiners use four basic methods: (a) tests, (b) observations, (c) rating scales, and (d) interviews.

Personality Tests

Two primary forms of tests are used in behavioral and emotional assessment: inventory scales and projective tests. Inventory personality scales are standardized; that is, norms have been obtained from a large number of persons, allowing evaluators to compare an individual child with other children of the same age. (The general standardization procedure described in the intelligence testing section is used.) Although most personality tests are designed for adults, a few are suitable for children and youth, including the California Test of Personality and the Minnesota Multiphasic Personality Inventory, Second Edition (MMPI-II) and the Minnesota Multiphasic Personality Inventory Adolescent Form (MMPI-A).

The California Test of Personality: The California Test of Personality is designed for both children (from kindergarten age) and adults. Five yes-no questionnaires provide scores in two major categories: personal and social adjustment. Each of these categories is divided into 6 parts, giving a score based on 12 subparts. The personal and social adjustment parts include self-reliance, sense of personal worth, sense of freedom, feeling of belonging, withdrawing tendencies, and nervous symptoms. The social adjustment sections consist of social standards, social skills, antisocial tendencies, family relations, school or occupational relations, and community relations.

Minnesota Multiphasic Personality Inventory: Although the Minnesota Multiphasic Personality Inventory is primarily designed for adults, it is normed for adolescents 14 through 17 years old. Composed of 550 statements covering a number of personality areas, MMPI-II items require a "true," "false," or "cannot say" response. Examples of items include "I like mechanics magazines" and "I find it hard to keep my mind on a task or job." The scale provides information on nine clinical scales, including Depression, Schizophrenia, and Social Introversion.

Projective Tests: Projective tests are used primarily by clinical psychologists but may also be used by some school psychologists and psychiatrists. None of these tests are standardized. Rather, they are based on the projective hypothesis that assumes that the way in which the examinee perceives and interprets test material reflects fundamental aspects of his or her personality (Rappaport, 1967). Projective techniques bring out the drives, motivations, desires, and conflicts that can affect a child's perceptual experience but that are often unconscious (Kamphaus & Frick, 1996). For some children and youth, these feelings are so disturbing that they are blocked from consciousness. To understand these unconscious feelings, therefore, projective techniques are used, usually in the form of ink blots, pictures with storytelling, drawings, and incomplete sentences to which persons must respond. Through their responses, individuals are thought to reveal their unconscious motivations and conflicts.

Projective procedures are categorized according to format. For example, *association* techniques require children to tell what they see when shown ink blots or to give the first word that comes to mind when presented a word by an examiner.

Probably the best-known association technique is the Rorschach Test. Consisting of 10 ink blots, this test is used to assess an individual's contact with reality, motivations, adaptiveness, and other personality qualities. Like other projective instruments, the Rorschach consists of ambiguous stimuli that the person under evaluation supposedly interprets according to his or her personal and emotional needs. The child being tested is instructed to tell what the blots look like, what they might be, or what they make the child think of. These spontaneous responses are followed by examiner questions regarding the location of each response and the properties that evoked them. In spite of its traditional acceptance and widespread use, the value of the Rorschach is questionable, particularly with regard to school and family problems.

Another, widely used projective test requires children and youth to create a story after being shown a picture. The Thematic Apperception Test (TAT) (Murray, 1943) consists of 31 drawings and photographs (e.g., a child staring at a violin). Certain items are designed for specific age and gender groups. Children are specifically instructed to indicate what is happening in the picture, what led up to the event, how the individuals involved felt, and how the story will turn out.

The underlying assumption of TAT and its counterpart, the Children's Apperception Test, designed for younger children, ages 3 to 10 years (Kroon, Goudena, & Rispens, 1998), is that the stories created will reveal personality qualities and conflict situations that children are otherwise unable to understand and talk about.

TAT and other projective tests are interpreted as such: Story interpretation is based on content—coherence and elaboration of the story and content—characteristics of the main character, forces in the environment, coping style, and outcomes (Kamphaus & Frick, 1996). Interpretation of responses is based on the central figure of each story, assumed to represent the child or adolescent under study. After generally characterizing the central figure of each story (e.g., hero: successful or frustrated), evaluators look for a basic and recurring theme or situation that confronts the central character. On the basis of this information, interpretations are made to identify the child's personality strengths and weaknesses and his or her ways of adjusting to the world and the people who make it up.

One 8-year-old boy who had been referred because of disobedience at home and academic and conduct problems at school repeatedly responded to the TAT cards presented to him with stories about children who were afraid of being abandoned. For example, in response to one scene, he noted, "The boy is wondering what he will do if his family puts him in an orphanage." These responses were considered significant in view of the divorce of the child's parents and placement of his stepbrothers and sisters with his father while he alone was assigned to live with his mother. As a result of this and other findings, the child was placed in a counseling program.

Another projective assessment procedure makes use of partially completed stories or sentences for which children and adolescents must form their own conclusions. One sentence-completion procedure consists of items such as, "When I am happy I . . ." "I get in trouble when . . ." "It makes me angry when . . ." and "When I grow up I want to be . . ." Particularly when combined with other information, responses such as these can provide valuable insights into personality, motivations, and conflicts.

Another projective approach requires a child to draw pictures of people or objects. This expressive form of projective testing commonly involves finger painting or drawing. For example, one frequently used method requires that children draw pictures of a person. Once the drawing, assumed to represent the child, is completed, the examiner asks questions about it. Another may ask the child to draw pictures of his or her family. Conclusions about personality and relationships are drawn on the basis of such information.

Observations

Behavioral observation methods, which sharply contrast with projective measures and other personality tests, are the most direct form of personality and behavioral evaluation. Direct observation makes no assumptions about the meaning of responses to artificial situations. Rather than attempting to determine if a child is angry and aggressive based on how he describes a picture or an ink blot, the child is directly observed in settings and at times when he might demonstrate his or her aggression.

This approach is based on the assumption that the environment in which an alleged problem occurs (e.g., home or school) is of crucial importance. Accordingly, when children and adolescents are evaluated using this method, the evaluator goes to their home, school, or other setting rather than having them come to the examiner's office.

One direct observation procedure requires that a trained observer watch a child in the classroom. Behaviors under study may include whether or not a child is attending to the assigned task or is engaged in any of several improper behaviors, including hitting or touching another pupil and being out of seat without permission. Observers watch a child for set periods of time (15–20 minutes) over several days. Although requiring substantial commitment from the persons conducting the evaluations, direct observation provides an effective and practical approach to understanding youngsters' problems.

Tests and other methods of understanding children's personality and emotional makeup are important, and so is direct observation. Indeed, we believe the most efficient way of understanding children and adolescents is to watch what they do in those settings where they are alleged to be experiencing problems. Thus, a child who is of concern because he hits and kicks other children at school without provocation will probably be best understood through direct observation, even though this method may not provide many clues to underlying dynamics involved. For this reason, parents and teachers should insist that persons conducting evaluations include direct observations in their assessment procedures.

Rating Scales

This form of assessment tool requires that someone familiar with a child or adolescent, usually a parent or teacher, evaluate their behavior using a structured form. Specifically, persons completing the forms are asked to rate children's behavior in comparison to other children or a hypothetical normal child. Ratings may take the form of "yes" or "no" responses or evaluations on particular dimensions (e.g., Does child fight with other children? never . . . occasionally . . . often . . . a great deal).

One popular behavioral rating scale, the teacher evaluation section of which is shown in Figure 4.2, is the Behavior Rating Profile. This rating scale allows information to be gathered from four sources: teachers, parents, peers, and the students themselves. Another behavior rating scale, the Behavior Assessment System for Children (BASC), includes rating scales for teachers and parents and self-report forms for children and adolescents to complete (Reynolds & Kamphaus, 1992). BASC evaluates information about adaptability, aggression, attention, conduct, depression, and social skills, for example (Reynolds & Kamphaus, 1992).

Behavioral ratings are used for evaluative purposes as well as treatment planning. That is, in addition to providing diagnostic personnel with an efficient and relatively easy method for evaluating a child's or youth's behavior, these measures can also direct the focus of treatment. For example, if a child is consistently perceived by others as being impulsive, this problem can be made a part of the treatment.

Interviewing

Interviews are designed to yield information that facilitates accurate diagnosis and treatment. Even though the content of the interview will vary depending on the focus of the person conducting the session (e.g., psychologist, educator, or psychiatrist) and the age and problems of the child or youth under study, certain basic procedures are generally followed.

(Text continues on page 74)

Figure 4.2   Teacher Rating Scale of the Behavior Rating Scale

BEHAVIOR RATING PROFILE
LINDA L. BROWN & DONALD D. HAMMILL

TEACHER RATING SCALE

Student's Name: _____

Birthdate: _____

Grade: _____

_____

Rater's Name: _____

Subject Taught: _____

School: _____

Date: _____

OTHER RELEVANT TEST SCORES:

_____

_____

_____

TEACHER'S COMMENTS AND OBSERVATION:

_____

_____

_____

_____

_____

_____

_____

_____

_____

_____

_____

_____

_____

Raw Scores may be converted into Standard Scores and Percentile Ranks by entering the table below.

Standard Score	Raw Scores for Students in Grades 1–4	5–12	Percentile Rank
1	0.4	0.2	1
2	5.11	3.10	4
3	12.17	11.28	1
4	18.27	29.31	2
5	28.31	32.37	4
6	35.45	38.46	9
7	46.56	47.51	16
8	57.64	52.58	25
9	66.71	59.65	37
10	72.78	66.69	50
11	79.84	70.76	63
12	85.87	77.82	75
13	88	83.87	84
14	89	88	91
15	90	89	96
16		90	98
17			99.1
18			99.6
19			99.9
20			99.5
M	70.6	66.2	M
SD	18.4	16.5	SD
N	387	568	N

Standard Scores Mean = 10, Standard Deviation = 3

Results:
    Raw Score _____
    Standard Score _____
    Percentile Rank _____

(Continued)

Figure 4.2 *(continued)*

INSTRUCTIONS

This behavior rating form contains a list of descriptive words and phrases. Some of these items will describe the referred student quite well. Some will not. What we wish to know is this. Which of these behaviors are you concerned about at this particular time and to what extent do you see them as problems?

Take for example item #1, "Is sent to the principal for discipline." If the child frequently is sent to the principal's office the rates might check the "Very Much Like" space. If the child is sent to the principal's office on an Infrequent but regular basis, the rates might check the "Somewhat Like" space. If the child has been sent to the principal's office on rare occasions, a check in the "Not Much Like" space might be appropriate. If the child never has been disciplined by the principal, the "Not At All Like" space would be indicated. These ratings should reflect your perceptions of the child's behavior. Please do not confer with other teachers in completing this form.

The student	Very Much Like the Student	Somewhat Like the Student	Not Much Like the Student	Not At All Like the Student
1. Is sent to the principal for discipline	☐	☐	☐	☐
2. Is verbally aggressive to teachers or peers	☐	☐	☐	☐
3. Is disrespectful of others' property rights	☐	☐	☐	☐
4. Tattles on classmates	☐	☐	☐	☐
5. Is lazy	☐	☐	☐	☐
6. Lacks motivation and interest	☐	☐	☐	☐
7. Disrupts the classroom	☐	☐	☐	☐
8. Argues with teachers and classmates	☐	☐	☐	☐
9. Doesn't follow directions	☐	☐	☐	☐
10. Steals	☐	☐	☐	☐
11. Has poor personal hygiene habits	☐	☐	☐	☐
12. Is passive and withdrawing	☐	☐	☐	☐
13. Says that other children don't like him/her	☐	☐	☐	☐
14. Can't seem to concentrate in class	☐	☐	☐	☐
15. Pouts, whines, snivels	☐	☐	☐	☐
16. Is overactive and restless	☐	☐	☐	☐
17. Is an academic underachiever	☐	☐	☐	☐
18. Bullies other children	☐	☐	☐	☐
19. Is self-centered	☐	☐	☐	☐
20. Does not do homework assignments	☐	☐	☐	☐
21. Is kept after school	☐	☐	☐	☐
22. Is avoided by other students in the class	☐	☐	☐	☐
23. Daydreams	☐	☐	☐	☐
24. Has unacceptable personal habits	☐	☐	☐	☐
25. Swears in class	☐	☐	☐	☐
26. Has nervous habits	☐	☐	☐	☐
27. Has no friends among classmates	☐	☐	☐	☐
28. Cheats	☐	☐	☐	☐
29. Lies to avoid punishment or responsibility	☐	☐	☐	☐
30. Doesn't follow class rules	☐	☐	☐	☐

Sum of Marks in Each Column =	_____	_____	_____	_____	Total Points
Multiply Sum by	X 0	X 1	X 2	X 3	Scored
Add Products	0 +	_____ +	_____ +	_____ =	_____

SOURCE: Brown, L. L., & Hammill, D. D. (1990). *Behavior rating profile, second edition (BRP-2)*. Austin: Pro-Ed.

Table 4.1   Comparison of IDEA and Section 504 of the Rehabilitation Act of 1973

Component	IDEA	Section 504
Purpose of law	Provides federal funding to states to assist in education of students with disabilities Substantive requirements attached to funding	Civil rights law Protects persons with disabilities from discrimination in programs or services that receive federal financial assistance Requires reasonable accommodations to ensure nondiscrimination
Who is protected?	Categorical approach Thirteen disability categories Disability must adversely affect educational performance	Functional approach Students (a) having a mental or physical impairment that affects a major life activity, (b) with a record of such an impairment, or (c) who are regarded as having such an impairment Protects students in general and in special education
Free and Appropriate Public Education	Special education and related services that are provided at public expense, meet state requirements, and are provided in conformity with the IEP Substantive standard is educational benefit	General or special education and related aids and services Requires a written education plan Substantive standard is equivalence
Least restrictive environment	Student must be educated with peers without disabilities to the maximum extent appropriate Removal from integrated settings only when supplementary aids and services are not successful Districts must have a continuum of placement available	School must ensure that the students are educated with their peers without disabilities
Evaluation and placement	Protection in evaluation procedures Requires consent prior to initial evaluation and placement Evaluation and placement decisions have to be made by a multidisciplinary team Requires evaluation of progress toward IEP goals annually and reevaluation at least every 3 years	Does not require consent; requires notice only Requires periodic reevaluation Reevaluation is required before a significant change in placement

(Continued)

Table 4.1 *(Continued)*

Component	IDEA	Section 504
Procedural safeguards	Comprehensive and detailed notice requirements Provides for independent evaluations No grievance procedure Impartial due process hearing	General notice requirements Grievance procedure Impartial due process hearing
Funding	Provides for federal funding to assist in the education of students with disabilities	No federal funding
Enforcement	U.S. Office of Special Education Programs (can cut off IDEA funds) Compliance monitoring by state educational agency	Complaint can be filed with Office of Civil Rights (can cut off all federal funding) Complaints can be filed with state's department of education

Source: Adapted from Yell (1997).

The information provided by children or adolescents can be predictive indicators of emotional and behavioral problems (McConaughy & Achenbach, 1996). Sessions may focus on many of the same areas as the parent interview. For example, children and adolescents may be asked to describe their problems, the causes of the reported difficulties, and their own feelings and those of their parents about these issues. Youngsters may also be encouraged to discuss their developmental history and personality traits; attitudes toward home, school, friends, and family; leisure-time activities; and likes and dislikes. Special attention may be paid to descriptions of their relationships with peers and school personnel and their academic successes and failures. Last, youngsters may be encouraged to discuss their personal goals and those of their parents for them and to describe their home and family life. In this connection, interviewers focus on differences between the responses of children and youth and those of their parents, teachers, and others. Such information will be considered in combination with other diagnostic data.

Consideration of Academic Abilities

Differences between children's or adolescents' intellectual abilities and their academic achievement rank among the best indicators of significant behavioral or emotional problems. Furthermore, since school-age emotionally and behaviorally disturbed youngsters almost always have significant academic problems, these difficulties must be identified and understood so that suitable remediation programs can be planned. Assessment of academic skills and abilities, therefore, must be a part of the overall evaluation, including classroom records and grades, and results of group tests and individualized academic measures (e.g., reading, math, spelling, language).

Decisions About Eligibility

If it is determined that a student has an emotional or behavioral disorder, certain laws and regulations come into effect to protect the student's rights. Three specific laws exist that help and protect individuals with disabilities. They are the Americans with Disabilities Act 1990 (ADA), the Individuals with Disabilities Education Act 1997 (IDEA), and Section 504 of the Rehabilitation Act of 1973. The purpose of ADA is to prohibit discrimination solely on the basis of a disability in employment, public services, and accommodations (Henderson, 1995). In educational settings, the student's "job" has been interpreted as participating in school. ADA also applies to child care settings (e.g., a child with a disability who bites others must be accommodated rather than dismissed from the setting; playground equipment must be made accessible to children who have disabilities).

The purpose of IDEA is to provide federal funding to state and local education agencies (school districts) to guarantee special education and related services to eligible students with disabilities (Henderson, 1995). If a student is identified and then labeled by an IEP committee as emotionally disturbed (ED), then IDEA provides safeguards and regulations to protect the student. Under IDEA, students who have ED are entitled to instructional support and numerous education-related services, including psychological counseling and differentiated discipline when violations are directly related to the student's emotional disturbance.

Section 504 is a civil rights law to prohibit discrimination on the basis of disability in programs and activities, public and private, that receive federal money (Henderson, 1995). IDEA maintains that to qualify, the child's disabling condition (documented by the multidisciplinary committee) "significantly interferes with the student's educational progress." If it does not, then the child does not qualify for special education services. Section 504 is commonly used in educational settings to protect students who have disabilities when a multidisciplinary team *cannot* document that the disabling condition is significantly interfering with educational progress. This law provides students with many similar accommodations as IDEA, such as modified assignments or untimed tests. It differs from special education, for example, in that students cannot receive instruction in the special education classroom. However, some students who are in need of additional instructional support are able to receive assistance through Title I reading programs or other programs designated for at-risk learners.

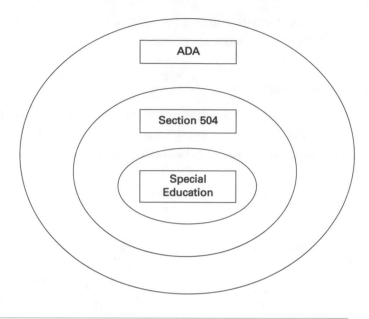

Figure 4.3   The Relationship Between ADA, Section 504, and IDEA.

Each of these laws protects different individuals, determines services provided, and has procedural safeguards, evaluation and placement procedures, and due process. Table 4.1 summarizes the aspects of each law that pertain most directly to children and youth with behavior disorders.

SUMMARY

Assessment is a significant part of meeting the needs of behaviorally disordered and emotionally disturbed children and adolescents. Even though personality and overall mental health is complex and difficult to evaluate, suitable and reasonably effective tests and procedures are available for this purpose. With skillful application of such methods, children and adolescents requiring professional attention can be identified and receive appropriate treatment.

REFERENCES

Americans with Disabilities Act of 1990, Pub. L. No. 101–336, §2, 104 Stat. 328 (1991).

Braden, J. P. (1997). The practical impact of intellectual assessment issues. *School Psychology Review, 26,* 242–248.

Gordon, M. (1998). Compare and Contrast. *Journal of Learning Disabilities, 31,* 613–614.

Henderson, K. (1995). A review of ADA, IDEA, and Section 504. *ERIC Digest E537.*

Individuals with Disabilities Education Act of 1997, Pub. L. No. 105–17, 20 U.S.C., Ch. 33, §§1400–1491.

Kamphaus, R. W., & Frick, P. J. (1996). *Clinical assessment of child and adolescent personality and behavior.* Boston: Allyn & Bacon.

Kroon, N., Goudena, P. P., & Rispens, J. (1998). Thematic apperception tests for children and adolescent assessment: A practitioner's consumer guide. *Journal of Psychoeducational Assessment, 16,* 99–117.

Kubiszyn, T. W., Meyer, G. J., Finn, S. E., Eyde, L. D., Kay, G. G., Moreland, K. L., Dies, R. R., & Eisman, E. J. (2000). Empirical support for psychological assessment in clinical health care settings. *Professional Psychology: Research and practice, 31,* 119–130.

McConaughy, S. H., & Achenbach, T. M. (1996). Contributions of a child interview to multimethod assessment of children with EBD and LD. *School Psychology Review, 25,* 24–39.

McLoughlin, J. A., & Lewis, R. B. (2001). *Assessing Students with Special Needs* (5th ed.). Upper Saddle River, NJ: Merrill.

Murray, H. A. (1943). *Thematic apperception test.* Cambridge, MA: Harvard University Press.

Ollendick, T. H., & King, N. J. (1999). Child behavioral assessment and cognitive-behavioral interventions in schools. *Psychology in the Schools, 36,* 427–436.

Rappaport, D. (1967). Principles underlying projective techniques. In M. M Gill (Ed.), *Collective papers of David Rappaport* (pp. 91–97). New York: Basic Books. (Original work published 1942)

Rehabilitation Act of 1973, 29 U.S.C. §794, Sec. 504.

Reynolds, C. R., & Kamphaus, R. W. (1992). *Behavior assessment system for children (BASC).* Circle Pines, MN: American Guidance Services.

Salvia, J., & Ysseldyke, J. E. (1998). *Assessment* (7th ed.). Boston: Houghton Mifflin.

Sattler, J. M. (1998). *Clinical and forensic interviewing of children and families: Guidelines for the mental health, education, pediatric, and child maltreatment fields.* San Diego, CA: Author.

Vonnegut, K. (1961). *Welcome to the monkey house.* New York: Dell.

Wechsler, D. (1989). *Wechsler preschool and primary scale of intelligence-Revised.* San Antonio, TX: Psychological Corp.

Wechsler, D. (1991). *Wechsler intelligence scale for children* (3rd ed.). San Antonio, TX: Psychological Corp.

Wechsler, D. (1997). *Wechsler adult intelligence scale* (3rd ed.). San Antonio, TX: Psychological Corp.

Wehby, J., Dodge, K. A., Valente, E., Jr., & Conduct Disorders Prevention Research Group. (1993). School behavior of first grade children identified as at risk for development of conduct problems. *Behavioral Disorders, 19,* 67–78.

Yell, M. L. (1997). *The law and special education.* Upper Saddle River, NJ: Prentice Hall.

Violence and Aggression in Schools

5

Sara Sibilsky and Paul Zionts

S everal tragedies in communities previously regarded as safe, such as West Paducah, Kentucky; Jonesboro, Arkansas; and, of course, Littleton, Colorado, have served to bring the issue of violence in our schools into the spotlight. Aggression and violence in schools seem to be on the lips of legislators, the general public, and school personnel alike. It is interesting that these concerns seem to contradict reports that indicate a decrease in school violence in recent years (Brooks, Schiraldi, & Ziedenberg, 2000; U.S. Department of Justice, 1999). Regardless, schools have developed policies and practices involving the management of students exhibiting aggressive and violent behaviors. Such policies and practices have major implications for the education of children and adolescents with EBD.

VIOLENCE AND AGGRESSION IN THE SCHOOLS

We distinguish between violence and aggression that occur in the general community and that which occurs in schools. We define those acts that result in significant harm or injury as *violent behavior*, as opposed to *aggression*, which, although serious and may continue over time, does not result in significant injury. Whether student behavior is considered aggressive or violent, communities and schools are called on to take a serious look at the behaviors of the students for whom they are responsible.

Juvenile crime has long been an issue for communities throughout our country. It is interesting that current crime statistics illustrate an overall decline in juvenile crime. In the years between 1973 and 1989, the rate of serious violence by juveniles (including robbery, aggravated assaults, and incidents involving rape and other sexual assaults) remained fairly stable (Snyder & Sickmund, 1999). However, beginning in the late 1980s, there was a dramatic increase in crime arrest rates for violent juvenile offenders. This increase led to a peak in 1994 (Snyder, 2000) before a dramatic decline thereafter. In fact, in 1999, the arrest rate for juvenile violence was the lowest in the decade (Snyder, 2000).

Formalized schooling has always required that school personnel provide discipline and manage student behavior. However, in recent decades, school discipline issues have increasingly involved behaviors that can be described as aggressive or violent. In this case, schools are *not* necessarily a microcosm of society. The U.S. Department of Justice (1999) reported the nature of crime to be far more serious and the likelihood of victimization greater (for students ages 12 through 18) while students are away from school. In fact, high school principals reported that the three most serious in-school problems were tardiness, absenteeism, and tobacco chewing (Barton, Coley, & Wenglinsky, 1998). It is interesting that these data present a stark contrast to the apparent perceptions of the general public.

Brooks et al. (2000) cited two studies that clearly illustrate declines in school-related aggression and violence between 1993 and 1997. The first study, conducted jointly by the Bureau of Justice Statistics and the National Center for Education Statistics, indicated that

- The total number of reported school crimes *declined* 29%.
- The total number of serious violent crimes *declined* 34%.
- The total number of violent crimes (including fighting) *declined* 27%.
- The total number of thefts *declined* 29% (Brooks et al., 2000, p. 9).

The second was conducted by the Centers for Disease Control. This study indicated that

- Student reports of physical fights on and off school grounds *decreased* by 14%.
- There was a 9% *decline* in students who reported being in a physical fight on school grounds.
- Student reports of being injured in a physical fight on and off school grounds *decreased* by 20%.
- Student self-reports of carrying a weapon in the previous 30 days *decreased* by 30%.
- There was a 25% decline in students who reported carrying a gun to school in the previous 30 days (Brooks et al., p. 8).

Although *most* crime in school is related to theft (U.S. Department of Justice, 1999), school homicide continues to generate greater public interest. Yet information in *The Annual Report on School Safety* (U.S. Department of Justice, 1999) indicated that homicides in school are extremely rare events. This report noted that of the more than 2,500 children across the nation who were victims of homicide or suicide between July 1997 and December 1997, less than 1% were victims while engaged in school or a school-related event.

Although the overall number of school-associated violent deaths has decreased, the number of homicide events involving *multiple victims* at school has increased. *The Annual Report on School Safety* (U.S. Department of Justice, 1999) reported that at least one multiple-victim homicide has occurred each year since the 1992–93 school year, with the exception of 1993–94.

Subsequently, events of school-associated violent death of this magnitude are imprinted into the minds of the American public through intensified media coverage. This has been exacerbated by the deaths of students in middle-class white communities. Such an outcry has not been heard regarding the deaths of students of color who reside in inner-city environments.

It is interesting that, as evidenced by data from self-reports, race and ethnicity have little influence on the overall proportion of nonfatal violent behavior despite the racial and ethnic differences in homicide arrest rates (Office of the Surgeon General, 2001). However, in spite of the recent multiple shootings involving suburban, middle-class white schools, those who continue to face the greatest risk of becoming victims or perpetrators of in-school violence are African American and Hispanic males who attend large inner-city schools serving extremely poor neighborhoods (Office of the Surgeon General, 2001).

In *The Annual Report on School Safety*, the U.S. Department of Justice (1999) detailed crime statistics involving teachers. These data indicated that, similar to students, most crime against teachers is theft related. It was reported that, on average, each year from 1993 to 1997, teacher-related school crime translated into a rate of 53 thefts for every 1,000 teachers in contrast to a rate of 31 violent crimes for every 1,000 teachers.

Regardless of the decline in incidence, problems with aggression and violence do exist in our schools. Many of the problems between students often originate outside of the schools but are brought to school grounds where they are likely to erupt (Guetzloe, 1995). In effect, more than half of all public schools have reported crimes on their premises (Barton et al., 1998). To this end, schools have a primary responsibility for ensuring student and staff safety. The Council for Children with Behavior Disorders (CCBD) and the Council of Administrators of Special Education (CASE) noted the requirement by state and federal law that school officials guarantee a safe and comfortable environment in which students can learn (CCBD/CASE, 1995). Unfortunately, this guarantee has done little to alleviate students' fears of school violence. Between 1989 and 1995, there was a 5% increase in the percentage of students (ages 12–19) who feared attack while traveling to and from school and a 3% increase in the percentage of students who feared they were going to be attacked or harmed at school (U.S. Department of Justice, 1998). According to Barton (2000), approximately 1 eighth grader in 10 feels unsafe in school, and students of Hispanic origin feel more unsafe in school than do students of white or African American origin. As educators, we know that students learn best in environments free of fear-related emotional stress and that the physical, psychological, and emotional well-being of students and staff is jeopardized by events of violence (National Association of School Psychologists, 1996). Consequently, it is critical for schools to increase efforts in improving the school environment so that students and staff feel a sense of security and comfort and the opportunities for teaching and learning are maximized.

Whether the data presented is perceived as encouraging or disheartening, events of aggression and violence continue in our schools. Not one newspaper article, TV report, chapter, or entire book can sufficiently capture the true and lasting *effects* of school violence. School personnel, students, parents, whole communities, victims, and perpetrators are each affected in a way that is never fully visible to the rest of the world.

THE ROOTS OF VIOLENT AND AGGRESSIVE BEHAVIORS IN CHILDREN AND ADOLESCENTS

Several theories pose explanations for violent and aggressive behaviors. These theories typically relate to *internal* influences, also referred to as *predisposing factors*, which are emotional difficulties, cognitive deficits, deficits in social skills, and so forth, and *external* influences, also referred to as *precipitating factors*, which include family stressors, abuse, neglect, exposure to violence, and so on (see Chapter 1 for further explanation of predisposing and precipitating factors). Theorists seem to agree that the origin of violent and aggressive behaviors cannot be pinpointed to one single factor.

In a 2-year study by the Office of Juvenile Justice and Delinquency Prevention's Study Group on Serious and Violent Juvenile Offenders, researchers examined current research related to risk and protective factors and the development of serious and violent criminal careers (Hawkins et al., 2000). Their research yielded the following factors that are predictive of youth violence. The list is organized into five domains related to the individual, family, school, peers, and neighborhood or community.

1. Factors Related to the Individual

- Stress during pregnancy or complications during delivery (Guetzloe, 1995; Hawkins et al., 2000; Verlinden, Hersen, & Thomas, 2000)
- Low resting heart rate (Hawkins et al., 2000; Verlinden et al., 2000)
- Internalizing disorders (Hawkins et al., 2000)
- Disorders that are neurophysiological, cognitive, or psychiatric in nature (Guetzloe, 1995; Walker, Colvin, & Ramsey, 1995)
- Hyperactivity, concentration problems, restlessness, and risk taking (Hawkins et al., 2000)
- Impulsivity, irritability, and hypervigilance (Guetzloe, 1995)
- Aggressive behavior (Hawkins et al., 2000)
- Initiation of violent behavior early in child's life (Hawkins et al., 2000)
- Involvement in other forms of antisocial behavior (Hawkins et al., 2000)
- Beliefs and attitudes approving of deviant or antisocial behavior (Hawkins et al., 2000)
- Victimization by others (Guetzloe, 1995)
- Reinforcement of violent and aggressive behaviors (Guetzloe, 1995)

2. Factors Related to the Family

- Family poverty or homelessness (Guetzloe, 1995; Walker et al., 1995)
- Inadequate family management (Hawkins et al., 2000)
- Poor discipline methods (i.e., limited supervision, physical punishment, child mistreatment; Guetzloe, 1995; Hawkins et al., 2000; Verlinden et al., 2000; Walker et al., 1995)
- Parental noninvolvement (Guetzloe, 1995; Hawkins et al., 2000; Verlinden et al., 2000)
- Poor bonding within the family and family conflict (Hawkins et al., 2000; Verlinden et al., 2000)
- Parental attitudes favorable to substance use and violence (Hawkins et al., 2000)
- Parental substance abuse (Guetzloe, 1995; Walker et al., 1995)
- Exposure to violence among family members (Guetzloe, 1995)
- Delinquent siblings (Hawkins et al., 2000)
- Criminality in family members (Guetzloe, 1995; Hawkins et al., 2000)
- Separation of parent and child (Hawkins et al., 2000)

3. Factors Related to School

- Academic failure (Hawkins et al., 2000)
- Weak bonding to school (Hawkins et al., 2000)
- Truancy and dropping out of school (Hawkins et al., 2000)
- School transitions on a frequent basis (Hawkins et al., 2000)

4. Factors Related to Peers

- Delinquent peers (Hawkins et al., 2000)
- Gang involvement or membership (Guetzloe, 1995; Hawkins et al., 2000)

5. Factors Related to Community

- Poverty (Hawkins et al., 2000; Verlinden et al., 2000)
- Disorganization with the community (Hawkins et al., 2000; Verlinden et al., 2000)
- Accessibility of drugs or weapons (Guetzloe, 1995; Hawkins et al., 2000; Verlinden et al., 2000)
- Neighborhood adults involved in crime (Hawkins et al., 2000)
- Racial prejudice or conflict (Guetzloe, 1995; Hawkins et al., 2000)
- Sociocultural expectations (expectations of family, community, and neighborhood or society; Guetzloe, 1995)
- Exposure to violence (Guetzloe, 1995; Hawkins et al., 2000; Walker et al., 1995)
- Violence exposure through the media (Guetzloe, 1995; Verlinden et al., 2000)

The extent to which each of these factors is involved in the development of violent or aggressive behaviors is unknown. Bronfenbrenner's (1979) Theory of Social Ecology offers clarity to this issue, as many of these factors are interrelated and interdependent. Moreover, it is through the complex interactions of these factors that we find one child who develops an EBD and another who may not. Why one does and the other doesn't is still perplexing to both parents and professionals. Mental health research conducted by national organizations, such as the National Institutes of Health, the Office of Juvenile Justice, and the Office of Special Education and Rehabilitative Services, will help to better understand the intricacies involved in understanding and predicting the problems of children and youth who show violent and aggressive tendencies. For example, Shubert, Bressette, Deeken, and Bender (1999) analyzed five highly publicized multiple school shootings that occurred in a 1-year period and found the following commonalities:

- All perpetrators were male, with some degree of alienation from others.
- All demonstrated some emotional difficulties that were obvious to their peers.
- All demonstrated a declining respect for life.
- All provided warnings of violence.
- Firearms were easily accessible to all (p. 100).

The problems of disconnectedness, emotional difficulties, distorted attitudes, and accessibility to weapons are evident in all of these cases. It would seem that serious consideration must be given to these factors for future study.

Clearly, the causality for violent and aggressive behaviors can be linked to myriad factors. Although we may not be able to pinpoint the exact etiology of particular aggressive or violent acts, we can be assured that violence is seldom truly random and lacking signals to warn us of impending difficulties and danger. Dwyer and Osher (2000), in cooperation with the U.S. Department of Education, developed a document that presents practical strategies to help educators create safe schools through community building; schoolwide planning; effective behavioral supports; and early intervention, prevention, and treatment with troubled students. Critical to early intervention is recognition of the following signs that serve as a warning to potentially aggressive and violent behavior:

- Social withdrawal
- Excessive feelings of rejection
- Being a victim of violence
- Feelings of being picked on and persecuted
- Low school interest and poor academic performance
- Expression of violence in writings and drawings
- Uncontrolled anger
- Patterns of impulsive and chronic hitting, intimidating, and bullying behaviors
- History of discipline problems
- History of violent and aggressive behavior
- Intolerance for differences and prejudicial attitudes
- Drug use and alcohol use
- Affiliation with gangs
- Inappropriate access to, possession of, and use of firearms
- Serious threats of violence (an imminent warning sign) (p. 17)

For a thorough description of these warning signs, readers should refer to the action guide. It should be mentioned that because all behavior is essentially an intent to communicate, we must carefully interpret these communications. There is a narrow path between responding to signs of a student who is in serious danger of hurting self or others and overreacting or labeling in a way that will be harmful to the student (Dwyer & Osher, 2000). Five principles are suggested for interpreting early warning signs: "do no harm, understand violence and aggression within a context, avoid stereotypes, view warning signs within a developmental context and understand that children typically exhibit multiple warning signs" (p. 18). These principles are not intended to be exhaustive; rather, they are intended as guidelines to assist in developing strategies for reaching students who exhibit potentially harmful behaviors. Dwyer and Osher also presented a list of *imminent warning signs*, to be considered as such:

- Serious physical fighting with peers or family members
- Severe destruction of property
- Severe rage for seemingly minor reasons
- Detailed threats of lethal violence
- Possession or use of firearms and other weapons
- Other self-injurious behaviors or threats of suicide (p. 19)

None of these behaviors should ever be ignored. All warrant immediate attention. Students exhibiting any of these behaviors should be considered at high risk for endangering self or others, and planned crisis intervention should be promptly enacted.

Notwithstanding their association to aggression and violence, the risk factors discussed in this chapter are also linked to *school achievement* and to difficulties in the physical, social, emotional, and mental health development of our children. Any and all of these factors may interfere with school success. We believe that schools and communities need to develop programs and services that enable students to fully benefit from their educational and life experiences despite the risk factors brought with them to school.

VIOLENCE, AGGRESSION, AND EBD

As we have discussed, our working definition suggests that aggression does not result in significant injury even though it may be serious and may take place over a long period of time. Individuals may demonstrate aggression as an isolated behavior or within the context of several behaviors commonly referred to as *antisocial behavior*. According to Walker et al. (1995), antisocial behaviors include "hostility to others, aggression, a willingness to commit rule infractions, defiance of adult authority, and violation of the social norms and mores of society" (p. 2). Most students who have been identified as antisocial are characteristically aggressive with violent tendencies (Rutherford & Nelson, 1995). In school, a student with antisocial behaviors might show disregard for classroom and school rules or policies, challenge adults (especially those in authority positions, such as teacher or principal), bully his or her peers, and engage in verbal and physical aggression toward others. When a pattern of antisocial behavior continues into adulthood, it is often referred to as an Antisocial Personality Disorder.

Antisocial behavior patterns are the foundation for the *clinical diagnosis* of Conduct Disorder. Conduct disorders are characterized by aggression toward people and animals, destruction of property, deceitfulness or theft, and serious violation of rules (American Psychological Association [APA], 2000). In school settings, antisocial behavior and conduct disorder are typically referred to as *social maladjustment* by educators (Walker et al., 1995). Students with social maladjustment may challenge authority, break school rules, and engage in behavior that is destructive to others in our schools. Debate continues related to the issue of providing special education support to students identified as having a conduct disorder or social maladjustment. In fact, most students with these identifications are typically excluded from services provided by special education. They are entitled to nonspecial education services and accommodations under Section 504 of the Rehabilitation Act. According to *DSM-IV-TR* of the APA (2000), there has been an increase in the prevalence of conduct disorder during the past 10 years from less than 1% to more than 10%, as derived from general population studies. Aggressive behaviors are often characteristic of students with EBD and those who have conduct disorders. Unfortunately, little research exists that describes in detail the nature and extent of specific aggressive behavior within school settings despite the serious impact it has on the lives of the students with EBD and others around them (Wehby & Symons, 1996).

Antisocial behaviors are not likely to decrease without intervention. Therefore, it is essential that both the community and the school work to address such behaviors to prevent potential graduation to more serious, violent behavior. Walker (1993) suggested early intervention as critical for breaking the pattern of antisocial behavior. He further indicated that antisocial behavior could be managed, much like diabetes or other chronic conditions where the treatment involves regulated, quality intervention (Walker, 1993). Practices related to early intervention and treatment, parent training, home-school communication and coordination of behavior supports, academic and social skill instruction needed for school success, and peer and teacher mentors have been found as key elements necessary for providing comprehensive service to students with antisocial behaviors (Walker, 1993).

There appears to be a misconception about who is perpetrating the violent and aggressive acts in our schools. Many people seem to believe that students with disabilities (especially those with EBD) are primarily responsible for such acts. Perhaps this belief stems from recent efforts to increase the integration of students with disabilities into general education settings. Or perhaps this is due to the overrepresentation of students with disabilities who are suspended or expelled from school. At any rate, the Council of Administrators of Special Education and the Council for Children with Behavior Disorders (1995) attempted to address this misconception by asserting, "The majority of the violent, aggressive or destructive students in American Schools are NOT students receiving special education, but rather, students whose behavior may be incidental to a particular emotional crisis" (p. 2). They go on to say, "Most students who have cognitive, emotional, social or behavioral disabilities are effectively managed and taught through their special education interventions, and as such, rarely exhibit violent behavior that places them and those around them in danger of harm" (p. 2).

In truth, there isn't any evidence to suggest that incidents of school violence are likely to be committed by students who have EBD. Previously, we mentioned that Shubert et al. (1999) analyzed five recent and highly publicized cases of school shootings. They found that in each case, the perpetrator (although indicated as having "emotional or peer-relation difficulties" and other problems that we may associate with EBD) was not receiving special education services. They further concluded that there is no correlation indicated between the attendance of special education students in a school and an amplified danger of random violence.

However, despite the lack of data suggestive of a connection between school aggression and violence and special education students, we cannot assert that the students doing the harm in our schools do not have EBD. Clearly, these students did have problems as they behaved in such extremely antisocial ways. Perhaps these students were not yet identified and could have been helped by a special education intervention. Perhaps if these students had not fallen through the proverbial cracks, their problems may have been appropriately addressed.

RESPONSES TO SCHOOL VIOLENCE AND AGGRESSION

A National Perspective

Legislators, policymakers, and other key governmental figures are becoming involved in the fight against community and school violence. Legislation is being proposed to deal with students who are aggressive. In many cases, the legislation attempts to exclude students from school, leaving them with no access to help. As mentioned earlier, the U.S. Department of Education has published documents addressing this issue.

Innovative programs are being developed to address the issue of school violence and aggression. For example, the American Psychological Association, as part of its public education campaign, collaborated with MTV (Music Television) to communicate information regarding the warning signs of violent behavior (Zabriskie, 1999). This effort yielded several different products: A 30-minute documentary on youth and violence was presented as part of MTV's "True Life" series (aired several times during April 1999), nationwide presentations by psychologists on the topic of violence to youth, and the publication of a guide titled *Warning Signs*.

The nation has begun to take a serious look at aggression and violence in schools. A report on youth violence by the Office of the Surgeon General (2001) investigated factors leading to violent behaviors and identified several effective, research-based strategies that are preventative in nature. And there are increasing numbers of organizations, professionals, and policymakers who are placing this issue at the forefront of their agendas. Even though the rates of aggression and violence have stabilized or decreased, the efforts must continue.

A Local Perspective

Local districts have responded to school violence in various ways. These include increased or improved school security measures, teacher training, and the development of school policies that specifically address violent and aggressive behaviors, assessment procedures of early identification of antisocial and dangerous behaviors, and prevention programs. Such responses have generally resulted in positive outcomes.

However positive, each has implications for students with disabilities, and unfortunately, many schools have neglected to account for such implications during the planning and implementation of these responses. Most policies do not take into account the needs of students with disabilities. Historically, this problem was exemplified in the 1988 case of *Honig v. Doe*, in which two students with EBD were expelled by the San Francisco Unified School District for demonstrating disruptive and violent behavior (Turnbull & Turnbull, 2000). This case, decided in the Supreme Court, clearly established that negative behaviors determined to be a manifestation of a disabling condition must be given special consideration in matters involving school disciplinary procedures. In the *Honig v. Doe* case, the two students who were expelled were found to exhibit behaviors caused by their disabilities. Disabilities that contribute to impaired cognitive, behavioral, and social functioning obviously put students at a disadvantage in school systems where there are rigid standards and consequences for misbehavior applied on a universal basis. Fortunately, current IDEA provisions clearly specify disciplinary procedures for students with disabilities that protect both the student and others within the school. Moreover, IDEA strongly encourages the use of management strategies that are proactive in nature (functional assessment, behavioral intervention) when addressing student misconduct (Turnbull & Turnbull, 2000). Essentially, this means that teachers and school administration plan for effective and appropriate management of students with EBD to avoid unnecessary disciplinary procedures that may be counterproductive to the education of the student.

Some schools are adopting a zero-tolerance stance. According to Skiba and Peterson (2000), there has been a dramatic increase in the establishment of zero-tolerance policies. These policies attempt to send a message that certain behaviors will not be tolerated under any circumstances, regardless of severity, and that such behaviors will warrant severe punishment (Skiba & Peterson, 1999). Although aimed at improving misbehavior, zero tolerance advocates a one-size-fits-all approach to dealing with student misbehavior (Brooks et al., 2000). This seems to violate the intent and spirit of the special education law regarding, among other principles, IEPs. It is important to note that school disorder was not reduced nor academic performance improved through zero-tolerance policy (Barton et al., 1998). There is a lack of data suggesting that school violence is reduced through the use of zero-tolerance policies. In fact, there is some evidence that suggests particular strategies may generate emotional harm or promote student dropout (Skiba & Peterson, 1999). A critical question becomes, "to what extent will zero-tolerance effects promote additional damage in students already experiencing emotional difficulties from mental illness, disturbance, and so forth?" If we believe that each student presents unique instructional and behavioral challenges, then most certainly, a one-size-fits-all approach would be ineffective and potentially harmful for students with EBD. It is our belief that zero incidence of violence and aggression in schools is desirable, but the extreme and rigid measures by which all students receive consequences, regardless of specific behavior, is inappropriate and illegal. Unfortunately, there have been examples of overreactions to zero tolerance. They include the following (Brooks et al., 2000):

In Ponchatoula, Louisiana, a 12-year-old who had been diagnosed with a hyperactive disorder warned the kids in the lunch line not to eat all the potatoes, or "I'm going to get you." The student, turned in by the lunch monitor, was expelled for two days. He was then referred to police by the principal, and the police charged the boy with making "terroristic threats." He was incarcerated for 2 weeks while awaiting trial (p. 23).

In Palm Beach, Florida, a 14-year-old disabled student was referred to the principal's office for allegedly stealing $2 from another student. The principal referred the child to the police, where he was charged with strong-armed robbery and held for 6 weeks in an adult jail for this, his first arrest. When the local media criticized the prosecutor's decision to file adult felony charges, he responded, "depicting this forcible felony, this strong-arm robbery, in terms as though it were no more than a $2 shoplifting fosters and promotes violence in our schools." The prosecution dropped charges when a *60 Minutes II* crew showed up at the boy's hearing (p. 24).

Alternatives to zero tolerance are programs such as Effective Behavior Support (EBS). EBS is a system of proactive, positive behavior support for *all* students. In essence, EBS provides a continuum of positive behavioral support (PBS) that recognizes the unique needs of each student. Lewis and Sugai (1999) describe the three broad levels of implementation as follows: At the first level, schoolwide management strategies provide *universal group behavior support* to meet the needs of the majority of students. At the second level, *specialized group behavior interventions* are provided for students who present critical risk factors (i.e., limited family or community supports, low academic achievement). At the third level, *specialized individual behavior support* targets those students for whom universal and group supports haven't been beneficial and who continue to demonstrate challenging behavior. Positive behavior supports are integral to programs aimed at managing student behavior (see Chapter 7 for a further discussion of PBS).

Another response by schools is heavy reliance on the juvenile justice system for management of students who demonstrate violent and aggressive behaviors. This growing reaction to direct misbehaviors that previously had been resolved in the principal's office is perhaps in response to the "post 'school shooting' world" (Brooks et al., 2000, p. 23).

This reaction has major implications for all students and especially students with EBD. The consequences are twofold. First, the message that is sent to these students is that the school is no longer willing to provide adequate support and care for them. This message may not be legal. A school that defers the misbehavior of a student with EBD to juvenile justice in lieu of providing appropriate behavioral intervention would be analogous to a school that refused to let a student who has paraplegia use a wheelchair.

Second, given IDEA (1997) provisions, intentional planning with regard to justice system involvement and exclusionary practices (i.e., suspension or expulsion) must take place to ensure due process for students with disabilities. This is not to say that juvenile justice services do not belong as a last-resort option for schools. Rather, we must develop collaborative partnerships with such community resources to enhance overall service provision to our students with disabilities (Chapter 9 further explores the relationship between the juvenile justice system and schools).

Remember, IDEA (1997) provides protections for students involved in school disciplinary incidents. Inherent to this process is the determination of the cause of the student misconduct. An IEP team (which includes the parents) must consider whether a student's misconduct is a manifestation of his or her disability when considering whether (a) the student's IEP and placement were appropriate, (b) the student understood the impact and consequences of his or her behavior, and (c) the student could control his or her behavior (Turnbull & Turnbull, 2000). If any of these conditions is not met, then the IEP team must conclude that the misbehavior was a manifestation of the student's disability and proceed according to disciplinary actions as outlined in IDEA.

Schools must have intentional, well-planned, and appropriate measures by which to assess students with (or at risk for) EBD as well as provide best-practice programs and services to meet their needs. Both reduction and prevention outcomes are more likely to occur when appropriate and effective academic and behavioral supports are provided.

REDUCING AND PREVENTING VIOLENCE AND AGGRESSION IN THE SCHOOLS

Reductive and preventative efforts must be addressed at all levels in society. Previously, we've discussed several initiatives at the federal and local levels. However, many of these initiatives have yet to be applied in many of our schools despite their efficacy (Quinn, Osher, Hoffman, & Hanley, 1998). In response to this problem, the Safe and Drug-Free Schools and the Office of Special Education Programs (both of the U.S. Department of Education) collaborated to examine three schools that had decreased student behaviors and improved the learning and behavior of all students:

1. Westerly, Rhode Island, restructured district and building policies to emphasize intervention and prevention.
2. South Florida, Project ACHIEVE (a schoolwide prevention and early intervention program) emphasized social skill development, problem-solving strategies, and anger-reduction methods to target students who were academically and socially considered at risk.

3. The Lane School and the Institute on Violence and Destructive Behavior at the University of Oregon successfully implemented early intervention, preventive intervention, and targeted intervention programs on a schoolwide basis (Quinn et al., 1998).

All of these programs provide examples of ways a theoretical research base can help prevent violence and aggression in our schools.

Early Intervention

Although no single program or strategy exists for the absolute prevention of violence, the literature clearly indicates that early intervention is extremely beneficial. Screening and assessment procedures may be very useful for preventing incidences of violence. In addition, although one cannot predict specific violent acts, many students typically offer warning signs that can serve as red flags for communities and schools (Dwyer, Osher, & Hoffman, 2000). Communities and schools must provide appropriate training to ensure recognition of these red flags.

Student Connectedness

The value of connectedness should not be underestimated in our efforts to understand as well as reduce and prevent violence. A national longitudinal study identified risk and protective factors of adolescent health and morbidity (Resnick et al., 1997). Results from this study concluded that health risk behaviors, with the exception of history of pregnancy, may be caused by a lack of parent-family connectedness and perceived school connectedness.

All human beings are susceptible to feelings of disconnection. Children and adolescents, especially those with EBD, may be especially vulnerable to these feelings. Student behavior, including behavior that is violent, is to a certain extent linked to the perceptions that students have regarding their school experience, and these perceptions are critically influenced by the quality of relationships between students and adults within the school (Jones & Jones, 2001). When school personnel (i.e., teachers, administrators, support staff, building staff), family members, and community members develop supportive relationships with children and adolescents, they increase the likelihood that a student who is in trouble will reach out to them (Dwyer & Osher, 2000). Thus, schools and communities must make intensive efforts to facilitate positive adult-student relationships.

Research has supported the development of what are called *caring schools*. In schools such as these, caring becomes the foundation on which all aspects of school culture, philosophy, and practice are based. To this end, Noblit, Rogers, and McCadden (1995) asserted that caring is a *value* that provides the foundation for instruction, discipline, classroom organization, and all other classroom pedagogy. They worked with two teachers during one school year to learn how caring was constructed in their classrooms. They discovered that the teachers incorporated caring into their relationships with every student and in the daily life of the classroom. The researchers concluded that caring cultivated the teacher-student connection and consequently created possibilities for students that may not otherwise have occurred. They suggested that many new teachers view control as the opposite of caring, rather than realizing that both control and caring must be intricately interwoven to create a positive classroom culture (Noblit et al., 1995). Last, creating caring families is as important as caring schools. Readers interested in learning about caring families should refer to Chapter 9.

How Teachers Can Connect With Students

Teachers can play a major role in the reduction and prevention of aggression and violence in their classrooms. Positive relationships with students provide the foundation for effective classroom management. Positive teacher-student relationships remain a critical factor in influencing the motivation, performance, and behavior of all students, especially students for whom school is challenging (Jones & Jones, 2001). Individual studies have examined the link between the teacher-student relationship and aggressive behavior (Coie & Dodge, 1997; Hughes, Cavell, & Jackson, 1999; Leff, Patterson, Kupersmidt, & Power, 1999). Hughes, Cavell, and Jackson (1999) described the teacher-student relationship in terms of its potential impact on aggressive behaviors in 61 second- and third-grade children. They found that the quality of teacher-student relationships helped reduce aggression. Among their recommendations was the importance of pairing aggressive students with teachers who are particularly well skilled in establishing and maintaining relationships with children who have learning and behavioral needs. They call for further research to identify teacher characteristics and teacher-child interactions that can be associated with positive developmental outcomes for aggressive children.

Children who are aggressive or violent often experience a history of conflict in their relationships with teachers and peers. The teacher's or student's feelings and beliefs about their relationship add fuel to their conflicts. If the teacher has negative perceptions regarding students, then their chances for success dwindle.

With the reauthorization of IDEA in 1997, schools began to increase efforts to meet least restrictive environment requirements through integration. Given this trend, general education teachers are required to improve classroom and behavioral management skills to meet the diverse needs of students with disabilities, including those with EBD. Their challenge is immense. Most of these teachers did not enter their profession with the belief that they have to teach students with these challenges. Consequently, it should be of little surprise that many of them have negative perceptions toward this population. Even so, all teachers must be prepared to manage these students with effective and appropriate behavior and classroom management strategies (see Chapter 7).

Understandably, teachers may feel initially overwhelmed by the intensity of the child problems and characteristics and the enormity of the community- and family-related issues at hand. However, several research-supported practices that teachers implement in their classrooms can and do have a positive impact on the behavior and emotional health of students (see Chapter 7 for examination of school-based interventions). It is hoped that, with support, they will rise to this challenge.

It is imperative that classroom behavior management systems based on positive-oriented approaches that promote behavior change are implemented in our schools. In fact, we know that when only punishing methods are used, problem behaviors are not reduced (Skiba & Peterson, 2000). Moreover, use of interventions that emphasize rules and punishments only serves to exacerbate violent student behavior (Jones & Jones, 2001). To this end, teachers must develop and apply best-practice strategies for behavior management when working with all students and especially those exhibiting violent and aggressive behaviors. There are several strategies for the management of students who exhibit violent and aggressive behaviors. They involve careful planning and preparation of all staff in crisis intervention training, management of the physical environment, establishment of a positive classroom climate and rapport with students, establishment of student behavioral expectations as well as consistent implementation of reinforcement and consequences for compliance and noncompliance, timely intervention with a disruptive student, demonstration of a calm and controlled presence by staff, and maintenance of a therapeutic attitude by staff (Myles & Simpson, 1994).

Skill-training approaches may serve to reduce aggressive and violent behaviors of all students, including those with EBD. It is essential that we incorporate prosocial skill instruction into our curriculums. We must provide students opportunities to develop competence in their interactions with peers and adults. To improve students' chances of staying in school, attaining school success, and increasing acceptance from peers and teachers, they must receive direct instruction of replacement adaptive behavior patterns (Walker et al., 1995).

The importance of appropriately developed, highly engaging curriculum that has been specifically tailored to meet the individual learning needs of each student cannot be understated. When students are involved in a meaningful, relevant, and exciting curriculum, there is less likelihood that they will become engaged in negative behaviors. Teachers must work to align district and state standards, the school curriculum, and individual IEP goals to best meet the educational needs of each student. After all, our primary goal is to provide students with instructional experiences that will ensure their success as adults (Quinn, Osher, Hoffman, & Hanley, 1998).

Time spent in school composes only about 25% of the student's day. It should follow that if the community can become involved in promoting positive mental health, than the battle would be better fought. Several strategies specific to community efforts at reducing and preventing aggressive and violent behavior in children and adolescents have been offered in the literature. Among these are the following:

- Provision of family support (Myles & Simpson, 1994)
- Provision of family therapy (Cornell, 1999)
- Facilitation of parent involvement (Myles & Simpson, 1994; Skiba & Peterson, 2000)
- Parent education programs (Cornell, 1999)
- Mentoring programs (Cornell, 1999)
- Supervised recreation (Cornell, 1999)
- Out-of-school programs that engage and support children when parents are unavailable (Schwartz, 1996)
- Employment assistance for young people (Schwartz, 1996)
- Restrictions on access to weapons (Kauffman & Spedtalk Participants, 1994)
- Community policing (Cornell, 1999)
- Campaigns designed to enhance antigang programs in schools (Schwartz, 1996)
- Abstinence from public displays of aggression (Kauffman & Spedtalk Participants, 1994)
- Efforts designed to address the conditions of daily life that cultivate aggression (Kauffman & Spedtalk Participants, 1994)
- Enhancement of cross-disciplinary collaboration to provide comprehensive services (institutional, social services, and other community-based agencies) to students (Myles & Simpson, 1994)
- Preschool programs (Cornell, 1999)

Whereas classroom teachers can affect their students, success for this population is more enhanced when the whole school embraces the task. On a *schoolwide level,* the following activities and programs can be effective in reducing school violence:

- Identification of early warning signs and screening procedures (Skiba & Peterson, 2000)
- Development of schoolwide and districtwide data systems (Skiba & Peterson, 2000)
- Enhancement of school security, safety policies, and crisis planning (Myles & Simpson, 1994; Schwartz, 1996; Skiba & Peterson, 2000)
- Schoolwide discipline and behavioral planning (Skiba & Peterson, 2000)
- Conflict resolution training (Skiba & Peterson, 2000)
- Violence prevention counseling (Cornell, 1999)
- Social skills development (Cornell, 1999; Skiba & Peterson, 2000)
- Bullying reduction programs (Cornell, 1999)
- Drug education programs (Cornell, 1999)
- Provision of a full continuum of services to meet academic and behavioral needs of students (Myles & Simpson, 1994)
- Functional assessment and individual behavior plans (Skiba & Peterson, 2000)
- Implementation of antiviolence programs (Schwartz, 1996)
- Implementation of antigang programs (Schwartz, 1996)

As overwhelming a task as reduction and prevention of aggression and violence may seem, we, as educators, are in key positions to advance peace in our classrooms on a daily basis. To this end, many of the foregoing recommendations begin with direct intervention and treatment with our children and youth. Aggression and violence reduction and prevention occur when we affect even just one student. Clearly, the list is as daunting as the problem. But it is no less challenging or time-consuming than the task of teaching somebody with dyslexia to read or somebody with significant mental retardation to navigate his or her world.

Appropriate and effective management of student behavior remains a critical factor in reducing and preventing student aggression and violence. All teachers are responsible for learning and practicing research-based, best-practice instructional and management strategies that keep students and staff safe as well as promote positive behavior change in students (see Chapter 7 for further management strategies).

SUMMARY

Because of isolated atrocities in some of our schools, the specter of violence and aggression has come to the forefront. Given these events, students, school personnel, and the general public alike question the level of safety in our schools. Accordingly, researchers have focused efforts on determination of features that relate to student aggression and violence. Through their work, we have learned of several factors that may be considered causal, although no single factor has yet been identified. More likely, violence and aggression can be caused by any number of factors.

At this time, there isn't any direct evidence linking students identified as having EBD to the violent episodes in our schools. Nonetheless, with improved identification procedures and a commitment to serve this under-identified population, we may be able to identify and help those students who exhibit dangerous behaviors and provide them with necessary services and supports. Legislators, policymakers, schools, and communities must focus their efforts on programs that decrease community crime, engage children and youth in positive activities outside of school, and support behavior change on a schoolwide and communitywide basis. Likewise, teachers must develop classroom management systems based on research-proven methods that involve a high level of student connectedness, prosocial skill instruction, and positive supports to foster behavior change. We are encouraged by new insights regarding violence reduction and prevention. There is a great deal we can do to better serve all students in our schools and especially those who present aggressive and violent behaviors. We are now faced with the challenging yet exciting task of implementing this knowledge in our classrooms, schools, and communities.

REFERENCES

American Psychiatric Association. (2000). *Diagnostic and statistical manual of mental disorders* (4th ed., Text Rev.). Washington, DC: Author.

Barton, P. (2000). *What jobs require: Literacy, education, and training, 1940-2006.* ED439136.

Barton, P. E., Coley, R. J., & Wenglinsky, H. (1998). *Order in the classroom: Violence, discipline and student achievement.* Princeton, NJ: Educational Testing Service.

Bronfenbrenner, U. (1979). *The ecology of human development: Experiments by nature and design.* Cambridge, MA: Harvard University Press.

Brooks, K., Schiraldi, V., & Ziedenberg, J. (2000). *School house hype: Two years later* [Online]. Available: http://www.cjcj.org/schoolhousehype/shh2.html [October 4, 2000].

Coie, J. D., & Dodge, K. A. (1997). Aggression and antisocial behavior. In N. Eisenberg (Ed.), *Handbook of child psychology: Vol. 3. Social, emotional, and personality development* (pp. 234–321). New York: John Wiley.

Cornell, D. G. (1999). *What works in youth violence prevention.* Unpublished manuscript, University of Virginia.

Council for Children with Behavior Disorders & Council of Administrators of Special Education. (1995). *A joint statement on violence in the schools.* Reston, VA: Council for Exceptional Children.

Dwyer, K., & Osher, D. (2000). *Safeguarding our children: An action guide.* Washington, DC: U.S. Departments of Education and Justice, American Institutes for Research.

Dwyer, K. P., Osher, D., & Hoffman, C. C. (2000). Creating responsive schools: Contextualizing early warning, timely response. *Exceptional Children, 66,* 347–365.

Guetzloe, E. (1995). Aggression and violence in the schools: What do we know about it? In L. M. Bullock & R. A. Gable (Eds.), *Perspectives on school aggression and violence: Highlights from the working forum on children and youth who have aggressive and violent behaviors* (pp. 12–15). Reston, VA: Council for Children with Behavioral Disorders.

Hawkins, J. D., Herrenkohl, T. I., Farrington, D. P., Brewer, D., Catalano, R. F., Harachi, T. W., & Cothern, L. (2000, April). *Predictors of youth violence* (Bulletin). Washington, DC: U.S. Department of Justice, Office of Justice Programs, Office of Juvenile Justice and Delinquency Prevention.

Hughes, J. N., Cavell, T. A., & Jackson, T. (1999). Influence of the teacher-student relationship on childhood conduct problems: A prospective study. *Journal of Clinical Child Psychology, 28,* 173–184.

Individuals with Disabilities Education Act of 1997, Pub. L. No. 105–17, 20 U.S.C., Ch. 33, §§1400–1491, [P.L. 105–17].

Jones, V. F., & Jones, L. S. (2001). *Comprehensive classroom management: Creating communities of support and solving problems* (6th ed.). Needham Heights, MA: Allyn & Bacon.

Kauffman, J. M., & Spedtalk Participants. (1994). *Violence and aggression of children and youth: A call for action* [Online]. Available: http://curry. edschool.virginia.edu/go/cise/ose/resources/papers.html/violence.html [October 4, 2000].

Leff, S. L., Patterson, C. J., Kupersmidt, J. B., & Power, T. J. (1999). Factors influencing teacher identification of peer bullies and victims. *School Psychology Review, 28,* 505–517.

Lewis, T., & Sugai, G. (1999). Effective behavior support: A systems approach to proactive schoolwide management. *Focus on Exceptional Children, 31,* 1–16.

Myles, B. S., & Simpson, R. L. (1994). Understanding and preventing acts of aggression and violence in school-age children and youth. *Preventing School Failure, 38*(3), 40–46.

National Association of School Psychologists. (1996). *Position statement: School violence.* Bethesda, MD: Author.

Noblit, G. W., Rogers, D. L., & McCadden, B. M. (1995). In the meantime: The possibilities of caring. *Phi Delta Kappan, 76*(9), 680–685.

Office of the Surgeon General. (2001). *Youth violence: A report of the surgeon general.* Washington, DC: Author.

Quinn, M. M., Osher, D., Hoffman, C. C., & Hanley, T. V. (1998). *Safe, drug-free, and effective schools for ALL students: What works!* Washington, DC: Center for Effective Collaboration and Practice, American Institutes for Research.

Resnick, M. D., Bearman, P. S., Blum, R. W., Bauman, K. E., Harris, K. M., Jones, J., Tabor, J., Beuhring, T., Sieving, R. E., Shew, M., Ireland, M., Bearinger, L. H., & Udry, J. R. (1997). Protecting adolescents from harm: Findings from the National Longitudinal Study on Adolescent Health. *Journal of American Medical Association, 278*(10), 823–832.

Rutherford, R. B., Jr., & Nelson, C. M. (1995). Management of aggressive and violent behavior in the schools. *Focus on Exceptional Children, 27*, 1–15.

Schwartz, W. (1996). *An overview of strategies to reduce school violence.* New York: Teachers College, ERIC Clearinghouse on Urban Education.

Shubert, T. S., Bressette, S., Deeken, J., & Bender, W. N. (1999). Analysis of random school shootings. In W. N. Bender, G. Clinton, & R. L. Bender (Eds.), *Violence prevention and reduction in schools* (pp. 97–101). Austin, TX: PRO-ED.

Skiba, R., & Peterson, R. (1999). The dark side of zero tolerance: Can punishment lead to safe schools? *Phi Delta Kappan, 80*, 372–376, 381–382.

Skiba, R. J., & Peterson, R. L. (2000). School discipline at a crossroads: From zero tolerance to early response. *Exceptional Children, 66*, 335–346.

Synder, H. N. (2000, December). *Juvenile Arrests 1999* (Bulletin). Washington, DC: U.S. Department of Justice, Office of Justice Programs, Office of Juvenile Justice and Delinquency Prevention.

Snyder, H. N., & Sickmund, M. (1999). *Juvenile offenders and victims: 1999 national report.* Washington, DC: U.S. Department of Justice, Office of Justice Programs, Office of Juvenile Justice and Delinquency Prevention. Also available online: http://www.ncjrs.org/html/ojjdp/nationalreport99/toc.html [October 4, 2000].

Turnbull, H. R., III, & Turnbull, A. P. (2000). *Free appropriate public education: The law and children with disabilities* (6th ed.). Denver, CO: Love.

U.S. Department of Justice. (1998). *Annual report on school safety.* Washington, DC: Author.

U.S. Department of Justice. (1999). *Annual report on school safety.* Washington, DC: Author.

Verlinden, S., Hersen, M., & Thomas, J. (2000). Risk factors in school shootings. *Clinical Psychology Review, 20*(1), 3–56.

Walker, H. (1993). Anti-social behavior in school. *Reclaiming Children and Youth, 2*(1), 20–24.

Walker, H. M., Colvin, G., & Ramsey, E. (1995). *Antisocial behavior in school: Strategies and best practices.* Pacific Grove, CA: Brooks/Cole.

Wehby, J. H., & Symons, F. J. (1996). Revisiting conceptual issues in the measurement of aggressive behavior. *Behavioral Disorders, 22*, 29–35.

Zabriskie, J. (1999). *APA teams with MTV to prevent violence* [Online]. Available: http://www.apa.org/monitor/feb99/mtv.html [October 4, 2000].

Adolescents Who Have Emotional and Behavioral Disorders and the Juvenile Justice System

6

Substantial numbers of the youth in our juvenile correctional facilities are adolescents who have EBD. Professionals must recognize the overlapping populations (EBD and juvenile offenders) in order to provide appropriate mental health and educational services to support these youth and their families. Professionals can intervene with or advocate for incarcerated youth who have EBD in four specific areas: (a) prevention, (b) concurrent appropriate special education services during incarceration, (c) psychiatric placements rather than incarceration, and (d) adequate transitional support for youth as they return to school and the community after incarceration.

There is a complex relationship between various predisposing or at-risk factors that lead adolescents into correctional facilities. Factors that seem involved can include low socioeconomic status, ethnicity, presence of EBD or another so-called mild disability, history of physical or sexual abuse, substance abuse, dropping out of school, and lack of parental supervision (Meisel, Henderson, Cohen, & Leone, 1998). Presently, the exact nature of how these factors interact to create an adolescent's success or failure in the school and community is not clear. Nor is it well understood how we can systematically alter the path of adolescents to support their success when we have identified the presence of several at-risk factors in their lives.

This chapter addresses what we *do* know about youth who have EBD and their presence in the mental health and juvenile corrections systems. It will describe facts about these youth that all professionals and parents who share a concern for adolescents with EBD should be aware of. Last, it will describe actions and advocacy issues for professionals and parents who want to make a positive difference in the lives of this marginalized and ignored group of teenagers.

BACKGROUND INFORMATION ON EBD
AND THE JUVENILE JUSTICE SYSTEM

Studies suggest that as many as 60% to 75% of incarcerated youth have a mental health disorder, 20% have a severe disorder, and as many as half have substance abuse problems (Cocozza, 1992). The percentage of incarcerated youth who qualify for special education services is estimated to be as high as 3 to 5 times that of teenagers who qualify for special education services in the public schools (Leone & Meisel, 1997). According to the National Longitudinal Transition Study of Special Education Students (Wagner et al., 1991), the arrest figures for adolescents who have EBD are nothing less than dismal. Nearly 20% had been arrested during their high school careers. The percentage of teenagers with EBD arrested within 2 years after leaving high school rises to 35%. And whereas nearly 50% of youth who have EBD drop out of high school, of those who drop out, 73% had been arrested at least once within 5 years after leaving school.

The specific types of EBD that are represented by youth offenders vary. For example, one study of juvenile youth offenders in California documented that 32% of males met the full criteria for posttraumatic stress disorder (PTSD) (Steiner, Garcia, & Matthews, 1997). A second California report evidenced that 4% of incarcerated females also met diagnostic criteria for PTSD (Cauffman, Feldman, Waterman, & Steiner, 1998). Otto, Greenstein, Johnson, and Friedman (1992) reviewed existing research on incarcerated youth who have EBD. They reported the following estimates of types of EBD among youth offenders:

- Mood disorders have been estimated in youth offenders at rates as high as 78% based on individual interviews.
- Schizophrenia or psychotic disorders were reported as occurring in 1% to 6% of all incarcerated youth.
- Conduct disorders that occur along with at least one other mental disorder were documented in 50% of youth offenders.

PERPLEXING ISSUES OF ETHNICITY, MENTAL HEALTH,
AND JUVENILE JUSTICE IN THE UNITED STATES

Issues of culture and ethnicity are inexplicably tied to mental health concerns, (special) education, and juvenile justice issues among youth in the

United States. Youth who are African American and Native American are statistically more likely to be labeled EBD than other youth (compared to numbers in the general school population). This fact is commonly referred to as the overidentification of minority youth for special education programs, meaning that more minority youth are identified for special education services than would be predicted based on the numbers of minority youth in the schools. Conversely, Caucasian and Asian American students are typically underreferred for EBD evaluation but overidentified for gifted and talented programs (compared to their numbers in the general school population; U.S. Department of Education, 1996).

Annual reports to Congress on the implementation of IDEA as well as other national studies have attempted to attribute problems with overidentification of minority students to socioeconomic status (U.S. Department of Education, 1996; Wagner, 1992). Identification of EBD does seem linked to economic status as the average youth identified as EBD has a family income level of approximately $12,000 (Woodruff et al., 1999). However, in the United States, socioeconomic status is also linked to ethnicity. Hence, the complicated nature of the problem surfaces.

Children of color are typically underserved by the mental health system. For example, African American teenagers are more likely to be referred to the juvenile justice system than the mental health system (Cross, Bazron, Dennis, & Isaacs, 1989). It is interesting that African American males who are incarcerated as teenagers are less likely than their Caucasian peers to have received mental health treatment before becoming incarcerated (Marsteller, Brogan, & Smith, 1997). Still, African American youth who do receive mental health services tend to be treated for more severe disorders than other youth. For example, they are hospitalized for psychiatric reasons at a rate as much as 2 times higher then their Caucasian peers (Myers, 1990). This would seem to indicate that African American youth are receiving needed early intervention for mental health disorders from neither school nor community. By the time they receive services, among those who do receive services, the emotional and behavioral problems have reached significant levels of disturbance.

African American males are not only overrepresented in special education programs for youth who have EBD, they are also overrepresented in the juvenile justice system (Drakeford & Garfinkel, 2000). Although the factors that interact to create this problem are clearly complex, biases within the mental health care system are suspected to account for a portion of the cause. Cohen (1991) studied African American youth who were incarcerated and those who were in psychiatric facilities. Although both groups of children had similar scores on the Child Behavior Checklist (Achenbach, 1981), 63% of the youth in the correctional facilities were African American, and 34% of youth in psychiatric facilities were African American.

Kaplan and Busner (1992) found similar mental health care biases in New York. Their results showed that 62% of the adolescents receiving inpatient mental health care were Caucasian, whereas only 23% were African American. Conversely, among adolescents who were in the juvenile correction facilities, 56% were African American and 28% were Caucasian.

Unfortunately, within the past decade, the problem has not abated (Drakeford & Garfinkel, 2000). In 1998, the Maryland Juvenile Justice Coalition (Richissin, 1999) reported some staggering figures within their own system: 120 Caucasian youth had been ordered to receive residential psychiatric treatment, whereas 223 Caucasian youth had been sentenced to a correctional facility; and during the same year, 132 African American youth were ordered to receive psychiatric treatment, whereas 672 were sentenced to prison.

ADDRESSING ISSUES OF ETHNICITY AND BIAS IN JUVENILE JUSTICE AGENCIES

The Juvenile Justice Agency has attempted to speak to the problem of ethnic overrepresentation through the 1988 amendments to the Juvenile Justice and Delinquency Prevention Act of 1974. These amendments made it a requirement that each state address the issue, yet a decade later, only 42 states had complied with the legislation (Hsia & Hamparian, 1998). In addition to the legislative attempts to deal with ethnic overrepresentation, the Office of Juvenile Justice and Delinquency Prevention (2000) awarded grants to five states in a program called the Disproportionate Minority Confinement Initiative (Devine, Coolbaugh, & Jenkins, 1998). The object of the program was to assist states in developing active system-level tracking and probing devices to better follow and understand the extent of overrepresentation.

Last, interagency collaboration has begun at a national level among the top agencies likely to deal with adolescents who have EBD. The U.S. Department of Education, the U.S. Office of Special Education, and the U.S. Office of Juvenile Justice and Delinquency Prevention (OJJDP) collaboratively sponsored the creation of a National Center on Education, Disability, and Juvenile Justice (EDJJ). Presently, the EDJJ is still in its infancy. However, it stands to become an important resource for the dissemination of pertinent and timely research on issues of overidentification of minority youth in correctional facilities as well as about mental health prevention and education that can have a strong impact on lowering the numbers of minority adolescents who receive correctional sentences rather than proper psychiatric care.

ADDRESSING THE MENTAL HEALTH NEEDS
OF ALL YOUTH IN THE JUVENILE JUSTICE SYSTEM

The National Mental Health Association (NMHA, 1998) has published a set of recommendations to improve services for this population (available online at (http://www.nmha.org/children/justjuv/calorij.cfm)). Their recommendations include several noteworthy suggestions: (a) improvement of systems of care through greater collaboration between mental health, juvenile justice, education, child welfare, and others who serve low-income youth and youth of color; (b) early identification, through psychological evaluation, on entering the juvenile justice system in order to access therapeutic treatment; (c) professional collaboration to address risk factors that affect the likelihood of juvenile justice agency involvement, such as family functioning, health care, housing, education, and racism in our communities; and (d) greater cultural competence among professionals who compose an integrated system of service delivery for youth who have emotional and behavioral disorders. In this set of recommendations, NMHA points out the importance of focusing on strengths and protective factors that affect culturally diverse youth and their families and extended families.

Many youth who have EBD are incarcerated for minor, nonviolent offenses. By providing mental health intervention rather than incarceration, these youth could be served in less restrictive settings. Programs such as wraparound services (described in Chapter 9) can provide needed collaboration among social service agencies, education, and the juvenile justice system. It is important that services provided to youth with EBD who have been in trouble with the law be appropriate, access the continuum of available services, and include the family to the extent possible. Other examples of services that may be appropriate for these youth include family support, counseling or cognitive behavioral therapy, inpatient care, clinic services, and day treatment programs. Certainly, special education would be in order for youth who have been formally identified as having EBD. Appropriate screening and identification of those suspected of having EBD should be undertaken so that appropriate special education can be provided to them as well. It should be noted that during the screening process, African American youth may seem less distressed by their confinement, but that should not influence their potential for mental health assessment (Drakeford & Garfinkel, 2000).

Mental health services should be consistently available to youth who have EBD, regardless of day or time. These services should include written arrangements with mental health facilities to care for youth who are or who become suicidal. Emergency services should be included in this arrangement, as should medication use as part of a treatment plan that is monitored by a trained mental health professional who has experience with youth.

In accordance with NMHA's recommendations (1998), another key consideration of appropriate care for incarcerated youth who have EBD is adequate staff training in crisis prevention and intervention techniques. The use of confinement, restraints, and seclusion should be subject to written policy and evaluative documentation. Although there may be instances in which these techniques are used to protect a youth, they should not be used to punish. The 1997 IDEA amendments requiring evidence of positive behavioral support interventions may assist educators, parents, and other concerned professionals in ensuring proper physical treatment of incarcerated adolescents who have EBD.

SPECIAL EDUCATION AND THE JUVENILE JUSTICE SYSTEM

The principles of IDEA (1997) apply to youth involved in the correctional system. A challenge to the successful implementation of IDEA principles in the juvenile justice system is the competing philosophies that typically exist between juvenile justice and education for youth offenders: punishment versus rehabilitation. Education programs in correctional facilities are often accountable to the administrators of the correctional institution, which limits their abilities to design and budget an effective educational program (Meisel et al., 1998).

Funding of Educational Programs in Correctional Institutions

Wolford (2000) indicated that of the 15 states he surveyed, 50% of them spent an average of $2,500 more per pupil to educate youth in correctional facilities than the average per-pupil expense in the public school setting. Wraparound services and the rehabilitative model of intervention for youth who have EBD seem to be supported by this data. Keeping youth in public school programs with appropriate services and supports is less expensive and contributes to outcomes that are more positive.

It should be noted that according to Coffey and Gemignani (1994), the largest sources of financial support for educational programs in juvenile corrections programs come from IDEA, the Carl D. Perkins Vocational Act of 1973, and Title I of the Improving America's Schools Act (formerly the Elementary and Secondary Education Act). Given that all states in Wolford's (2000) study were using federal education funds from these three sources, it would seem easier to ensure that students would receive equitable educational services and supports from the correctional facilities or, at a minimum, that they would comply with the federal laws that accompany federal dollars.

Youth Who Have EBD, FERPA Rights, and the Juvenile Justice System

A communication problem is caused by school district misinterpretations of the Families' Educational Rights and Privacy Act (FERPA) of 1996, also known as the Buckley Amendment. (See Puritz & Scali [1998] for a complete discussion of *Smith v. Wheaton*, a ruling that demonstrates how IDEA principles apply to juvenile offenders in correctional institutions.) Educators report an unwillingness to share educational information about youths with the corrections agencies, to maintain what they interpret as the requirements of FERPA regulations (Slayton, 2000). FERPA was created by the federal government in order to protect families' and student's rights to privacy by protecting record-keeping practices in schools and ensuring parents' rights to inspect all written records about their child.

However, when schools do not share educational records of youth with EBD with the correctional system, the youth's mental health needs must be discovered and prescriptive interventions designed by staff within the juvenile justice system. This process of identification and program development can take considerable time away from proper mental health intervention for an adolescent who has potentially serious emotional and behavioral needs. Leone (1994) indicated a backlog of over 4 months for processing just the students who had previously been identified as having EBD, without considering the needs of those for whom information was not available. Incidentally, a related problem, but not due to FERPA, is the difficulty of attaining student records for youth with EBD who have a history of non-attendance or a number of school placements (Meisel et al., 1998).

FERPA was amended to better specify that collaborations between juvenile justice and the educational system are indeed permissible. The Improving America's Schools Act of 1994 also indicates that information sharing between juvenile justice and education is encouraged. In an effort to increase interagency collaboration, OJJDP has created a free pamphlet for schools titled *Sharing Information: A Guide to the Family Educational Rights and Privacy Act and Participation in Juvenile Justice Programs*. It is available through the U.S. Office of Education and through OJJDP.

Principles of IDEA in Correctional Facilities

The principles of IDEA (1997) are applicable to correctional facilities. There have been many obstacles to implementing IDEA in juvenile justice programs, including program resistance, lack of communication, professional biases about the role of mental health interventions for juvenile offenders, and lack of training and awareness among correctional facilities' staff of special education needs. Multiple court cases have challenged IDEA principles in juvenile justice facilities, and after lengthy trials, the courts have consistently upheld the student's rights under IDEA (*Andre H. v. Sobol*, [1984], lasted 7 years [Leone & Meisel, 1997]; *Smith v. Wheaton* [1987] lasted 11 years [Becker, 1999]).

One principle of IDEA (1997) that is frequently underused in correctional facilities is that of child find. The child-find principle requires that states and local education agencies actively seek out all youth with disabilities and provide them with special education services as needed. To justly serve youth who have EBD, NMHA (1998) advocates that all youth should be screened for mental health and substance abuse problems when they are first admitted to correctional facilities.

In fact, OJJDP, in its *Juvenile Justice Bulletin* on "Special Education and the Juvenile Justice System" (Burrell & Warboys, 2000), make clear the importance of intake evaluations for all youth. They state,

> It is important to understand that youth may have a variety of impairments that are not readily apparent. Numerous checklists and screening instruments are available to help recognize signs of disabilities and to determine eligibility for special education services (National Council of Juvenile and Family Court Judges, 1991). (p. 2)

IDEA Principle: Free and Appropriate Public Education

The principle of free and appropriate public education is applicable but difficult to monitor. The 1997 amendments to IDEA loosened requirements for special education in correctional facilities by allowing states the option of not providing services to 18- to 21-year-old offenders who were not identified as having a disability before they were incarcerated or those who did not have an active IEP in place at the time they became incarcerated (Burrell & Warboys, 2000). However, *Green v. Johnson* (1981) firmly established that students who have disabilities do not forfeit their rights to an appropriate education when they enter the correctional system. In addition, NMHA has advocated on behalf of incarcerated youth who have EBD by invoking the 8th Amendment, which prohibits cruel and unusual punishment, in this case, by refusing adequate mental health treatment to youth who have been identified as having EBD (NMHA, 1998).

Leone (1994) described several studies that demonstrate that youth who have disabilities have a higher occurrence of disciplinary actions than nondisabled peers. A frequent type of discipline is confinement, which would constitute a removal from the special education services. Youth who have EBD may spend up to 20% of their time in confinement, which is a greater percentage than other youth who have disabilities and far greater than youth who do not have disabilities (12.3% and 5.6%, respectively; Leone, 1994). Disciplinary provisions within IDEA (1997) may be used in some situations to protect youth who have EBD and discourage correctional facilities from the overuse of segregation or confinement. For example, Burrell and Warboys (2000) pointed out that if the disciplinary action were related to behavior that occurred during educational instruction, then the confinement would constitute a removal from the regular educational placement. Such a change in placement would subsequently require an IEP meeting at which a review of behavioral intervention plans, functional assessments, manifest determinations, and time limits on exclusion may apply. And furthermore, students and parents would have the due process rights to challenge any change in placement or modification to the IEP.

IDEA Principle: Least Restrictive Environment

Another common principle of IDEA (1997) that is problematic for correctional facilities is the issue of least restrictive environment (LRE). (For an in-depth discussion of determination of least restrictive environment in public school settings, see Chapter 8.) Nothing in IDEA prevents schools from reporting crimes committed by a child with a disability to appropriate authorities. The 1997 amendments to IDEA make clear that a youth's rights under IDEA in no way supercede criminal law nor the juvenile justice agencies from prosecuting the youth under the law. According to Burrell and Warboys (2000), at least one court ruling since the enactment of the amendments has confirmed that the juvenile courts have jurisdiction over students with disabilities "even when the school is attempting to evade its special education responsibilities" (p. 2).

An interesting problem of LRE arises when youth who have EBD are incarcerated for minor offenses but, due to their disability, are not able to succeed in the juvenile corrections programs and are then sentenced to a longer stay in the correctional facility. According to Burell and Warboy (2000), the reason for youth failure could be twofold: (a) The student's disability may make it difficult for the youth to understand procedures and comply with rules, or (b) the youth's misbehavior may be interpreted as a poor attitude, disrespect for authority, or a failure to show appropriate remorse for his or her misdeeds. In fact, the nature of the EBD disability is also believed responsible for the very detainment of the youth. It is hypothesized that the lack of social skills and the language-communication deficits that commonly occur with EBD create problems for the youth when interacting with the arresting officer, intake officers, and at the detention hearing. The youth, due to his or her disability, presents an impression of hostility, disrespect, and impulsivity. The need for increased professional education about the *disability* of EBD and for greater advocacy by parents and professionals is clear.

IDEA Principle: Parental Participation

A last IDEA (1997) principle is that of parental involvement in the child's IEP process. For many parents who have youth in correctional facilities, distance from home to the facility is the greatest limitation to participation in the special education process. However, other restrictions to parental participation may apply (Garfinkel, Jordan, & Kragthorpe, 1999). For example, parents may resist participation because they feel that they are being judged for their child's behavior by the courts and the school. They may have disabilities similar to their child's and have had similarly negative experiences in schools and court systems. They may simply lack experience dealing with the many professionals involved in the court and educational systems and lack information on how to best participate, or they may feel overwhelmed by the process.

Several strategies have been published to attempt to gain greater participation from parents of incarcerated youth who have EBD. Meisel et al. (1998) recommend scheduling IEP conferences during family visitation to the facility, the use of speakerphones for participation in conferences, and implementing surrogate procedures.

IDEA (1997, §330.20) provides clear information about parent participation. It defines a *parent* as being at least one of the following:

- A natural or adoptive parent of a child
- A guardian but not the state if the child is a ward of the state
- A person acting in the place of a parent (such as a grandparent or stepparent with whom the child lives or a person who is legally responsible for the child's welfare)
- A surrogate parent who has been appointed in accordance with Section §300.515

Foster parents may act as parent if natural parents' authority to make educational decisions on the child's behalf has been extinguished under state law and if the following conditions are met:

- The foster parent has an ongoing, long-term parental relationship with the child.
- The foster parent is willing to make educational decisions required of parents under the Act.

- The foster parent has no interest that would conflict with the interests of the child (§330.20).

IDEA (1997) also mandates particular processes for the use of parent surrogates in the event that a person is not available to serve as the parent (child advocate) in the IEP process. Each public agency shall ensure that the rights of a child are protected if

- No parent (as defined in §300.20) can be identified
- The public agency, after reasonable efforts, cannot discover the whereabouts of a parent
- The child is a ward of the state under the laws of that state (§300.515)

The criteria by which a person can be appointed as a surrogate parent are clearly defined in the law, although states are left with the opportunity to establish their own procedures for appointing and selecting a surrogate parent. The criteria include the following:

- The person is not an employee of the state education agency, the local education agency, or any other agency involved in the education or care of the child.
- The person has no interest that conflicts with the interest of the child he or she represents.
- The person has knowledge and skills that ensure adequate representation of the child (§300.515).

For youth who have EBD in our correctional facilities, finding a parent or even a parent surrogate who can fulfill the federally designated criteria may be problematic. Advocates for youth who have EBD must attend to providing input at the state level as to the actual processes that will be used to determine surrogate parents. Furthermore, strong advocates may well be wise to organize a formal network by which advocates who are willing will step forward to serve in the parent-child advocate role through the IEP process for incarcerated youth.

JUVENILE JUSTICE AND YOUTH WHO HAVE EBD: INTERVENTION AND REINTEGRATION STRATEGIES

Effective Intervention Services and Strategies

According to NMHA (1998), several treatment programs have demonstrated success with juvenile offenders. Cognitive-behavioral therapy approaches are used in many programs. It has been shown to be effective with youth in the juvenile justice system as well as youth who have problems with anger in general. The basic notion of this approach is that one must recognize how reactions and thoughts or interpretations of a situation affect one's behaviors and actions. In this way, one can modify those reactions and thereby modify one's actions.

Another effective model identified by the NMHA (1998) is multi-systemic therapy. In this model, the therapist is responsible for working with the family to identify factors in the youth's family, peers, and school that are problematic and addressing them through specific interventions. A third model is that of integrated systems of care, described in more detail in Chapter 8. In brief, it consists of the collaborative planning and implementation of programs through a coordinated body of social, school, and community service.

Other recommendations made by the NMHA (1998) included the following: (a) Treatment programs are recommended that are structured, intensive, and focused on changing specific behaviors; (b) community-based treatment programs are recommended over institution-based programs; and (c) justice authorities must involve parents and family members in the treatment and rehabilitation of their children.

Meisel et al. (1998) also endorsed the integrated model of service delivery. Their recommendations extended those set forth by NMHA (1998) in the following ways:

- An emphasis on competency-based curriculum that includes many academic levels (i.e., literacy and functional skills, academic skills, general educational development courses, and prevocational and vocational education courses)
- Direct and peer-mediated instructional strategies
- Functional, curriculum-based assessment
- Prosocial skills curriculum (and conflict resolution)
- Business and community involvement (as mentors, tutors, surrogate parents, and work exploration opportunities)
- Leadership and advocacy (including administrative leadership, and teacher and program accreditation)
- Ongoing professional development for staff in curriculum, behavior management, special education accommodations, functional assessment, and collaboration

The Comprehensive Community Mental Health Services for Children and Their Families Program (Woodruff et al., 1999) is another source of helpful information for designing effective intervention programs for incarcerated youth who have EBD. The final reports of several of their sponsored integrated-services programs for youth who have EBD were reviewed, and the following common characteristics were noted: (a) Clinicians or some other student support providers in the schools worked with students, families, and school staff; (b) school-based and school-focused wraparound services supported learning and reintegration; (c) school-based case management linked families to services and advocated for change as needed; (d) schoolwide prevention and early intervention programs assisted students with or at risk of EBD to manage their own behavior; (e) centers within the schools linked families with the entire system of care to meet their needs; (f) family liaisons empowered families in their children's education (p. xiii).

Effective Reintegration Services and Strategies

Reintegration is a term used to discuss the transition of youth back into the community after incarceration. This transition is the most challenging (Leone, 1994), but it is also the most ignored aspect of correctional education programs, according to the National Center on Education, Disability, and Juvenile Justice (1998). Stephens and Arnette (2000) summarize reintegration strategies that have been effective for students who have EBD as they prepare to exit the correctional system and reenter their home communities and schools. One of the strongest recommendations they make is for the process to be gradual and systematic. In addition to individual case planning from a family perspective (a familiar theme), Stephens and Arnette (2000) observed that common elements of successful reintegration programs included "a mix of intensive surveillance and services, a balance of incentives and graduated consequences coupled with realistic, enforceable conditions, and service brokerage with community resources linked to social networks" (p. 4).

At times, transitional educational settings are necessary for youth who have been incarcerated (Stephens & Arnette, 2000). These settings may include alternative campuses or other educational programs that will allow a temporary intermediate zone of supervision and structure while students make the necessary and often difficult adjustment from confinement back to the community. This placement offers many benefits to the youth, including the opportunity for educational assessment and proper placement in academic programs and a way to avoid becoming lost in the shuffle as they leave a very structured environment.

As an integrated-services or IEP team plans for the youth's imminent reintegration, several specific issues must be anticipated (Stephens & Arnette, 2000). First, curriculum should be coordinated with that of the school the student will use when he or she returns to the neighborhood school. Failing to provide the student with exposure to the community school curriculum will jeopardize his or her ability to meet the challenge of a midsemester return.

On a related note, it is important for the integrated-services or IEP team to begin discussions on the next least restrictive environment for the youth several months before the student exits the correctional facility. At the point that a school placement is made, juvenile justice representatives should provide the school officials with information about the student, his or her behavioral and other therapeutic programs, and his or her academic levels of ability. The school and the juvenile justice representative should begin work on how they will jointly monitor the student's behavior, attendance, activities, and achievement.

A prerelease visit to the school by the student and a juvenile justice representative should be arranged to ease pressure and establish expectations for both school and student. The student should have the opportunity at that time to meet his or her classroom teacher and principal and to tour the school (if he or she is new to the environment). Such a visit can also alleviate concern in the minds of school personnel.

Transitional counseling can be provided to the youth after his or her release. A phone call or visit during the first 2 weeks and additional contacts made at 6-month intervals can ease the strain on a youth who is adjusting to new individuals, environments, and expectations after his or her release. Recruiting a well-trained adult mentor to work with the student can also be a beneficial strategy for helping the student reacclimate to the community school. Classroom teachers should be carefully selected for the first semester. Last, the school should provide space on campus for the juvenile probation officer and work closely with the officer and the presiding judge.

The reintegration process is an important piece of the successful comprehensive mental health care program for youth who have EBD and who have been incarcerated. On release, it will be critical that proper wraparound services are available to support both the youth and his or her family. Without a systematic plan for supporting the youth who has EBD, the stress and sudden lack of structure can create chaos in his or her life. Youth who have been afforded a solid reintegration plan with careful follow-up by an integrated system of services have demonstrated lower recidivism rates than youth who did not receive this type of care.

SUMMARY

This chapter examined the juvenile justice system as it affects youth who have EBD. Several aspects of the system were explored, including what subtypes of EBD are represented within the population of incarcerated youth and the role of ethnicity on the mental health care and juvenile justice systems.

In addition, this chapter described how the principles of IDEA (1997) are applied to juvenile justice facilities. It provided examples from case law as well as from leading mental health advocacy groups and researchers to support the status of youth with EBD in correctional facilities in terms of their educational programming.

Last, this chapter provided strategies and recommendations from effective programs for intervention with incarcerated youth who have EBD and strategies for their reintegration to community schools.

Parents and professionals are the people most responsible for advocating for just treatment of children and youth who have EBD. This means advocating for appropriate mental health care treatments rather than incarceration for youth who have committed minor offenses. It means continuing to advocate for ethical treatment of youth who have EBD in their education, physical care, and mental health intervention during their incarceration. Last, it means serving as an advocate in whatever capacity is needed: (a) for policy and practice changes at the local, state, and national levels, (b) as a surrogate parent for incarcerated youth who have EBD, (c) as an agency representative who will take leadership to establish wraparound services in the community, or (d) as a mentor to a recently reintegrated youth in need of support. Each of us has a part to play in creating a more secure future for youth who have EBD.

REFERENCES

Achenbach, T. M. (1981). *The child behavior checklist.* Burlington, VT: University of Vermont Department of Psychiatry.

Andre H. v. Sobol. (1984). No. 84-3114 (S.D.N.Y., filed May, 1984).

Becker, E. (1999). Juvenile justice system under scrutiny. *APA Monitor Online, 30* (4) [On-line Serial]. Retrieved October 12, 2001, from http:www.apa.org/monitor/apr99/jn.html.

Burrell, S., & Warboys, L. (2000). Special education and the juvenile justice system. *OJJDP Juvenile Justice Bulletin (July).* NCJ 179359 Washington, DC: Office of Juvenile Justice and Delinquency Prevention.

Carl D. Perkins Vocational Rehabilitation Act of 1973, Section 504, 29 U.S.C. §794(a) (1973), as amended by Act of 1978 (Section 504 regulations concerning education can be found at 34 C.F.R. §104 [1990]).

Cauffman, E., Feldman, S., Waterman, J., & Steiner, H. (1998). Posttraumatic stress disorder among female juvenile offenders. *Journal of the American Academy of Child and Adolescent Psychiatry, 37,* 1209–1216.

Cocozza, J. J. (Ed.). (1992). *Responding to youth with mental disorders in the juvenile justice system.* Seattle, WA: National Coalition for the Mentally Ill in the Criminal Justice System.

Coffey, O., & Gemignani, M. (1994). *Effective practices in juvenile correctional education: A study of the literature and research 1980–1992.* Washington, DC: National Office for Social Responsibility.

Cohen, R. (1991). To prisons or hospitals: Race and referrals in juvenile justice. *Journal of Health Care for the Poor and Underserved, 2,* 248–249.

Cross, T. L., Bazron, B. J., Dennis, K. W., & Issacs, M. R. (1989). *Towards a culturally competent system of care: A monograph on effective services for minority children who are severely emotionally disturbed.* Washington, DC: CASSP Technical Assistance Center, Georgetown University Child Development Center.

Devine, P., Coolbaugh, K., & Jenkins, S. (1998). Disproportionate minority confinement: 1997 update. *Bulletin.* Washington, DC: Department of Justice, Office of Juvenile Justice and Delinquency Prevention.

Drakeford, W., & Garfinkel, L. F. (2000). Differential treatment of African Americans. *Reclaiming Children and Youth: Journal of Emotional and Behavioral Problems, 9*(1), 51–52, 61.

Families' Educational Rights to Privacy Act (1996). 34 C.F.R. Part 99.1.

Garfinkel, L. F., Jordan, D., & Kragthorpe, C. (1999). *Unique challenges, hopeful responses: A handbook for professionals working with youth with disabilities in the juvenile justice system.* Minneapolis, MN: Pacer Center.

Green v. Johnson, 513 F. Supp. 965 (D. Mass. 1981).

Hsia, M., & Hamparian, D. (1998). Disproportionate minority confinement: 1997 update. *Bulletin.* Washington, DC: Department of Justice, Office of Juvenile Justice and Delinquency Prevention.

Improving America's Schools Act of 1994 (formerly the Elementary and Secondary Education Act), Pub. L. No. 106–554, 20 U.S.C.S. §§6421, §1(a)(4), 114, Stat. 2763 (2000).

Individuals with Disabilities Education Act of 1997, Pub. L. No. 105–17, 20 U.S.C., Ch. 33, §§1400–1491 (1997).

Juvenile Justice and Delinquency Prevention Act of 1974, Pub L. 102–586, 42 U.S.C.S. §5662 (2001).

Kaplan, L. S., & Busner, J. (1992). A note on racial bias in the admission of children and adolescents to state mental health facilities versus correctional facilities in New York. *American Journal of Psychiatry, 149,* 768–772.

Leone, P. (1994). Education services for youth with disabilities in a state-operated juvenile correctional system: Case study analysis. *Journal of Special Education, 28,* 43–58.

Leone, P. E., & Meisel, S. M. (1997). Improving education services for students in detention and confinement facilities. *Children's Legal Rights Journal, 17*(1), 2–12.

Marsteller, F., Brogan, D., &, Smith, I. (1997). The prevalence of substance use disorders among juveniles admitted to regional youth detention centers operated by the Georgia Department of Children and Youth Services. *Center for Substance Abuse and Treatment (CSAT) Final Report.* Atlanta: Georgia Department of Human Resources.

Meisel, S., Henderson, K., Cohen, M., & Leone, P. (1998). Collaborate to educate: Special education in juvenile correctional facilities. In *Building collaboration between education and treatment for at-risk and delinquent youth* (pp. 59–72). Richmond: Eastern Kentucky University, National Juvenile Detention Association.

Myers, H. (1990). Urban stress and mental health in Afro-American youth: An epidemiological and conceptual update. In R. Jones (Ed.), *Black adolescents*. Berkeley, CA: Cobb & Henry.

National Center on Education, Disability, and Juvenile Justice. (1998). *Transition planning and services*. Washington, DC: Author.

National Mental Health Association. (1998). *NMHA position statement 37: Children with emotional disorders in the juvenile justice system*. Alexandria, VA: Author.

Office of Juvenile Justice and Delinquency Prevention. (2000). *Special education in correctional facilities*. Washington, DC: Author.

Otto, R., Greenstein, J., Johnson, M., & Friedman, R. (1992). Prevalence of mental disorders among youth in the juvenile justice system. In J. Cocozza (Ed.), *Responding to the mental health needs of youth in the juvenile justice system* (pp. 7–48). Seattle, WA: National Coalition for the Mentally Ill in the Criminal Justice System.

Puritz, P., & Scali, M. A. (1998). *Beyond the walls: Improving conditions of confinement for youth in custody*. Washington, DC: Office of Juvenile Justice and Delinquency Prevention.

Richissin, T. (1999, June 25). Race predicts handling of many young criminals: Care vs. punishment of mentally ill youth correlates with color. *The Baltimore Sun*, p. IA.

Slayton, J. (2000, March). *Establishing and maintaining interagency information sharing* (Juvenile Accountability Incentive Block Grants Program Bulletin NCJ 178281). Washington, DC: Office of Juvenile Justice and Delinquency Prevention.

Smith v. Wheaton, No. H-87–190 (TPS) 29 IDELR 200 (D-Conn., 1998).

Steiner, H., Garcia, I., & Matthews, Z. (1997). Post-traumatic stress disorder in incarcerated juvenile delinquents. *Journal of the American Academy of Child and Adolescent Psychiatry, 36,* 357–365.

Stephens, R. D., & Arnette, J. L. (2000). *From the courthouse to the schoolhouse: Making successful transitions* (OJJDP Juvenile Justice Bulletin NCJ 178900). Washington, DC: Office of Juvenile Justice and Delinquency Prevention.

U.S. Department of Education. (1996). *Eighteenth annual report to Congress on implementation of the Individuals with Disabilities Education Act*. Washington, DC: Author.

Wagner, M. (1992). *What happens next? Trends in postschool outcomes of youth with disabilities. The second comprehensive report from the national longitudinal transitional study of special education students*. ED356603.

Wagner, M., Newman, L., D'Amico, R., Jay, E. D., Butler-Nalin, P., Marder, P., & Cox, R. (1991). *Youth with disabilities: How are they doing? The first comprehensive report for the National Longitudinal Transition Study of transition study*. Menlo Park, CA: SRI.

Wolford, B. I. (2000). *Juvenile justice: Who is educating the youth?* Richmond: Eastern Kentucky University, Center for Educators of At-Risk and Delinquent Youth.

Woodruff, D. W., Osher, D., Hoffman, C. C., Gruner, A., King, M. A., Snow, S. T., & McIntire, J. C. (1999). The role of education in a system of care: Effectively serving children with emotional and behavioral disorders. In *Systems of care: Promising practices in children's mental health* (1998 Series, Vol. 3). Washington, DC: Center for Effective Collaboration and Practice, American Institutes for Research.

Part Two

Helping Students Who Have Emotional and Behavioral Disorders

Treatment of Emotional and Behavioral Disorders

7

Treatment and intervention methods are of primary concern to persons who work with children and youth having emotional and behavioral problems, including parents, family members, and teachers. Current treatment methods are not based on a perfect science, as evidenced by children who fail to develop productive behavior in spite of professional intervention. Most individuals with emotional and behavioral problems can and do improve, however. Gains do not occur by accident, and rarely do children outgrow their problems. Rather, behavioral and emotional improvements result from carefully formulated intervention programs and strategies. Several major treatment methods are discussed in this chapter, including behavior modification, counseling-psychotherapy, and schoolwide management programs. Psychopharmacology, the intervention commonly associated with the dispersing of medication, will be discussed in Chapter 9. Each of these procedures has been successfully used with children and adolescents, and each offers unique advantages and disadvantages.

BEHAVIOR MODIFICATION

Behavior modification, also known as the *behavioral model, applied behavior analysis, learning theory,* and *operant conditioning,* is used to describe a set of principles and procedures for understanding and systematically changing behavior. There have been many excellent books written on this subject. In this section, we have used the following sources that we also highly recommend for further study: Jenson, Sloane, and Young (1988), Maag

(1999), Malott, Malott, and Trojan (2000), Martin and Pear (1999), Zionts and Simpson (1988), and Zirpoli and Melloy (2001).

Most educational programs for behaviorally disordered and emotionally disturbed children and youth are based on behavioral procedures. Likewise, many therapists use behavioral procedures when working with children and adolescents.

Unlike traditional therapeutic approaches, such as psychoanalysis, which considers maladaptive behavior a symptom of underlying psychological and emotional problems, behavior modification views problem behaviors as targets for change. Behavior modification proponents do not support the notion that problem behaviors are signs of deep-seated emotional conflict but, rather, consider them learned patterns of maladaptive behavior. According to this model, developing maladaptive behaviors is no different from learning adaptive responses. Thus, children may learn that they are able to manipulate their parents through tantrums or parents learn that they are able to manipulate their children by paying them allowances for completing chores.

Behavior modification principles are used to decrease maladaptive behaviors and increase adaptive responses that have been occurring infrequently. In the preceding examples, throwing tantrums and hitting are viewed not as signs of unconscious or deep-seated problems but as *the problems themselves*, and procedures are subsequently developed to modify these behaviors.

As mentioned, a basic rule of behavior modification is that maladaptive behaviors are learned and maintained in the same way as adaptive behaviors. Accordingly, maladaptive behaviors of behaviorally and emotionally disturbed children and youth can be unlearned and replaced with more adaptive behaviors.

As a result of this fundamental principle, behavior modification deals with specific, observable behaviors. Behaviors identified for change, therefore, must be overt (e.g., taking out the trash, handing in math papers, hitting another child) and measurable. *Measurable* refers to behaviors that we can count or measure. Thus, instead of targeting *hyperactivity* for change (*hyperactivity* means different things to different people, making it difficult to measure), the target for change might be being out of seat without permission at school. Being out of seat without permission at school is a behavior that can be seen, agreed on, and measured.

Another principle of behavior modification suggests that it is not necessary to assign a diagnostic label (e.g., emotional disturbance, schizophrenia) to children in order to treat them. Therefore, behavior modification practitioners attempt to improve behaviors that interfere with a child's adjustment without regard for how the child is diagnosed. For example, a child whose excessive pouting interferes with peer relationships would be exposed to procedures designed to reduce pouting and increase appropriate peer interactions. Whether or not the child had previously been identified as emotionally disturbed would not affect the manner in which the program would be applied.

Behavior modification also maintains that the effectiveness of behavior change methods is not known until they have been tried. Thus, a procedure that has proven effective with one child cannot automatically be assumed to work equally well with another. Only by systematically applying and evaluating a behavior management procedure can its effectiveness be determined.

A final assumption of behavior modification is that most behaviors are affected by events and experiences that happen before and after them. A child's tantrums, for example, might be the result of parental attention to crying and screaming. The significance of this principle for successfully modifying behavior is great: If we can isolate the actions or reactions of others that support a behavior identified for change (e.g., one aimed at attention getting or manipulation of others), behavior problems may be replaced with more adaptive behavior.

Teachers, therapists, and parents can use behavior modification procedures. Although successful use of these methods requires training and guidance, one need not be a professional to use them. In fact, children often show the greatest gains when a variety of persons, including parents and family members, make consistent use of behavior modification.

Behavior Modification With Children and Adolescents

Four primary steps underlie successful behavior modification procedures: (a) identify, define, and measure the behavior to be increased or decreased; (b) determine where, when, and with whom the target behavior occurs; (c) identify events that may be promoting or maintaining the target behavior; and (d) apply intervention procedures. As noted earlier, these steps may be applied by a number of persons, including parents.

Identifying, Defining, and Measuring a Behavior for Change

In accordance with the notion that problem behaviors are not symptoms of unconscious or underlying difficulties, behavior therapists attempt to modify (i.e., increase or decrease) the behaviors that interfere with a child's or adolescent's adjustment. Thus, *specific, precisely defined behaviors* are identified for change. Examples include failure to follow parents' or teachers' commands, talking out without permission at school, or kicking another person. All these behaviors may be measured; a teacher, therapist, or parent can count the number of times they occur and can share with others their observations and interventions without the interference of subjective interpretation and misunderstanding.

As part of thoroughly understanding a target behavior, the person attempting to bring about a change must be familiar with the setting in which the behavior occurs and the circumstances surrounding it. For example, a child who displays negative behavior only in the presence of a baby-sitter would probably undergo a different intervention program than a child who displays such behavior around a number of people. Similarly, an adolescent who is considered a problem only during the dinner hour or in gym class at school would be dealt with differently than somebody who tends to have problems across different times and settings.

Identifying Events That May Promote or Maintain a Problem Behavior

As noted earlier, behavior modification is based on the assumption that we learn from experience to do particular things in particular ways. Thus, a toddler may learn that banging his head against a wall is an excellent way to gain his parents' attention (i.e., whenever he bangs his head, someone attends to him) or that hitting effectively allows him to control a situation. Not all behaviors are so simply analyzed; however, identifying factors associated with the occurrence of a problem behavior is important. Accordingly, behavior modification involves attempts to uncover those factors that may be controlling a child's behavior and, subsequently, establish the most effective and efficient intervention program. Identifying these antecedent and consequent variables is associated with the process of creating functional behavioral assessment and functional behavior analysis.

Intervention Procedures and How They Are Used With Children and Adolescents

The responses of children and youth with EBD can be changed by systematic use of consequences. *Consequences* refer to positive or negative events that happen *after* a child engages in a behavior that someone wants to increase or decrease. For example, a child may receive additional free time in the classroom *after* she successfully finishes her daily math assignments. Similarly, a student may lose his recess whenever he fights on the playground. Successful use of consequences requires that an agreed-on intervention plan be followed each time a specified behavior occurs. Consequences can be of three types: (a) reinforcers, (b) planned ignoring (extinction), and (c) punishers (negative consequences).

Reinforcers are consequences that increase the likelihood of future occurrences of a behavior; children and youth are rewarded for specified behaviors in the hope that positive consequences will increase the chances that the desired behavior recurs. For example, a teacher may verbally praise a child each time he holds up his hand to speak or a youngster may be allowed to play a computer game at school when she completes an assignment within a specified time. In the preceding examples, the teacher's praise for seeking permission to talk and playing with a computer for successfully completing an assignment function as reinforcers if they increase the specified target behavior.

Reinforcers for children and adolescents usually fall into three categories: (a) social rewards (e.g., hugs and verbal praise for desired behavior); (b) tangible rewards (e.g., edibles and toys for displaying specified behavior); and (c) contingent activities (e.g., recess and free time for completing school assignments, or a special dessert or evening family board game for following directions at home). It is fundamentally important to understand that what one person finds reinforcing may be utterly unenjoyable or unimportant to another person. It takes time and careful observation of a child to know what he or she truly enjoys or would be likely to find reinforcing. When a teacher or parent cannot identify what is reinforcing, the parent may be tempted to state that positive reinforcement does not work for the child. That usually means that the correct reinforcer just hasn't been located yet. Teachers and parents have found many unexpected preferences among children and youth, including baseball trading cards, lunchtime with a friend from another class, 2 minutes to visit a favorite teacher, or spending time with Dad shooting hoops, to name a few. There are several ways to identify potentially useful reinforcers: One approach is to use checklists or fill-in-the-blank worksheets that ask the child to identify what they like. Sample items may include, "What is your favorite television show or music group?" "When you do something good, what does your parent usually do or say?" "If you had five dollars, what would you do with it?" Offering a menu of choices as the reinforcer is another way to get started. When the child earns a reinforcer, he or she can select something from a few options. Or before beginning to work on a skill, a child can make an agreement with the parent or teacher in advance that when a certain level of success in completing the activity or using the skill has been reached, he or she will earn a specific desired reinforcer.

Some people have equated offering reinforcers to bribery. Nothing could be farther from the truth. Bribes are money or items received for illegal activities, whereas reinforcers acknowledge a job well done. It may help to think of paychecks, grades, or praise as types of reinforcers generally appreciated by adults.

Children and youth often seek attention by displaying unacceptable behavior. For example, a student may get out of his assigned school seat without permission to gain teacher attention or throw a tantrum to control his parents' actions. *Planned ignoring* (extinction) involves systematic withdrawal of attention for unacceptable behavior followed by replacement of attention for desired behavior. Using this approach, a child may be ignored when she pouts but attended to when she engages in acceptable social behavior. Extinction may not work with every child. However, for children who are motivated by attention, it may be an effective consequence.

When using planned ignoring, it is important to recognize that if the behavior has helped the child get his way in the past, it will probably make him feel upset when you begin ignoring the behavior. He will probably continue to do it or even do behaviors that seem worse when you begin ignoring. If you have anticipated that this will happen and have a plan prepared for how to keep ignoring even when he is behaving badly or what to do if his behavior gets significantly worse, then you will increase the likelihood that you will be successful using this method. Once children understand that you will not pay attention to them until they are demonstrating appropriate behavior, they will change how they behave. There are three important rules to using planned ignoring:

1. Have a plan for how to keep ignoring even when the behavior starts to get to you.
2. Ignoring will not work if the child is not trying to get your attention (for example, if laughter from peers or siblings is encouraging the behavior, not attention or ignoring from you).
3. If the behavior could injure the child or someone else or damage property, then ignoring is not a good option.

Punishment means different things to different people. It may create an image of a "trip to the woodshed" for some and withdrawal of privileges for others. As part of behavior modification, *punishment* (or negative consequences) refers to any event that decreases a behavior it follows. For example, a child who reduces the number of fights he gets into as a result of losing bicycle privileges for fighting is said to have his behavior modified through negative consequences. Punishment programs for behaviorally disordered children and adolescents typically involve three types of negative consequences: response cost, time-out, and overcorrection. Spanking and other forms of corporal (physical) punishment are rarely considered appropriate forms of behavior modification punishment.

Response cost refers to systematic removal of rewards when specified unacceptable behaviors occur. For example, children may lose TV or other privileges for failing to abide by established rules and regulations. It works in the same manner as positive reinforcement, described earlier.

When using negative consequences (or any of the negative-consequence procedures), adults must plan in advance what the appropriate consequences will be for certain behaviors. Whatever the consequences, they should be (a) equal to the infringement (not more than or less than the offense) and (b) consistently applied by all adults who interact with the child and without regard to excuses or differing sets of expectations. An advantage of using this type of systematic approach to changing children's behavior is the preplanned aspect.

Children who have behavior disorders can at times become challenging, frustrating, or hurtful (psychologically or otherwise). The safest, fairest, and most protective action, for self and child, that adults can do is to plan ahead (cooperatively) how they will react to the behaviors of the child. Acting in the heat of the moment is most often counterproductive to all. When advanced planning has occurred, and all adults as well as the child know what the consequences of certain acts will be, then you have leveled the playing field so that everyone involved knows what to expect.

Time-out involves removing children from reinforcing situations whenever they display specified maladaptive behaviors. Time-out may require children and youth to sit quietly away from the group (but close enough to see them) for short periods of time following unacceptable behaviors or otherwise restrict them from participating in reinforcing activities or being in reinforcing environments. One child was required to quietly lay his head on his desk for 3 minutes whenever he threw an object in class. Time-out is a popular intervention that has been used successfully by both professionals and parents. However, many professionals have observed that to be effective, time-out must be structured properly. Time-out can only be effective if the child finds the group activity interesting or positively reinforcing. It would not be a good option if the student is bored by the activity, finds it too difficult, or is embarrassed in front of peers by his or her performance in skills required by group participation. Exclusionary time-outs, where the child is entirely removed from the room without adult supervision or in any way restrained or confined during the time-out process, are not advocated.

As a behavioral intervention procedure, overcorrection consists of two main parts, *restitution* and *positive practice.* The first, restitution, requires that individuals who disturb or destroy things clean up or otherwise restore a situation to its original state. For example, an adolescent who purposefully throws food on the floor may be made to clean the soiled area. Positive practice, in turn, requires that a child or youth practice an appropriate behavior related to a maladaptive response. Thus, the youngster who throws food may be required to transfer blocks from one container to another for several minutes. Or it could mean having the adolescent work in the cafeteria serving food for a day to make up for throwing food on the floor. In this case, transferring blocks is an alternative behavior to throwing, which the youth is required to practice. Overcorrection is often a time-consuming and complex process; however, it offers an effective management procedure for children and youth with severe behavior problems.

EXAMPLES OF TWO BEHAVIOR MODIFICATION PROGRAMS

Two sample behavior management programs for emotionally disturbed children follow. The first uses a reinforcement system; the second, a punishment procedure.

Example 1. Positive Reinforcement

The participant was a 10-year-old boy in treatment at a center school for students with significant EBD. He had been placed in the program as a result of extreme acting-out behavior. Although the child had made good progress, his teacher observed that he was slow and inconsistent in completing daily academic assignments, and that he had not responded well to attempts to motivate him to improve in this area.

As a result, the professional staff began to monitor the boy's completion of daily classroom assignments. Specifically, the target behavior was completion of daily spelling, history, and math papers on the day they were assigned and within the appropriate class period. Observations revealed that over a 5-day period, the child completed about 20% of his assignments.

To increase the boy's schoolwork output, a reinforcement program was used consisting of (a) verbal praise following the submission of assignments and (b) earning the privilege of being "staff man" on those days when at least 90% of his assignments were completed. As staff man, the boy had an opportunity to aid the teacher in a variety of tasks.

This reinforcement program greatly increased the child's work output. Within the first week of the program, he was completing almost all his assignments. Because failure to hand in school assignments and follow adult directions were primary reasons for the child's original treatment referral, the intervention program was considered important to the youngster's overall well-being.

Example 2. Punishment Program: Response Cost

The subject of the program was a 4-year-old boy who was a residential patient in a state-operated psychiatric facility. The child was admitted to the program because his parents were unable to control his behavior.

As a part of his treatment plan, the child was assigned to a preschool classroom. School progress was slowed by his tendency to leave his seat without permission. The classroom teacher observed that whenever the youngster was not being attended to by an adult, he would leave his seat and wander around the room. Several behavior modification programs, developed specifically to deal with this problem, had proven unsuccessful.

Last, a response-cost punishment intervention was tried. The program consisted of notifying the child that the 5-point star he and his classmates received at the end of each school day would be altered if he did not stay in his seat. He was told that he would be given a mark each time he got out of his seat without teacher permission. The marks were placed next to his name on the chalkboard. After he had received three marks, the teacher would take a pair of scissors and cut one of the points from his star. No loss of privileges was associated with the cutting of points from the star; however, staff praised the boy when his star was complete.

This response-cost program successfully reduced the child's out-of-seat problem. Furthermore, once he began staying in his seat, his other behavior problems also subsided.

SCHOOLWIDE DISCIPLINE: POSITIVE BEHAVIORAL SUPPORTS

Counseling-Psychotherapy

Counseling or psychotherapy refer to any type of psychological or psychiatric treatment that is based on verbal or nonverbal communication. Whereas different types of counseling-psychotherapy exist, they all rely on a discussion and interaction process. They aim at improving behavior and mental health by means of having the person talk about personal issues and concerns. Thus, children are treated through discussions of their behavior, feelings, and motivations. Discussions may take place in individual sessions with a therapist or in groups of children having similar problems. A trained counselor, teacher, psychologist, or psychiatrist may assume the role of the therapist.

With children for whom talking does not come easily or who are too young to discuss their problems, play is used to allow them to express their feelings, conflicts, and concerns. These intervention methods differ from drug treatment and other procedures that do not primarily rely on counseling, discussions of feelings, communication, and interaction programs. The information in this section was obtained from some of the many valuable sources that are currently available (e.g., Seligman, 2001).

It is difficult to say what actually occurs during counseling-psychotherapy because it may take many different forms. Most types share several features, however. First, counseling-psychotherapy relies on trust and a positive relationship between children and their therapist. Therefore, therapists can be expected to invest time in developing a positive atmosphere. They may tell children that information shared during sessions will remain confidential, including being unavailable to parents and teachers. Therapists will also avoid being critical of a child, choosing instead to understand and accept the child's behavior and feelings. Such an atmosphere is needed for children to benefit from the therapy.

Second, counseling-psychotherapy relies on both children and therapists to be involved in the process. Children cannot sit back and expect the therapist to do all the work. Rather, both parties must try to understand the nature and basis of disordered behavior. Similarly, both children and therapists are involved in identifying appropriate solutions to problems.

Third, most counseling-psychotherapy programs focus on one's feelings and emotions. Children and adolescents will be encouraged to talk about how they feel about certain events and circumstances (e.g., their resentment at a parent's remarrying and the subsequent problem of having to share a bedroom with a new stepbrother).

Fourth, counseling-psychotherapy is based on self-understanding. Therefore, attention is focused on making children and adolescents aware of who they are and why they engage in certain behaviors, including responses considered maladaptive. Based on the underlying assumption that positive change can only occur with accurate self-understanding, children and adolescents are helped to understand their relationships with significant individuals in their lives, particularly parents.

Fifth, counseling-psychotherapy emphasizes an individual's unique perception of the world, recognizing that children and youth may interpret their worlds and the people with whom they interact in an individual manner. Accordingly, therapists often attempt to understand and accept children's perceptions of their world as opposed to directly trying to change such views, based on the belief that intervention must build on a child's or adolescent's unique feelings and perceptions.

Last, much of what occurs in counseling-psychotherapy has its roots in psychoanalysis, although the latter may not constitute the treatment. An example of what one may find in therapy follows:

> One 3-year-old girl, whose parents sought professional help because their daughter began to have sleeping and eating problems, was assisted through play psychotherapy. In sessions with a professional therapist, the child was able to reenact an experience with a relative who had stayed with her while her parents were out of town. The child was able to express, without fear of betrayal or retribution, the anger and confusion she felt toward the relative who had sexually molested her.

Counseling-Psychotherapy and Psychoanalysis

Psychotherapy is a general term used to describe a number of verbally based therapeutic and counseling methods, including play therapy. Much of counseling-psychotherapy has it is roots in *psychoanalysis,* which refers to a specific form of psychotherapy. Sigmund Freud, considered the founder of psychoanalysis, and the psychoanalytic method, developed in the 19th century, continue to have a significant influence on the manner in which children are educated and treated.

The History and Theory of Psychoanalysis

Psychoanalysis is based on the notion that maladaptive behaviors are the result of underlying problems. *Underlying* is used here to describe conditions that cannot be seen (e.g., anger, resentment, personality conflict) but that cause overt problems. For example, parents may complain about a child's poor motivation in school, low grades, and inability to maintain friends. According to a psychoanalytic interpretation, these *surface* behaviors (i.e., the overt problem behaviors of concern to parents and teachers) are caused by an underlying conflict or feeling of which the child may not be aware. Thus, psychoanalytic treatment does not focus on the immediate maladaptive behaviors, adhering instead to the belief that significant and long-term improvement will come only as a result of understanding and removal of the underlying problem.

Psychoanalysis places great importance on children's early years, particularly their relationships with parents. An early trusting relationship between parent and infant is crucial, and children's relationships with their mothers is considered especially important in determining their future interpersonal dealings. Consequently, children who fail to establish trusting relationships with their parents may struggle with this issue throughout life. In addition, unresolved conflicts or psychological crises during critical phases of development may set the stage for future problems.

Other significant characteristics of psychoanalysis include an emphasis on (a) unconscious motivation, (b) structure of personality, and (c) stages of personality development. Psychoanalytic theory and thought are somewhat complicated, and an in-depth discussion is beyond the scope of this book. Readers wishing more information on psychoanalysis are encouraged to obtain books on this topic from their public library.

A major assumption of psychoanalytic theory is that all of us (including children and adolescents) do things for reasons of which we are unaware. The origin of this part of psychoanalytic theory stems from Freud's belief that conscious motivation and awareness account for only a small portion of our behavior. Using the analogy of an iceberg, with the conscious awareness being the small part showing above the water and the unconscious the major portion of the iceberg below the surface, Freud believed that the unconscious largely determines our behavior. In psychoanalysis, therefore, the unconscious is most important for understanding and correcting emotional and behavioral problems. Psychoanalytic treatment programs, accordingly, involve attempts to make children and adolescents more aware of the reasons for their behavior.

According to psychoanalytic theory, children may become fixated or arrested at certain stages of development. Disturbed behavior is thought to result from an inability to resolve a conflict at a particular developmental stage or to pass through a stage at the appropriate time.

Counseling-psychotherapy with children and adults may be a lengthy process, sometimes (although rarely) lasting up to several years. A child may be seen by a therapist several times a week. In addition, the child's parent(s) are typically also seen by a therapist at regular intervals in the course of the child's treatment. During this process, therapists attempt to help children gain insight, that is, to recognize, understand, and accept their feelings and motivations, including urges and drives, and thereby gain improved emotional health and behavior. To achieve such insight and understanding, children and youth examine past emotional experiences, some of which they may not be conscious of.

One 12-year-old boy received therapy because of severe anxiety and fear of abandonment by his father and stepmother. Through therapy, the boy was helped to understand and accept his feelings associated with his biological mother leaving the family to live with another man. He believed that his feelings caused his mother to leave the family. Furthermore, guilt over the situation led him to believe that his family would eventually banish him. The boy learned to understand his feelings, including his repression of the incident (pushing thoughts and feelings about the matter to an unconscious level).

Counseling-Psychotherapy in Schools

The psychoeducational approach to educating children and adolescents with emotional and behavioral problems adapts psychoanalytic (and psychotherapeutic) principles for educational use. Accordingly, classroom personnel not only concentrate on teaching traditional academic content areas (e.g., reading, math), they also attempt to understand the underlying motivation for their students' behavior. In addition, because it is assumed that children's emotional well-being and their ability to learn in school are closely connected, attention is given to both students' feelings and their learning ability.

A teacher using a psychoeducational approach will concentrate on accepting students' feelings and attempt to bring such feelings to conscious awareness along with helping them understand how their feelings relate to their classroom behavior. For example, the teacher may ask a child, "You seem angry today; does it have anything to do with spending the weekend with your father?"

One specific psychoeducational approach is *life-space interviewing*, whereby teachers or other adults help children deal with difficult situations or work through problems. Life-space interviewing involves children talking about what happened in a situation and finding alternatives so as to avoid the same problem in the future.

Educators using a psychoeducational approach view crises as opportunities for helping children and adolescents learn more productive behavior patterns. For example, one child who verbally provoked another youngster during recess was knocked to the ground. When the injured child complained to his teacher, he was shown, through the teacher's use of a life-space interview, how his actions (taunting another student) resulted in his injury and how future occurrences might be avoided.

COGNITIVE BEHAVIOR THERAPY

Cognitive behavior therapy (CBT) is a combination of psychotherapy and behavior modification. Developed by psychologists (Ellis & Harper, 1975; Meichenbaum, 1977), CBT is designed to integrate elements of the behavioral and traditional psychotherapeutic approaches. Based on the notion that people are disturbed because of their inaccurate perceptions of reality rather than arrested or delayed psychosexual development, CBT focuses on conscious rather than unconscious thoughts and the present rather than the past. As a result, teachers and therapists attempt to show children and adolescents that their perceptions are inaccurate, that they are not true. For example, some children may believe that others should not tease them or that teachers must be fair. Although these expectations are desirable, the reality is that other children do tease, and that some teachers may on occasion be unfair.

CBT involves aiding children in identifying thoughts that upset them and analyzing why they are bothersome. Once these thoughts are understood, efforts are made to change them. In some cases, understanding one's thinking process will encourage changes in behavior. However, for most people, understanding is not enough. For example, most people understand that weight gain is associated with eating certain types of food, such as ice cream and candy. Nevertheless, many people who are concerned about their weight do not change their diet. This is where the behavior modification approach is used in cognitive behavior therapy. Subsequent to thought restructuring, children and youth must practice their new patterns of thinking. Thus, many of the techniques described in the behavior modification section are used to encourage behavioral changes.

Professionals who use CBT work toward many of the same goals as do proponents of behavior modification. The major difference is that those who use CBT want children and youth to understand that their thinking patterns are often the cause of their problem behavior. Such understanding is thought to reduce similar problems in the future. CBT may be broken into several different types, including rational emotive behavioral therapy, reality therapy, and cognitive behavior modification (Nichols, 1999; Vernon, 1998; Zionts, 1996).

School Implications for the Treatment of Behavior and Emotions

Behavior modification, counseling-psychotherapy, and their various permutations reflect earnest attempts to help students with emotional and behavior disorders to learn to control their feelings and behaviors whenever possible. Acknowledging that EBD is a disability, most caregivers realize that it may be permanent and impossible to cure. Regardless, like those who educate individuals who have other disabilities, their goal is to teach students to manage their disabilities as best as they are able and to use techniques that will allow them to navigate their worlds despite their disability. It is critical to understand that these efforts may not be the same and in fact may conflict with current management and discipline practices that are displayed in many of our schools.

During the reauthorization hearings of IDEA in 1997, much attention was devoted to discipline. At least part of this focus was a reaction to the violent tragedies that had recently occurred in some of our schools (see Chapter 5). Legislators passed laws that reflected this concern (e.g., Gun-Free Schools Act), and school boards enacted zero-tolerance policies that immediately dealt with infractions with impunity.

A representative example of schoolwide classroom management was offered by the American Federation of Teachers (1997) in their publication *Setting the Stage for High Standards: Elements of Effective School Discipline*. They suggested that the following six components must be considered:

1. Promote effective classroom management: The heart of effective classroom management rests on ensuring that the instructional techniques, classroom arrangement, and classroom rules and

procedures are all well thought out and supportive of the instructional program and students' learning (p. 5).

2. Enact a districtwide discipline code: This includes parental, community, and staff involvement, applying consequences to all misbehaviors, distinguishing between minor and severe offenses (with appropriate matching consequences), and requiring removal of dangerous and chronically disruptive students from educational environments.

3. Enforce the discipline code: This needs to be done consistently with backing (including resources) from the school board. This involves providing the critical infrastructure necessary to maintain and communicate about the program's efficacy.

4. Implement programs to modify student misbehavior: Provide behavior specialists for students who do not respond to the traditional rule systems.

5. Establish alternative placements for chronically disruptive and violent students: These settings will help students with behaviors, academics, and other supervisory needs. Also, provide a continuum of alternatives, including specialists, of in-school crisis centers (short duration), in-school suspensions (medium duration), and off-campus alternatives.

6. Support the work of families, religious institutions, and communities in developing sound character in children, which has repercussions in their behavior: The purpose of this element is to recognize and reinforce the values of these institutions.

It is important to note that these components are designed to provide a culture that enables all students to learn and thrive in schools although students with EBD may not have the ability to comply with them. However, when students with EBD are not punished because of their disability, it is often considered a double standard. The same double-standard label is not applied when there are special considerations for those who have learning disabilities or mental retardation. Some teachers, students, and communities prefer to disregard the fact that EBD is as valid a disability as those two if it is for this reason that programs such as positive behavior support systems are implemented.

Positive Behavioral Supports

Characteristics of students who exhibit acting-out behaviors are that they are more likely to have had a life situation of poverty and illiteracy and a history of acting out that may have been exhibited when they were toddlers than were their normally developing peers. School reactions to these students typically have been excluding them from either the classroom or the school settings. Unfortunately, this response only exacerbates the problem as the more time that these students are out of the classroom setting, the less they learn, and the more frustrated the student and teachers become, creating the breeding ground for more inappropriate behaviors.

Emanating from the 1997 reauthorization of IDEA was a major initiative called Positive Behavior Supports (sometimes called Positive Behavior Instructional Supports). The philosophy of positive behavior supports (PBS) is to create a fair, preventative, schoolwide behavior management program that uses many of the principles discussed in the sections on behavior modification as well as creating an environment that meets the learning needs of students with disabilities. In a guide for administrators, the Office of Special Education and Rehabilitative Services (2001) provides the following explanation of PBS:

- Positive behavior support is the application of positive behavioral interventions and systems to achieve positive change.
- Positive behavior support is an approach to discipline and intervention that is proving both effective and practical in schools.
- Positive behavior support is the application of the science of behavior to achieve socially important change. The emphasis is on behavior change that is durable, comprehensive, and linked to academic and social gains.
- As a general principle, positive behavior support should be applied before any child is excluded from school due to problem behavior.
- The development of positive behavioral interventions and plans that are guided by functional behavioral assessment (FBA) is a foundation on which positive behavior support is delivered.
- FBA is a systematic way of identifying problem behaviors and the events that predict occurrence, nonoccurrence, and maintenance of those behaviors.
- Strong, active administrative leadership, supports, and participation are needed for effective efforts.
- Positive behavior support considers multiple contexts: community, family, district, school, classroom, nonclassroom, and individual.

A proactive perspective is maintained along a continuum, using primary (what we do for all), secondary (what we do for some), and tertiary (what we do for a few) prevention and interventions (p. 4).

It is important to consider that there may be two types of students who disturb others: those that are products of their environments and those who behaviors and emotions may have nothing to do with their status in life. If special education students' behaviors are a result of their disability, than manifest determination decisions are made. If the students' behaviors are those that can be predicted from their disability, then those students should not be treated in the same manner as the general education population. When this occurs, these students will need to be educated either in the general education environment or in an interim alternative educational setting.

Functional behavioral assessment is designed to fully understand why students behave the way they do (what the behavior's function is for the student) and then develop a hypothesis to teach the students new behaviors (Sasso, Garrison-Harrell, & Doelling, 1997; Sugai, Lewis-Palmer, & Hogan, 1998). Those who use functional behavioral assessment typically follow the steps outlined in the behavior modification section, although there are some who pay attention to the counseling-psychotherapy approach (Kaplan, 2000).

Keeping a Watchful Eye

On July 25, 2000, a letter was written to all concerned by the Office of Civil Rights and the Office of Special Education and Rehabilitative Services (Cantu & Heumann, 2000) that had the explicit intent of informing their readers regarding disability harassment. Specific to the content in this chapter, "harassing conduct may take many forms, including verbal acts and name calling, as well as nonverbal behavior, such as graphic and written statement or conduct that is physically threatening, harmful, or humiliating" (p. 3). Two specific examples by the authors have implications for teachers and administrators:

> Several students continually remark out loud to other students during class that a student with dyslexia is "retarded" or "deaf and dumb" and does not belong in the class; as a result, the harassed student has difficulty doing work in class and her grades decline (p. 3). This example pertains equally to those students who cannot behave well because of their disability. Teachers (and students) are not allowed to defame a student regardless of their behavior if they have EBD.

> A teacher subjects a student to inappropriate physical restraint because of conduct related to his disability; with the result that the student tries to avoid school through increased absences (p. 3).

Teachers are not allowed to manage students who have EBD in ways different from other students unless expressly written in the student's IEP. Certainly, any intervention must be examined for its documented effectiveness; and most certainly, if it results in increased student absences, it should be deemed ineffective. Equally important was the intent of the letter to inform teachers, parents, and administrators that schools will be held accountable for the actions of the individuals inside the building, adult and child alike. The courts have ruled in favor of students and their families in harassment cases (and allowed large settlements) when it can be documented that teachers or administrators knew of the harassment and failed to protect the child by stopping the persecutors (for more information, see *Nabozny v. Podlesny*, 1996).

SUMMARY

In this chapter, we have identified and discussed major ways to deal with the emotional and behavioral problems of children and youth. In spite of the value of each, no single approach is complete or adequate with every child. The best treatment results occur when a combination of procedures is used. Thus, children and adolescents who are helped by cross-sections of professionals (e.g., educators, mental health workers, medical personnel) using a variety of treatment approaches (e.g., psychotherapy, behavior modification) based on the children's needs make the best progress. In addition, for optimal progress, parents and families must play an integral part in the overall treatment and education process.

REFERENCES

American Federation of Teachers. (1997). *Setting the stage for high standards: Elements of effective school discipline*. Washington, DC: Author.

Cantu, N. V., & Heumann, J. E. (2000, July 25). *Memorandum on harassment based on disability*. Washington, DC: U.S. Office of Special Education Programs.

Ellis, A. E., & Harper, R. A. (1975). *A new guide to rational living*. Hollywood, CA: Wilshire.

Jenson, W. R., Sloane, W. R., & Young, K. R. (1988). *Applied behavior analysis in educaton: A structured teaching approach*. Columbus, OH: Prentice Hall.

Kaplan, J. S. (2000). *Beyond functional assessment*. Austin, TX: PRO-ED.

Maag, J. W. (1999). *Behavior management: From theoretical implications to practical applications*. San Diego, CA: Singular.

Malott, R. W., Malott, M. E., & Trojan, E. A. (2000). *Elementary principles of behavior* (4th ed.). Columbus, OH: Prentice Hall.

Martin, G., & Pear, J. (1999). *Behavior modification: What it is and how to do it* (6th ed.). Columbus, OH: Prentice Hall.

Meichenbaum, D. (1977). *Cognitive behavior modification*. New York: Plenum.

Nabozny v. Podlesny, 92 F. 3d 446 (7th Cir. 1996).

Nichols, P. (1999). *Clear thinking: Talking back to whispering shadows*. Iowa City, IA: River Lights.

Office of Special Education and Rehabilitative Services. (2001). *Prevention research and the IDEA discipline provisions: A guide for school administrators.* Washington, DC: Author.

Sasso, G. M., Garrison-Harrell, L., & Doelling, J. E. (1997). Functional analysis and treatment of problematic behavior. In P. Zionts (Ed.), *Inclusive strategies for children and youth with behavioral disorders.* Austin, TX: PRO-ED.

Seligman, L. (2001). *Systems, strategies, and skills of counseling and psychotherapy.* Upper Saddle River, NJ: Merrill Prentice Hall.

Sugai, G., Lewis-Palmer, T., & Hogan, S. (1998). Using functional assessments to develop behavior support plans. *Preventing School Failure, 43,* 6–13.

Vernon, A. (1998). *The passport program: A journey through emotional, social, cognitive, and self-development. Grades 1–5.* Champaign, IL: Research Press.

Zionts, P. (1996). *Teaching disturbed and disturbing students* (2nd ed.). Austin, TX: PRO-ED.

Zionts, P., & Simpson, R. L. (1988). *Understanding children and youth with emotional and behavioral disorders.* Austin, TX: PRO-ED.

Zirpoli, T. J., & Melloy, K. J. (2001). *Behavior management: Applications for teachers* (3rd ed.). Upper Saddle River, NJ: Merrill Prentice Hall.

School-Based Placements

8

It is important to understand that it is difficult to predict how any one school district will program and place students who have emotional disturbances or behavioral disorders. Although laws have been developed to guide the educational system, different schools have different interpretations of those laws. The purpose of this chapter is to present the possible public education placement options for these students.

AFTER IDENTIFICATION

The placement of students with EBD is as significant as diagnosis and assessment. Professional evaluations and their purposes were discussed in Chapter 3 to help you understand this complicated and, oftentimes, confusing procedure. Identification of the child, however, is only half of the process as placements may be handled differently from school district to school district. The cornerstone of all placements should be guided by the spirit of the least restrictive environment philosophy stated originally in the Education for All Handicapped Children federal law and reiterated in the current law (IDEA). The information presented in this chapter represents one interpretation of the least restrictive environment that would ensure what we define as the best possible education for special education students.

DETERMINING APPROPRIATE EDUCATIONAL GOALS

After eligibility for special education has been determined, an appropriate program must be developed. It is critical that educational goals are discussed first. This is frequently easier said than done. The reason for the difficulty is the often conflicting goals that stakeholders bring to the table. Some participants believe that the most critical goals are those that promote social integration. Consequently, their placement recommendations tend to be the general education classroom, even when it appears that the student and environment may be incompatible at the time. Others believe that academic progress should be the priority. These people may argue that the students should be in an environment where the students are in the best academic placement for academic growth—which may not be the general education setting.

The ideal solution would be an environment where both goals are being met. Unfortunately, for many students who have EBD, both goals cannot be met in one setting. The general education setting may not have the supports to teach the student with EBD well. By definition, these students will need help in the emotional, behavioral, and social domains. This can be an overwhelming task as these students may take an enormous amount of time and teacher attention.

We believe that the least restrictive environment can be defined as the setting in which a student's disability does not interfere with his or her learning. For example, the least restrictive environment for severely emotionally disturbed students who do not have the ability to control their behaviors might be a very structured setting, such as a residential or day school that is separate from the public school. (Later in this chapter, the functions of the many types of placements will be discussed.)

Rarely are students with EBD placed in the general education classroom without supports because the teacher most likely will not have the time nor the necessary skills to teach or manage them. Furthermore, the academic curriculum for students with EBD tends to be on a significantly lower level than that of the other students. This is, at least in part, due to an inability on the part of the student to complete class assignments owing to behavior and emotional issues, which is different from many students who receive special education to receive greater or different cognitive instruction. Some students who have EBD have the capability to perform well academically, given the proper social and behavioral supports.

With the large number of general education students in many general education classrooms, teachers usually teach to the majority of the students, leaving less instructional time for the special education students. It is also possible that the general education teacher has not been trained to meet the special needs of students who have EBD. Last, these students may have a disturbing influence on other students by exhibiting behaviors that normally lead to such disciplinary actions as exclusion from class, detention, and suspension, all resulting in less teaching time for all students. And equally important, when these students are removed from a setting because of their behavior, they too are missing significant academic instruction, which can result in their falling behind. Needless to say, this can become a cycle that becomes failure laden.

Consequently, the general education classroom is usually not the least restrictive environment for many students who have EBD. In fact, it is a setting that can be very restrictive to such students' academic and behavioral growth.

THE LEAST RESTRICTIVE ENVIRONMENT

The least restrictive environment for special education students is determined through careful examination of the students' needs and selection of the program that most effectively helps meet these needs. Placements, hopefully, are dictated by students' needs: Assessment information, both formal and informal, should determine what programs and placements are needed so that students are not handicapped by their disabilities in their educational pursuits. School district placement options are associated with many factors. The size of the school system, its location, relative wealth, and its commitment to education each has an impact on the quality and quantity of available placement choices. For example, larger urban areas place fewer students in the general education setting than smaller rural districts (U.S. Department of Education, 1997). These differences are due to resources and the numbers of students served.

IDEA (1997) is very clear about the appropriateness of placements for any student who has a disability. It states that, to the maximum extent appropriate, children with disabilities, including children in public or private institutions or other care facilities, are educated with children who do not have disabilities. Furthermore, special classes, separate schooling, or other removal of children with disabilities from the regular educational environment occurs only if the nature or severity of the disability is such that education in regular classes with the use of supplementary aids and services cannot be achieved satisfactorily (34 CFR 300.550). Practically speaking, the IEP team, after discussing the strengths and needs of the students, should then consider their most appropriate placements. A simple and fair process would be to regard all of the available options. Should one of the available options not be the least restrictive for a student and the school, then an exploration of other possibilities must begin (this may range from the creation of a program to transportation to another school district to possible placement in a residential program).

For example, consider the placement description about "Joe" (see pages 151-152). Is the general education setting appropriate for Joe? Is the setting, with accommodations (things that will be altered in the classroom to help Joe), an environment where he will not be handicapped because of his disability? If the answer is "no," then go down the continuum to the next option. Can Joe receive an appropriate education if the general education teacher has access to a consultant? Continue through the continuum until the most acceptable setting is determined. Remember that the most acceptable setting may not be the placement where Joe can reach his potential (an understandable goal); rather, it is the placement that *will not prevent him from learning*, when compared to his peers. It is important to understand that a placement is only as good as the services it provides to the students. Two factors must be considered: specially designed instruction and the actual classroom itself (the specific teacher, peers, and physical room).

IDEA is quite clear about specially designed instruction. In fact, it defines special education as

> Specially designed instruction, at no cost to the parents, to meet the unique needs of a child with a disability. Furthermore, it must . . . address the unique needs of the child that result from the child's disability and to ensure access of the child to the general curriculum so that he or she can meet the educational standards within the jurisdiction of the school district/public agency that apply to all children. (34 CFR 00.26)

In other words, special education students must have instruction, if needed, that is different from that for general education, and also, it should reflect the general curriculum (they should have access to the same information). Related services may also be included as part of the students' specially designed instruction. These are services that are traditionally offered or are available in many schools or school districts. They may reflect anything from access to school to specialized therapy in any of the following placement options. For example, related services can include

- Transportation to school
- Speech and language intervention
- Hearing services
- Psychological services
- Physical or occupational therapy
- Counseling

The personnel staffing of any of the aforementioned services is critical to placement. Are they capable of carrying out the IEP? Obviously, this can be a very sensitive issue but one that needs to be addressed for a successful placement to be achieved.

THE CONTINUUM OF SERVICES: PLACEMENT OPTIONS

The following options contain both in-school and out-of-school options. Given the foregoing discussion, we recognize that in an ideal environment, there would not be a need for out-of-school options. However, these placements, especially within the EBD community, are viable and are being used in virtually every region of our country.

The General Education Classroom

The general education setting is often perceived as the least-restrictive option. Some have argued that many professionals may be too hasty in automatically excluding students with EBD from consideration for this option. In fact, there have been very few studies that have compared the effectiveness of general education placements with other settings for students with EBD (Clarke, Schaefer, Burchard, & Welkowitz, 1992).

Support for general education teachers is critical for all students to succeed. General education teachers may receive help from behavioral or instructional consultants who are hired by the school, available for consultation with the teacher and possibly the parent(s). Consultants may offer specific techniques or general programs to help remediate the students' problems. They may provide direct services to the student or simply give the information to the teachers for their use.

Other support services that may be included in the general education setting are cooperative or coteaching with a special educator. These teachers may plan and teach together for all or part of the school day (especially during the more academic classes). Another option that has been used more frequently is the use of special education instructional aides (sometimes called *paraprofessionals*) that stay in the general education classroom to help with behavior and instruction. However, it is critical that these people are involved in more than just behavioral control. These supports are allowing more students with EBD to succeed in the general education setting than ever before.

If students are placed in a general education classroom, with the special assistance, they should be able to learn. Many general education teachers are responsible for teaching 20 to 35 students, and it may be unrealistic to expect that much of their time can be devoted to one or two students who have disabilities without negatively affecting academic progress and classroom morale.

Consequently, this placement, as with the others, has a very important "reality" component: It is important to determine if appropriate support services are available to the teacher before it is recommended for a particular student. Also, before making this placement, it must be determined if the teacher has the time during the day to receive consultation and if a consultant has time available to consult. In some cases, support may include help in a particular academic or skill area. Some districts have used very broad wording in the student's IEP goals, which allows the student to participate in the general education setting "with modifications." We advocate that when general education placements are recommended, the goals and objectives to be achieved in that setting are clearly delineated, for the good of the student as well as the benefit of the general education teacher, who may have little special education training. For example, when behavior is an issue, it may take priority over the academic content. The student's goal for the general education classroom may be related to the behavior rather than content. In that case, the written goal would not only specify the behavior to be taught but may also specifically narrow the focus of academic achievement for the student in order to provide guidance to the general education teacher about how to best balance the needs of the student in special education with the needs of the general education students. An example might be that a student achieves a major social or behavioral goal while mastering 80% of the general education social studies content. Which 80% of the curriculum is to be mastered would be determined collaboratively by the special education and general education teacher, *not* by maintaining an overall 80% course grade average.

Last, and most important, it will need to be decided if the classroom teachers can and will actually make the accommodations necessary for the student. Some researchers have been cynical regarding the prospects of teachers making changes in their teaching (Fuchs & Fuchs, 1998).

Part-Time Placement in the Special Education Classroom

This option has been traditionally described as the *resource room*. Students assigned to resource rooms spend most of the school day in the general classroom; however, they receive services in a special education classroom for as much as 3 hours per day (50% of the school day). Resource rooms may serve a heterogeneous group of students with varying mild disabilities and of different ages, grades, and abilities all together during instructional times. Implementation of this program option also differs from district to district as well as being influenced by the level of school (e.g., elementary, middle, secondary).

Resource rooms may also differ according to the philosophies of the teachers. For example, many resource rooms function as supplements to general education classrooms. Special education teachers, with consultation from general educators, arrange the students' program so they can stay in the general setting as much as possible and still have their needs met in those subjects with which they encounter most difficulty. The special education teachers might tutor the students in particular subjects or provide additional instructional time in those skills that allow them to compete in the general education setting—for example, reading.

The problem with this philosophy is, again, the reality factor. The resource room may be filled with many students, each having his or her specific problems. For example, there might be three students from each grade in the resource room at the same time, each for a different reason (e.g., reading, math, or social skills training). The resource room teacher has the difficult task of consulting with all the students' teachers and teaching each student within a very narrow time frame.

Critics of the resource room concept claim that it is difficult for one teacher to meet all students' needs, even with the help of an aide. Thus, to be able to manage a resource room, special education teachers may have to resort to a large amount of seatwork, leaving little time for teaching. Seatwork often takes the form of dittos and workbooks, resulting in little motivation to learn on the part of the students. Yet, teachers in these programs may have little choice of teaching style because it would be virtually impossible for them to teach each student individually. In addition, the demands for the student to maintain a minimal level of competence in the general education content can create a situation that leaves little time for the teacher to spend teaching critical remedial skills that provide the foundation for success in the general education curriculum.

Not all resource rooms present such a bleak picture. In some schools, especially in the upper grades, teachers teach the same subject matter to the entire class (e.g., reading, social studies) and individualize instruction based on students' learning styles. This is much more manageable and effective than trying to teach everybody everything at once. When discussing placement options for a particular student, it is important to be aware of the activities and design of the programs in the student's building.

Full-Time Special Classroom

Students in this setting attend a special education classroom in the general education school for most or all of the day. They may be integrated into general education settings for a few class periods. Many times, the classes the students attend with their nondisabled peers are so-called specials, such as industrial education, art, music, and physical education. However, students who show academic strength in particular subject areas may attend general education sections for those classes.

Parents and professionals should be cautioned not to place students in classes that are designated as specials simply because they are not traditionally academic in nature. Some of these specials require skills that some students have not been able to demonstrate in other settings, such as the ability to control frustration, which may result in tools being broken or thrown, or the ability to read, which may result in failing music. In fact, many of these specials provide less structure than many general education classrooms, creating problems for all concerned. For example, behavioral expectations in an art class or wood shop area are often more relaxed, or at least more independent, than those for the general class. These different expectations may give rise to more problems for both students who have EBD and their teachers.

School systems may have different names for this type of setting. It may be called *special ed* or the *self-contained* classroom. This is a more restrictive setting than those discussed thus far. Yet it is not too restrictive for students requiring a highly structured program.

Sometimes, people perceive self-contained special class settings as negative. Because of their restrictiveness from interactions with general education students, self-contained classrooms are chosen with some hesitation. It is hoped that students who are placed in such settings are those who have demonstrated that their disabilities have prevented them from learning in less restrictive settings and are students who will benefit from this placement option. Placing students in an inappropriate less-restrictive placement because it seems "more normal" does not take into consideration the feelings of insecurity and frustration that students experience when they cannot learn or behave in the manner expected of them.

Public or Private Special Day School

If the students' behavior cannot be managed or remediated in a general education school setting, placement outside a traditional public school may be necessary. There are a variety of options from which to choose, and in addition to selecting the program that best meets a student's needs, accessibility to the school is an important consideration (distance from the home and cost of transportation).

Day schools may take the form of alternative schools, nonpublic schools (student tuition is paid by several participating districts, but enrollment is not open to the public), day treatment centers, charter schools, or hospital outpatient programs. In each of these settings, students with EBD have the same educational rights that are due to them as if they were in a public school. If the adolescent student has a severe emotional disturbance, a sheltered workshop experience may be appropriate. Sheltered workshops allow the student to learn simple vocational tasks. If there is convenient access to a residential school, the student might attend the school portion of the program and return home daily.

Residential School, Hospital Setting, or Treatment Center

Students may receive their education in residential schools, in-patient hospitals, or treatment centers for short- or long-term stays. Their behavior is too intense for most general education settings. Medical or psychological services are frequently needed for students who are placed in these environments. Some students may spend their weekends at home. It is not unusual for some students in these settings to be integrated into nearby public schools.

A student may be placed in a residential setting for two reasons: lack of access to a viable community program or when the student's home life contributes to his or her problems. Many communities do not have the resources necessary to help students with severe problems. In other instances, the home life may contribute to the students' problems. However, removing them from their home settings should only happen as a last resort. Whenever possible, students must be taught to cope with their home life. When the home life is so destructive that removal is therapeutically necessary, it is important that students understand that removal from their home does not necessarily mean it is their fault that the family has problems. There are also situations where the severity of the student's behaviors makes safety at home a critical issue (i.e., when the student is suicidal or when the student has physically attacked or harmed family members). Most schools are reluctant to make such placements because they are very expensive.

Several types of residential placements, including foster homes and group homes, allow students to live in the same or a different community while attending a public school. In that school, they may be placed in a special education setting. Other types of residential placements include 24-hour care facilities that may be either medical (psychiatric or psychological) or educational in nature.

Homebound Instruction

The most obvious reason for this, hopefully temporary, placement would be if a student became bedridden because of a physical ailment. Homebound teachers visit students in their homes to give them the instruction they are missing in school. Because of the complexity involved in teaching any student, let alone one with emotional problems, high-quality homebound instruction can be difficult to secure.

It would be inappropriate to use this placement for students who exhibit severe behavioral problems in school, thereby making it serve as a type of school suspension. Rarely are homebound services equivalent to those offered in a full-day program. Students with emotional and/or behavioral problems have a disability, meaning, they do not behave in an unacceptable manner by choice. To deny them access to a viable school program is to deny them their right to an equal education because of their disability.

Detention or Correction Facilities

This placement is usually not a school option. That is, students who receive their education in a detention center are not usually given a choice regarding where they receive an education, and the judicial system is involved in the students' education. Some students with emotional or behavioral problems express their feelings in ways that get them into legal trouble. For others, one would argue that it is equally often due to their impulsivity, lack of judgment, and strong risk-taking behavior combined with social skills deficits (i.e., they get caught) that land them in jail. Thus, some researchers have reported that up to 40% of those labeled as juvenile delinquents have also been found to have EBD.

Students who are labeled delinquent may have committed acts that would not get them into trouble if they were adults. Such acts include truancy, inability to get along with parents, and use of alcohol or drugs. Many people believe that students should not be incarcerated or adjudicated if they exhibit such behaviors. If children or adolescents commit crimes for which they would be arrested in the adult world, they would probably not be placed in a less-restrictive setting (see Chapter 6 for a more complete discussion of this issue).

Mental Health Clinics

In some instances, a child's problems can be best dealt with outside the public school. Sometimes, clinics not only provide help from specialists who are not available in schools (e.g., clinical psychologists, social workers), but they can also offer opportunities for group counseling where students can meet and work with others having similar problems. Another benefit of clinics is that their services may be provided to students without having to take the students out of the general school routine. Some students may receive services both at school and from a clinic. This placement may supplement any of the previously listed services. Students may be referred to clinics as part of their school program or as an after-school activity. Professionals from clinics may also work with students during the school day.

Psychologists, psychiatrists, social workers, guidance counselors, and youth workers are some of the staff who may be affiliated with clinics with which a school may contract for services. They are rarely full-time employees of the school system, although many clinics have established long-term relationships with school districts.

AN IMPORTANT CAVEAT ABOUT PLACEMENTS

Remember that before an educational placement can be determined, a multidisciplinary team must identify the most appropriate program for the student. Identification of the students and selection of their placements are only two, albeit very important, concerns. The most important issue to consider is the type of program the student will receive in a given setting. A particular placement does not guarantee availability of a program that meets a specific student's needs.

For example, let's say that Joe needs to be placed in a setting that is very nurturing. He has a difficult time accepting orders from authority figures, including simple teacher demands, such as, "Joe, please sit down. Class is starting." When given such instructions, Joe may shout at the teacher, screaming that he or she is not his parent, and so forth.

Yet Joe is intelligent, almost to the point of being gifted, and if left alone, he can accomplish a considerable amount of work. His behavior is such that he could not function well in a traditional general class, and he needs help in the emotional-behavioral area. A special education teacher trained to work with Joe might help him deal with authority figures and control verbal aggression. Accomplishing these goals would be more beneficial to Joe's future work and relationship opportunities than prioritizing his academic progress (which his abilities indicate can be more easily advanced than his behavior).

Consequently, a multidisciplinary evaluation team might recommend a special education placement for Joe. Specifically, it would be suggested that Joe be assigned to a special education classroom on a part-time basis, and attend those general classrooms where his behavior would not interfere with his learning. Although this is a logical recommendation, one very important ingredient is being overlooked—the philosophical makeup of the particular part-time special education setting.

Different approaches to treating students with emotional or behavioral problems exist. It is at this point in the placement process that these approaches take on particular significance. In the example of Joe, the part-time special education classroom may be very structured, with rules and consequences clearly stated and consistently followed. Furthermore, the teacher may believe that students need to learn to follow rules in order to succeed in general education classrooms. Most important, the teacher may believe that if she is inconsistent in following classroom rules, if she bends them for some of her students, then the students will receive messages that rules are only for some students.

Enter Joe. His needs cannot be met because of the philosophy of the classroom. Joe has difficulty taking directions and will openly rebel if they are given. The teacher, to demonstrate to her class that she is fair, feels that she must follow her behavioral orientation. Furthermore, she believes that if she changes the classroom program for Joe, she will do major harm to the other 12 students in her room. If Joe is placed in this classroom, either he or the program—or both—is likely to suffer. This is a case where the use of a part-time special classroom seems to be appropriate, but the actual implementation will probably not work.

Other instances where this problem could occur are when students' learning styles dictate a specific approach and the classroom teacher does not use that approach. For example, in many resource rooms, teachers serve a variety of students who study different subjects at the same time. These teachers have to resort to such teaching and management techniques as worksheets, workbooks, and other types of seatwork for students who are not being directly taught at a given time. Yet many of these students are placed in the setting because of their inability to sit still, complete seatwork, and so forth—students who need to have lessons explained or demonstrated to them in order to understand difficult concepts.

It is crucial that parents and professionals consider not only the label of children and their placements but also the expectations of the teachers in those placements. Thus, it is the academic, social, and behavioral programming for the student, and not the placement, that should be adapted for the child to be successfully placed in the least restrictive environment.

As mentioned earlier, a student is usually referred to a residential treatment center as a last resort. Inadequate community treatment options are one reason for such placement. This is not unusual in small communities. Remembering the least restrictive environment concept, the real issue behind having students live someplace else is their inability to learn and live in their current placement or environment.

Some students may have problems that are so severe that continued living at home and public school attendance are simply out of the question. Also, and this is an equally sensitive issue, some family situations, either intentionally or unintentionally, may contribute to the students' problems in such a way that a change is necessary, at least a temporary one. A placement away from the home can provide time-out from a very difficult situation, allowing those involved to examine critical issues that may be causing problems and hopefully allowing them to work on remediating those problems.

There is also the possibility that some students need more intensive help in either or both the academic or emotional domains. Although there are trade-offs to consider when making the decision of a residential placement, the notion of placing individuals in settings where they can learn to deal with their disabilities and not be handicapped by the setting itself should be of primary importance.

Early in this book, we mentioned that one of the least productive reactions to dealing with a child with emotional problems is blame. It is very easy to blame children for their behaviors and emotions. It is also easy for parents to blame themselves for the way children develop and, likewise, to blame the educational system for failing to "fix" the child. Quite simply, what has happened has happened. To examine and cross-examine the whys and wherefores only takes attention away from the main issue: how best to support the youth so he or she can develop more effective social, academic, and behavioral skills and reach higher levels of independence.

POSSIBLE PARENTAL REACTIONS TO PLACEMENT OPTIONS

Parents may react in a variety of ways to the placement options that have been discussed. Parents who have children with behavioral problems perhaps get the least empathy, of all of the disabilities. The public's reaction to these parents is not the same as that for parents who have children with other disabilities. Furthermore, these parents may have a more difficult time in rearing these children because of the effect on the family, community, and school. Parents of children and youth who have EBD have reported feeling blamed, confused, and patronized, as if their feelings are discounted by the professionals dealing with their child, and as if they are not treated with cultural sensitivity (Duchnowski, Berg, & Kutash, 1995). It should certainly be no surprise, then, that parents of children and youth who have EBD are often reluctant to be involved in the child's educational planning process.

Difficult decisions must sometimes be made to plan appropriately for children and youth who have EBD, such as placements in residential or hospital settings. Perhaps, with the decision to send a child to a residential school, parents feel shame ("What will others think of me if Joe is sent to a residential school?") or guilt ("Maybe this wouldn't have happened if . . ."). If these feelings are very strong, we recommend counseling. Many other families of children with EBD share the same feelings and problems. Sometimes, support groups are available, or family counseling is an option. Many residential schools, recognizing the need to include families in the remediation process, welcome family input and provide services to families. Collaborative programs involving families, community mental health programs, and schools are described in a later chapter. Resources for support and advocacy for parents and families of children and youth with EBD are also described in the final chapter of the book.

A common misconception about placing students in residential schools is that the process involves locking someone away in some medieval institution. Currently, many residential facilities can be inviting and caring places, with more than adequate educational and living facilities. On the family's first visit to the school, it should be evident that Joe isn't being sent away to some "crazy" house. Last, guilt and shame may only add to the problems Joe is having. It is probably going to be a very difficult transition for Joe, which will only be compounded by also having to deal with the guilt or shame his family feels.

CHANGING PLACEMENTS BECAUSE OF BEHAVIOR

One of the characteristics of students who have EBD is behavior that is not acceptable in the general education setting. Depending on the school setting, these characteristics may be anything from using profanity to carrying a weapon. The reactions of the schools to these behaviors vary, with one possible solution being a (temporary) change of placement. Here is what IDEA (1997) says about any change of placement: Schools cannot remove "a child for more than 10 consecutive school days" or for a "series of removals that constitute a pattern because they cumulate to more than 10 school days in a school year" (34 CFR 300.519).

The implications of the law are these: If students with EBD are being removed from their placement for more than 10 days, they are not in the least restrictive environment. This means that their current placements need to be altered (a different intervention, more accommodations) or that they need to be in a different setting.

There may be rare instances when a student with EBD has a weapon, drugs, or other contraband. If this occurs, the school district may place students in an alternative placement for not more than 45 days. IDEA (1997) goes on to state, "It would be reasonable to expect that the IEP team, during the period of time the child is in the interim alternative setting, would meet to determine future strategies for dealing with the child's challenging behaviors" (34 CFR 300.522).

It is incumbent on the IEP team to determine if the students' behavior is a result of their disability. This process is called *manifestation determination*. If the behavior is *not* a result of their disability, then they are subject to the same disciplinary measures as their general education peers (which may mean suspension or expulsion for terms longer than described).

It should be noted that due to the acts of violent behavior among general education students in public schools, legislators have attempted to change the federal law so that *all students* (general and special education) may be subject to suspension and expulsion if they exhibit any of a wide range of behaviors, including aggression, a characteristic that may be a result of EBD.

A FEW WORDS ABOUT INCLUSION

Readers familiar with trends in general and special education may notice that the term *inclusion* has not been used (yet) in this chapter. This is a term that means different things to different people. Some people believe that inclusion means, under all circumstances, participation in the general education classroom; this is sometimes called *full inclusion*.

We believe that if the concepts that have been discussed are followed, when appropriate, individualized inclusion has occurred. Students will be included in the least-restrictive placement to the extent possible. We have made clear that we believe that the general education setting is not always the least-restrictive setting nor is it the most appropriate setting for some students who have EBD.

SUMMARY

Many school-related placement options are available to children and youth with emotional and behavioral problems. It is crucial to remember that gaining access to special education programs is only one hurdle to jump. Basic to any placement decision is that educational programs be designed to meet the individual needs of the students. It is from determining these needs that an appropriate placement can be chosen.

REFERENCES

Clarke, R., Schaefer, M., Burchard, J., & Welkowitz, J. (1992). Wrapping community-based mental health services around children with a severe behavior disorder: An evaluation of Project Wraparound. *Journal of Child and Family Studies, 1*, 241–261.

Duchnowski, A., Berg, K., & Kutash, K. (1995). Parent participation in and perceptions of placement decisions. In J. M. Kauffman, J. Wills Lloyd, D. P. Hallahan, & T. A. Astuto (Eds.), *Issues in educational placement for students with emotional and behavioral disorders* (pp. 183–195). Hillsdale, NJ: Lawrence Earlbaum.

Fuchs, L., & Fuchs, D. (1998). General educations' instruction adaptation for students with learning disabilities. *Learning Disability Quarterly, 21*, 23–33.

Individuals with Disabilities Education Act of 1997, Pub. L. No. 105–17, 20 U.S.C., Ch. 33, §§1400–1491.

U.S. Department of Education. (1997). *Nineteenth annual report to Congress on the implementation of the Individuals with Disabilities Act*. Washington, DC: Author.

Supporting Students With Emotional and Behavioral Disorders Outside the Public School Setting   9

This chapter provides an overview of considerations that affect the child or youth who has EBD and may be treated by professionals outside of the traditional public school setting. Although these supports and approaches to treatment fall outside of the school day, they are important topics for parents and professionals to contemplate. This chapter discusses (a) medications (interchangeably referred to as *psychotropic* and *psychopharmacological* drugs) typically used with children and youth who have EBD, (b) the specific roles of psychiatric and non-school-psychology specialists in the child's or youth's comprehensive educational program, and (c) the importance of interagency collaboration in developing a comprehensive treatment program for children and youth who have EBD.

MEDICATIONS FOR EMOTIONAL AND BEHAVIORAL DISORDERS: PSYCHOPHARMACOLOGY

The use of medications to treat children and youth who have EBD is confusing and controversial. It appears to be an area in which educators (Singh, Epstein, Luebke, & Singh, 1990) and physicians (Tinsley, Shadid, Li, Offord, & Agerter, 1998) all desire further training and knowledge. Medications can have a profound impact on behavior and mental health. Their use in the treatment of children and youth who have EBD is steadily increasing (Gadow, 1997), probably due to the greater good that can come from the proper use and close monitoring of psychotropic medications. Recent figures show that not only are youth with EBD being prescribed medications more often than in the past but, in fact, so are all youth in and out of the special education system. For example, it has been documented that between 40% and 60% of youth in residential treatment centers are treated with medication (Bastiaens, 1998; Gadow, 1997) and that 15% to 20% of special education students may be receiving daily medication (Barkley, 1990; Forness & Kavale, 1988; Forness, Swanson, Cantwell, Guthrie, & Sena, 1992). Moreover, as many as 5% to 7% of the nondisabled children in the Medicaid system receive psychiatric treatment, which often includes the use of psychotropic drugs (Buck, 1997).

In fact, pediatricians are currently diagnosing psychosocial problems in typically developing children at a rate that has almost tripled between 1979 and 1997 (6.8% up to 18.7%; American Academy of Pediatrics, 2000). It is interesting that some studies have found that HMOs and other managed health care systems have set levels of severity for treatment of serious emotional disturbance higher than can be legitimately defended. For example, a study by Costello, Angold, and Keeler (1999) showed that every level of childhood behavioral disorder predicted serious emotional disturbance in adolescence. Therefore, the researchers concluded that childhood disorders not severe enough to meet HMO or insurance company treatment criteria can still act as consistent indicators of severe emotional disturbance later in adolescence. Although many children and youth are recognized as having emotional problems, only a portion of them are treated with the range of treatment options that currently exist.

One reason that HMOs and insurance companies seem to fail to provide children with adequate early intervention is the expense involved in mental health treatment. In a study of nondisabled Medicaid patients, the total costs for mental health care recipients was more than 3 times higher than for other pediatric patients (Buck, 1997). This is because hospital stays are typically much longer (an average of 44–60 days), psychopharmacological medications can be costly, and even outpatient and clinic care can last from 3 months to a year or much longer. Still, proper treatment of mental health needs in children and youth who are at risk for developing EBD, and certainly for those who already display characteristics of EBD, is of the utmost importance and priority. Informing policymakers of the importance of proper and early mental health intervention for youngsters is an advocacy role that parents and professionals can fill together.

Guidelines for Medication Use
With Children and Youth Who Have EBD

Medications can have profound impacts on health and behavior. Accordingly, drug treatment must be considered a viable option for helping problem children and youth. However, drugs are not a cure for social and emotional problems; therefore, they must be used only to support a comprehensive treatment plan. Other treatments, such as behavior modification or counseling-psychotherapy, must be part of the treatment program to produce positive lasting changes to the quality of the child's life. In addition, drugs are not appropriate or effective with all children. Consequently, systematic evaluation and monitoring *must* constitute an important part of any drug treatment effort. For every child or adolescent treated with psychotropic medications, medical personnel, educators, mental health workers, and families must work closely together to determine the drug's benefit.

A Range of Problems, a Range of Solutions

Medications can be used to address a variety of childhood psychiatric disorders and other problems. These include anxiety, depression, ADHD, eating disorders, enuresis, autism, psychosis, bipolar disorder (manic-depression), severe aggression, and sleep problems.

The Need to Learn About Psychopharmacology

As noted at the opening of this chapter, pediatricians and psychiatrists have expressed an interest in learning more about the rapidly growing use of medication to treat mental illness, EBD, or other psychosocial problems in children and youth (Tinsley, Shadid, Li, Offord, & Agerter, 1998). In recent years, physicians and EBD and mental health organizations have recognized the need to better inform parents and other lay professionals about the psychotropic medications commonly used with children and adolescents, their intended benefits, their possible side effects, and complications that can occur. For example, the American Academy of Child and Adolescent Psychiatry (AACAP) has created both print and online brochures to assist families in locating psychiatric care for their child, as well as to assist them in talking with doctors about medications that may be recommended. The National Association for Mental Illness (NAMI) has also established online resources to assist parents and professionals in learning about medications that may be recommended for a child. Some important questions to ask a pediatrician or psychiatrist (whether you are a parent, teacher, or other invested professional or caretaker) include the following:

- What is the name of the medication? Does it have other names (e.g., generic)?
- What changes can I expect to see in the child's behavior, cognition, or emotions?
- What side effects may occur with this medication?

- How often should the medication be taken? How long does it take after ingestion before it reaches its most effective point? How quickly will it wear off?
- What diet or other recommendations would you make while the child is taking this medication?
- How long can I expect the child to be taking this medication?
- How can I best provide information that can help monitor the medication use (i.e., diary observations)?
- What should I do if I notice something unusual or if a problem occurs while the child is taking the medication? (AACAP, 1995)

Notes to Professionals About the Use of Psychotropic Medications With Children and Youth

Any person who spends substantial time with a child or adolescent who is being treated with psychopharmalogical medications has a moral and ethical obligation to monitor the child's mental, affective, and physical changes and communicate them to the parent, IEP team, or physician. Ongoing medical assessment should be a part of the comprehensive plan for treatment but is not intended as a separate function from the daily observations and feedback from teachers, school nurses, tutors, or other related professionals.

The side effects that can be present with the use of psychotropic medications can range from bothersome (e.g., dry mouth or sleepiness) to very serious (e.g., kidney failure or permanent liver damage) (Sweeney, Forness, Kavale, & Levitt, 1997). It is important that communication among the parents, physician, and IEP team be maintained to carefully monitor all changes in the child so that dosages, dietary considerations, or alternate medications or therapies may be considered as needed.

Some types of medication monitoring or evaluation that a teacher, caregiver, or other related professional may be asked to provide may include formal checklists, rating scales of behaviors or affect, and informal logs of more subjective observations. The first two provide more objective or even standardized forms of evaluation for the physician, parent, and IEP team. Maintenance of an informal journal or log of observations of the youth may prove extremely helpful in that it is more readily incorporated within the busy school or caregiving environment. Such a log should include time and date information as well as any observations of the affective, physical, or behavioral characteristics exhibited by the youth while in your care.

Parents can be a great source of information about the medication and its intended (and not-intended) effects. They should be consulted first when there are questions about the youth or his or her medications. If they do not know the answers to the questions you may have, they can communicate with the youth's doctor and report the information shared. If a child needs frequent medication adjustments, the IEP team may elect to determine a more formal process by which observational monitoring will be conducted. The team should also consider creative and manageable ways professionals' observations can be documented and a means by which regular, frequent feedback can be shared with parents or physician (or both) in a timely manner.

Notes to Parents About the Use of Psychotropic Medications With Children and Youth

As useful as medications can be for children and youth who have EBD, it is important for parents to learn as much as they can about the potential benefits and risks of any given medications being considered for their child. A physician who recommends medication treatment for a child should be experienced in treating mental illnesses in children as well as in using medications to treat them.

Medication treatments should only be one part of a comprehensive mental health plan for the child or adolescent (AACAP, 1999; Forness et al., 1999). In addition to psychopharmacology, cognitive-behavioral therapies or psychotherapies must also be implemented (see Chapter 7). Parental guidance sessions should be a routine part of the comprehensive plan as well.

When medications are appropriately prescribed, taken as directed, and carefully monitored and adjusted, they can greatly improve the everyday life of the child. However, just as there are many benefits to using medications, each has its own side effects, potential health risks, and other complications. It is important to learn about these and to maintain close communication with the child's prescribing doctor (as well as the other people who work closely with the child) to monitor the effects the drug is having. Because every child is different, they can have different reactions to the same medication. It is important to observe all possible changes in affect, physical state, and behavior and to communicate them to the physician in a timely manner. It is also important not to stop or change a medication dosage without first consulting the prescribing physician.

In dealing with teachers and school personnel about a child's medication(s), it is important to know that many teachers have not received training in children's medication issues and that those who have report that they feel underprepared to deal with children's medications (Singh et al., 1990).

For this reason, it will be important for parents to communicate to them (perhaps in writing so they can refer to it later) the type of medication being used, the exact dosage (including times of dosage), implications (what it is intended to affect), possible side effects, and any dietary restrictions. Dietary restrictions are important to know about when certain foods could possibly be ingested either at lunch or during school or classroom social events. It will also be valuable to provide or ask those who interact with the child to provide a brief observation journal of any cognitive, affective, or physical changes that occur (including the exact time and date, activities, and specific descriptions of the child's changes or states). This information can be very helpful to the physician to know when adjustments are needed.

Types of Medications Used, Side Effects, and Benefits

We authors are not physicians, and the information included in this chapter is intended to provide initial information that can prompt conversations and inquiries of treating physicians. Currently, there are several categories of medications used: (a) stimulants, (b) antidepressants, (c) antipsychotics, (d) mood stabilizers and anticonvulsants, (e) antianxiety medications, (f) sleep medications, and (g) miscellaneous (AACAP, 2000).

Stimulant medications are often used to treat ADHD. Examples of stimulants are Dexedrine, Ritalin, and Cylert. Stimulants are one of the more common categories of psychopharmacological treatments used with children. The only two FDA-approved uses of stimulants in children and youth are for ADHD and for narcolepsy. Stimulants are being prescribed to treat ADHD-like symptoms in children who have other coexisting problems, such as Tourette's syndrome and pervasive developmental disorders (Sweeney et al., 1997), but further formal study of their effects and side effects is still needed.

Antidepressant medications are used for many purposes, such as panic attacks, depression, school phobias, bed-wetting, obsessive-compulsive disorders, and personality disorders. Antidepressants are divided into four subtypes. Tricyclic antidepressants (TCAs) are one type. Common brand names are Elavil and Pamelor. A second subtype is serotonin reuptake inhibitors (SRIs), which include Prozac, Zoloft, and Paxil. A third subtype is the monoamine oxidase inhibitors (MAOIs); examples are Nardil and Parnate. The final subtype of antidepressant is known as *atypical antidepressants*. This final category includes brand-name medications, such as Wellbutrin, Desyrel, and Remeron.

In general, there are a few issues to be aware of when considering the use of antidepressant medications. One is the choice of one category of antidepressant over another. A psychiatrist or prescribing physician can provide the rationale for his or her recommendation for a particular child. However, some general considerations are that SRIs tend to have fewer negative side effects than TCAs. TCAs tend to carry a risk of liver damage as a possible side effect, hence underscoring the need for careful monitoring to ensure safe dosage and usage. TCAs have been commonly used in combination with other psychotropic medications to treat children and youth (Wilens, Spencer, Biederman, Wozniak, & Connor, 1995). Combined medications can have positive effects for children and youth. However, one study found that over 50 different combinations of medications were used to treat 83 children and adolescents in a residential setting (Conner, Ozbayrak, Harrison, & Melloni, 1998). This information only serves as a reminder of the importance of coordinating care, treatment, and information among all professionals who deal with a child or youth who is using medication as part of his or her treatment plan.

Antipsychotic medications may be used to treat a wide range of disruptive or aggressive disorders as well as self-injurious behaviors. Specifically, these medications may be used to treat psychosis, aggressive behavior, mania, Tourette's syndrome, hallucinations, delusions, and disorganized thinking. Examples of these medications include Thorazine, Mellaril, Haldol, Clozaril, Risperdal, and Zeldox.

This category of medication carries with it some concerns about possible severe neurological and developmental side effects that may influence socialization and learning. However, newer varieties, such as Risperdal, have demonstrated positive effects while minimizing negative side effects. A final concern about this category of medications is the possible side effects to the extrapyramidal system, which controls movement, posture, and balance, among other things. Adolescents who have used clozapine, in particular, have responded well with fewer extrapyramidal problems than other medications (Birmaher, 1996). Parents and professionals who know a child is using this category of medication should be aware of possible effects on movement control, posture, and balance and make note of irregularities to inform the physician.

Mood stabilizers and *anticonvulsants* are useful in the treatment of manic-depression, severe mood swings, impulse control disorders, and schizoaffective disorders. Lithium is a commonly used mood stabilizer. Anticonvulsants may include Depakote, Depakene, Tegretol, Dilantin, and Neurontin. Each of the primary anticonvulsant medications (Depakene, Tegretol, and Dilantin) has potentially serious negative side effects, so a common recommendation is the short-term use of these medications for nonepileptic disorders (Forness, Sweeney, & Toy, 1996).

Antianxiety medications are often prescribed to treat severe anxiety. This category of medications may include Zanax, Ativan, Valium, and Klonopin. Also included in this category are antihistamines such as Benedryl and Vistaryl. A final group of medications included in this category are atypical antianxiety medications, such as Ambien and Buspar. The FDA has yet to grant approval for the use of drugs such as Buspar (a.k.a. buspirone) for children and youth, yet it is being more frequently prescribed due to its limited sedative effects and low potential for abuse (Sweeney et al., 1997).

Sleep medications may be used to treat short-term sleep problems. Desyrel, Ambien, and Benedryl can each be used for this purpose (AACAP, 2000). The typical use of these medications for children and adolescents is to treat temporary or situational anxiety. Tolerance to these medications develops quickly, so their use should only be seen as short term. Long-term usage may predispose patients to substance abuse (Sweeney et al., 1997).

The final category of medications to be outlined in this chapter is *miscellaneous medications* (AACAP, 2000). These are medications used to treat a variety of symptoms, such as the use of clonidine to treat severe impulsiveness and tenex to treat so-called flashbacks in children.

Medication use is a serious issue with many complicating factors ranging from intended effects to additional positive side effects, possible negative side effects, and unknown reactions, given an individual's nature and body chemistry. The child's or adolescent's treating physician or psychiatrist is the most informed member of the treatment team in this aspect of the comprehensive mental health intervention plan. Parents and professionals have an obligation to become well informed regarding the medications prescribed for the child or youth and to stay in close communication with the physician regarding the proper dosage and course of treatment. Often, the initial medication choice, dosage or, administration schedule must be modified to find the best match for the child and family.

Adolescent Medication Treatment Issues

When dealing with adolescents, an issue that deserves mention is the fact that medications will only work as well as they are administered. Often, teenagers resist taking greatly needed psychotropic medications for a variety of reasons that may include not wanting to seem different from peers or reporting that they "feel fine," so they do not think they "need medicine." Some report that the negative side effects of the medication are worse than the symptoms treated by it.

When teenagers fail to take the properly prescribed dosage at the designated intervals, the medication will be less useful at best, and can be dangerous at worst. Teens offer many reasons why they do not take medications properly and over long periods of time (as examples: troubling side effects, not wanting to feel "different" from peers, and being tired of the "routine"). This was illustrated in a study of adolescents who were treated in a residential facility and then released, with medication as part of their continued intervention and treatment, that reported that only 38% continued to take their prescribed medication at a 14-month follow-up. Only 23% of the teenagers that were not taking their medication reported that they stopped taking it due to negative side effects. The others failed to follow many aspects of the treatment plan (of which medication was only a part), and several had developed postdischarge substance abuse problems (Lloyd et al., 1998). This study indicates the importance of teaching teenagers how the medications work, the importance of the medication in their treatment, and careful monitoring for substance abuse.

As stated earlier, we authors of this are in no way medication experts. Furthermore, many physicians are not children and youth experts. The information included in this chapter is intended to provide information that can prompt conversations, collaboration, and inquiries of the treating physicians.

THE ROLE OF PSYCHIATRIC AND JUVENILE JUSTICE PROFESSIONALS ON THE IEP TEAM

Typically, students with EBD receive limited, if any, services from community mental health agencies (Steinberg & Knitzer, 1992). However, one of the criteria for assigning the label of EBD is evidence of pervasive problems across multiple environments. When designing an educational plan for a student who has emotional or behavioral disorders, it is important to maximize the benefits of having multidisciplinary team members who may not be school-based, because of their expertise and connections within the community.

The Psychiatric Consultant

In addition to contributing to the evaluation process, an important role for psychiatric team members is that of team educator. The professional with expertise in mental health issues is well suited to provide the IEP team with education about mental illness and emotional and behavioral problems. This education will assist the team to make accurate identification and intervention plans for children and youth who are being considered under this disability category. Several authors have documented the need for school personnel to be better educated in emotional and behavioral issues (Mattison, 1999; Shapiro, 1991; Steinberg & Knitzer, 1992).

Organizations such as the Council for Children with Behavior Disorders have recently begun working collaboratively with their parent group, the Council for Exceptional Children, to educate professional organizations nationwide regarding the disability considerations that fit within the label of emotional disturbance. There is a common tendency to treat children and youth with EBD differently than children with other types of disabilities, with less accommodation and less effective treatment (see Chapter 7 for a more detailed discussion of these points).

A related role for the psychiatric consultant on the IEP team is that of translator: This person can be particularly effective in assisting the IEP team to translate the DSM or other diagnostic criteria used to determine the child's special education label into teachable components of the IEP document, or into specific placement recommendations, or critical considerations for behavior intervention plans.

The psychiatric consultant can also make recommendations regarding the types and levels of support that may be useful from community mental health agencies. For a variety of reasons, school personnel and parents are often unaware of mental health programs or resources in the community. Likewise, the psychiatric consultant may be the best team member to recommend necessary family interventions as part of the comprehensive treatment plan. This professional most likely has received greater training in parent communication, family patterns, and interactions that negatively or positively affect EBD in children and youth. The psychiatric consultant is in a strong position to model effective collaboration with families and community agencies.

For the past two decades, the federal government has recognized the need for psychiatric and education professionals to work together to provide the services needed to support students who have EBD. There are many reasons why this collaboration has proven challenging. The following section examines how the mental health and educational systems can effectively work together to provide a seamless and integrated program of services for children and youth with EBD and their families.

COLLABORATIVE EFFORTS BETWEEN MENTAL HEALTH AGENCIES AND THE EDUCATIONAL SYSTEM

Building collaborative efforts between schools and mental health agencies has been a national goal for the past three decades. As early as 1969, the Joint Commission on Mental Health of Children presented evidence that children with emotional disorders were underserved, and those who were receiving services were being served in overly restrictive settings (such as residential settings). More than a decade later, the Children's Defense Fund published *Unclaimed Children* (Knitzer, 1982), a report that asserted that two thirds of the children in the United States who had emotional disturbance were either not receiving appropriate services or were receiving no services at all.

In 1984, Congress formally recognized the need for combining resources and services to provide appropriate, efficient, and cost-effective care for children and youth with EBD. They authorized the National Institute of Mental Health to start the Child and Adolescent Service System Program to help states develop integrated systems of care for youth with EBD and their families. However, this goal of collaborative services across agencies has been difficult to attain for a variety of reasons that include professional resistance, differences in system priorities, and different ways of operating, among others.

In 1994, Congress recognized the shortcomings of their efforts through the publication of *National Agenda for Achieving Better Results for Children and Youth with Serious Emotional Disturbance* (Chesapeake Institute, 1994). This document reiterates national priorities as (a) strengthening comprehensive, collaborative systems of care (partnerships among agencies serving children and youth with EBD); (b) addressing diversity; (c) collaborating with families; and (d) promoting appropriate assessment, promoting ongoing skill development, and strengthening school-community capacity. The most recent development in this continued effort to coordinate care was the Surgeon General's, who hosted a national conference on children's mental health in September 2000. The result of this 2-day conference was the *Report of the Surgeon General's Conference on Children's Mental Health: A National Agenda.* (U.S. Public Health Service, 2000). The agenda represents a major undertaking by the Department of Health and Human Services, the Department of Education, and the Department of Justice. A related meeting, "Psychopharmacology for Young Children: Clinical Needs and Research Opportunities," was hosted in October 2000 by the National Institute of Mental Health and the Food and Drug Administration. The results from both conferences compose a national action agenda. In the words of David Satcher, Assistant Secretary for Health and Surgeon General,

> There is no mental health equivalent to the federal government's commitment to childhood immunization. Children and families are suffering because of missed opportunities for prevention and early identification, fragmentation of services, and low priorities for resources. . . . Responsibilities for children's mental healthcare is dispersed across multiple systems: schools, primary care, the juvenile justice system, child welfare and substance abuse treatment. But the first system is the family, and this agenda [Surgeon General's National Action Agenda] reflects voices of youth and family. The vision and goals outlined in this agenda represent an unparalleled opportunity to make a difference in the quality of life for American children. (U.S. Public Health Service, 2000, p. 2)

A call for the voices of children and youth with EBD and their families in the formulation of service provision models has been made in the professional literature, seen as a missing and important link in developing a successful collaborative system.

SYSTEMS OF CARE

The systems-of-care approach is a notion of community-based collaborative efforts among agencies that provide care and services for children and youth with emotional disorders and their families. This philosophy is built on several key tenets:

- Interagency collaboration among systems that provide services for youth with EBD
- Treatment provided in the least-restrictive setting for the child or adolescent
- Services individualized and based on family and individual strengths
- Service teams having access to flexible funding and approaches
- Cultural competence and family centeredness
- A balance of formal and informal supports and resources

Using a systems-of-care approach can take several forms. *Wraparound services* is one model (Behar, 1985; Knitzer, 1993). It provides leadership from the mental health community in most cases. This approach to coordinated services operates from the premise that it is more effective and cost-efficient to provide services to support a family and child in the home or community than to provide residential care. In this type of system, a coordinated team of professionals plans services and supports designed to allow a student to function in a more normal environment. Although some might refer to this as the least restrictive environment, we encourage you to recall that *least restrictive* is a subjective term relative to the individual (see Chapter 4 for an in-depth discussion of the least restrictive environment). Regardless of terminology, as student needs increase in the more normal setting, more intensive and creative supports are provided before removing the student to a more specialized setting.

According to *The Comprehensive Community Mental Health Services for Children and Their Families*, as reported by Burns and Goldman (1999), 88% of states and territories report the use of a wraparound approach, serving an average of 3,800 students per state. The success of the wraparound model is dependent on several factors, especially the existence of adequate community services (e.g., counseling options, a range of clinical services, respite care). At this point, evaluation of such models, although positive, has been primarily confined to program-level observation (e.g., program coordination and provision of services) as opposed to outcomes for clients (e.g., mental health improvements, increased quality of life for student and family).

INSURANCE, MANAGED CARE,
MEDICARE, AND SYSTEMS OF CARE

As is the case of medication and inpatient care, the provision of systems-of-care services, such as wraparound services, is influenced by insurance, Medicare, and managed care policy. The nationwide Health Care Reform Tracking Project (Stroul, Pires, & Armstrong, 1998) provided an excellent discussion of the impact of managed care on systems-of-care services for children and youth who have EBD. They report that youth who have EBD are among the greatest challenges for managed care systems due to the in-depth and wide range of services required to provide adequate care. Stroul et al. (1998) reported that overall managed care seems to have increased access to basic mental health care for children and youth with EBD. Among the concerns reported about managed care were as follows:

- Managed care could result in limits on the number of services or time in which services may be provided to a child (as typical of traditional insurance).
- Without attention to effective risk management for serving the most expensive patients, there is little incentive for managed care systems to serve students who have EBD.
- Numerous Medicaid programs are being managed by private, for-profit managed care companies that do not understand nor have provisions to meet the needs for many Medicare clientele (e.g., fewer clients have telephones; more have important needs for baby-sitting in order to participate in family intervention or planning sessions; many need transportation; some parents have limitations in academic skills, such as reading, that pose significant challenges to comprehending or completing paperwork).
- Families of children who have EBD will have less input in the decisions about their own children and fewer options for the planning and operation of the supports available to them.
- Managed care systems have relied on public agencies (e.g., child welfare, juvenile justice, special education) to provide services to children who are at highest risk in terms of financial investment, for those who do not qualify for Medicaid, and for those who have exhausted insurance limits.

A lack of coordinated efforts among child welfare, juvenile justice, and education with those of managed care systems was also cited by Stroul et al. (1998). This is particularly out of step with federal efforts to coordinate services and care for children and youth who have EBD and their families.

Cultural Competence and Systems of Care

The philosophy of systems-of-care services requires family involvement at every level of development and organization. Cultural competence was a concern for families of children and youth who have EBD before managed care became an issue (National Mental Health Association, 1989). However, even those states with strong family advocacy organizations reported that their own managed care systems did not initially employ this philosophy (Stroul et al., 1998). Several states have set requirements that managed care providers incorporate cultural competence. Examples of states that are meeting this kind of requirement include Washington and Arizona, who require that culturally and linguistically diverse providers be options within the selection of service providers (Stroul et al., 1998).

It has been challenging for mental health providers who cater to families of color to thrive in an age of managed care, despite the public recognition for their specialized and valuable perspectives. Increasing requirements for mental health providers associated with managed care or Medicaid programs to have advanced degrees (in some states, above an MA level) have limited the numbers of service providers of color, who are fewer at the postbaccalaureate level.

In addition, families who participate in Medicaid-eligible programs are often families of color due to U.S. demographics that place more people of color in lower socioeconomic levels. Providers who offer services that meet the needs of families who participate in Medicaid programs often struggle with lower levels of financial stability. For that reason, these providers are often forced to merge with larger, profit-driven companies to maintain their practices or to remain competitive. When this occurs, bureaucracy often limits flexibility and nontraditional perspectives.

Systems of Care: Implementation Guidelines

In 1999, the Center for Effective Collaboration and Practice published a series of monographs that provide extremely useful information for professionals who are interested in learning more about how to establish a systems-of-care approach in their community (e.g., Burns & Goldman, 1999; Woodruff et al., 1999). This series was funded by the Center for Mental Health Services Substance Abuse and Mental Health Services Administration (U.S. Department of Health and Human Services). In addition, although considerably briefer, the Council for Children with Behavior Disorders published a minilibrary booklet (Skiba, Polsgrove, & Nasstrom, 1996) that describes well the systems-of-care approach and provides specific recommendations for schools that would like to establish a wraparound-services model.

As pointed out by Skiba et al. (1996), systems-of-care models can be established either outside schools or in them. In the former situation, educational services are coordinated with other community services, such as juvenile justice, child welfare, and mental health. In the latter, services from the participating agencies are housed within the school building. Both models have produced effective results.

SUMMARY

This chapter has addressed out-of-school concerns relevant to professionals and families who support youth with EBD. Medications are an increasingly common part of a comprehensive treatment plan but create confusion and controversy among parents, professionals, and society as a whole. It is important that all adults who work with children and youth who have EBD take responsibility for (a) learning (from the treating physician) about the medications and their possible side effects; (b) carefully observing and reporting to parents and physicians any behavioral, cognitive, or physical changes in the student while using medications; and (c) ensuring that medications are only one part of a comprehensive plan of treatment. The plan may also include individual or family counseling, cognitive behavioral therapy, or other behavioral interventions to support the youth's improved quality of life.

In addition to understanding medication as a part of an intervention plan, parents and professionals should be aware of the need for increased advocacy for unified and collaborative systems of care for youth who have EBD. It has been recognized at the highest levels that coordinated care for youth with EBD and their families is the most effective and efficient delivery mechanism we have developed to date. These systems need careful planning and organization as well as continued documentation, and further evaluation in terms of outcomes for youth and families (as opposed to provision of services or effective collaboration among agencies). Several sources exist that provide information for how to implement a coordinated systems-of-care program in your local community.

REFERENCES

American Academy of Child and Adolescent Psychiatry. (1995). Psychiatric medication for children and adolescents. Part 3: Questions to ask. *Facts for Families*, # 51. Washington, DC: Author.

American Academy of Child and Adolescent Psychiatry. (1999). Psychiatric medications for children and adolescents, Part 1: How medications are used. *Facts for Families, #21*. Washington, DC: Author.

American Academy of Child and Adolescent Psychiatry. (2000). Psychiatric medications for children and adolescents, Part 2: Types of medications. *Facts for Families, #29*. Washington, DC: Author.

American Academy of Pediatrics. (2000, June 5). *New study shows increased psychosocial problems in children* (Press release). [Online] Available: http://www.aap.org/advocacy/archieves/junphys.html [September 27, 2000].

Barkley, R. A. (1990). *Hyperactive children: A handbook for diagnosis and treatment.* New York: Guilford.

Bastiaens, L. (1998). Pediatric psychopharmacology in a capitated managed care system: How do patients fare? *Journal of Child and Adolescent Psychopharmacology, 8*(2), 115–124.

Behar, L. (1985). Changing patterns of state responsibility: A case study of North Carolina. *Journal of Clinical Child Psychology, 14*, 188–195.

Birmaher, B. (1996). Clozapine for child and adolescent schizophrenia. *Child and Adolescent Psychopharmacology News, 1*(3), 1–4.

Buck, J. A. (1997). Utilization of Medicaid mental health services by nondisabled children and adolescents. *Psychiatric Services, 48*(1), 65–70.

Burns, B. J., & Goldman, S. K. (Eds.). (1999). Promising practices in wraparound for children with serious emotional disturbance and their families. In *Systems of care: Promising practices in children's mental health* (1998 Series, Vol. 3). Washington, DC: Center for Effective Collaboration and Practice, American Institutes for Research.

Chesapeake Institute. (1994). *National agenda for achieving better results for children and youth with serious emotional disturbance.* Washington, DC: U.S. Department of Education, Office of Special Education Programs.

Costello, E. J., Angold, A., & Keeler, G. P. (1999). Adolescent outcomes of childhood disorders: The consequences of severity and impairments. *Journal of American Academy of Child and Adolescent Psychiatry, 38*(2), 121–128.

Conner, D. F., Ozbayrak, K. R., Harrison, R. J., & Melloni, R. H. (1998). Prevalence and patterns of psychotropic and anticonvulsant medications used in children and adolescents referred to residential treatments. *Journal of Child and Adolescent Psychopharmacology, 8*(1), 27–38.

Forness, S. R., & Kavale, K. A. (1988). Psychopharmacologic treatment: A note on classroom effects. *Journal of Learning Disabilities, 21*(3), 144–147.

Forness, S. R., Kavale, K. A., Sweeney, D. P., & Crenshaw, T. M. (1999). The future of research and practice in behavioral disorders: Psychopharmacology and its school treatment implications. *Behavioral Disorders, 24*, 305-318.

Forness, S. R., Swanson, J. M., Cantwell, D. P., Guthrie, D., & Sena, R. (1992). Response to stimulant medication across six measures of school-related performance in children with ADHD and disruptive behavior. *Behavioral Disorders, 18*, 42–53.

Forness, S. R., Sweeney, D. P., & Toy, K. (1996). Psychopharmacologic medication: What teachers need to know. *Beyond Behavior, 7*(2), 4–11.

Gadow, K. D. (1997). An overview of three decades of research in pediatric psychopharmacoepidemiology. *Journal of Child and Adolescent Psychopharmacology, 7*(4), 219–236.

Knitzer, J. (1982). *Unclaimed children: The failure of public responsibility to children and adolescents in need of mental health services.* Washington, DC: Children's Defense Fund.

Knitzer, J. (1993). Children's mental health policy: Challenging the future. *Journal of Emotional and Behavioral Disorders, 1*(1), 8–16.

Lloyd, A., Horan, W., Borgaro, S. R., Stokes, J. M., Pogge, D. L., & Harvey, P. D. (1998). Predictors of medication compliance after hospital discharge in adolescent psychiatric patients. *Journal of Child and Adolescent Psychopharmacology, 8*(2), 133–141.

Mattison, R. E. (1999). Use of psychotropic medications in special education students with serious emotional disturbance. *Journal of Child and Adolescent Psychopharmacology, 9*(3), 149–155.

National Mental Health Association. (1989). *Children in need of mental health care.* Alexandria, VA: Author.

Shapiro, E. S. (1991). Training school psychologists for service delivery to children with severe emotional disturbance. *School Psychology Review, 20,* 485–497.

Singh, N. N., Epstein, M. H., Luebke, J., & Singh, Y. N. (1990). Psychopharmacological Intervention. I: Teacher perceptions of psychotropic medication for students with serious emotional disturbance. *Journal of Special Education, 24*(3), 283–295.

Skiba, R., Polsgrove, L., & Nasstrom, K. (1996). *Developing a system of care: Interagency collaboration for students with emotional/behavioral disorders.* Reston, VA: Council for Children with Behavioral Disorders.

Steinberg, Z., & Knitzer, J. (1992). Classrooms for emotionally and behaviorally disturbed students: Facing the challenge. *Behavioral Disorders, 7,* 145–156.

Stroul, B. A., Pires, S. A., & Armstrong, M. A. (1998). *Health care reform tracking project: Tracking state managed care reforms as they affect children and adolescents with behavioral disorders and their families—1997 impact analysis.* Tampa: University of Florida, Florida Mental Health Institute, Louis de la Parte Research and Training Center for Children's Mental Health.

Sweeney, D. P., Forness, S. R., Kavale, K. A., & Levitt, J. G. (1997). An update on psychopharmacologic medication: What teachers, clinicians, and parents need to know. *Intervention in School and Clinic, 33*(1), 4–21, 25.

Tinsley, J. A., Shadid, G. E., Li, H., Offord, K. P., & Agerter, D. C. (1998). A survey of family physicians and psychiatrists: Psychotropic prescribing practices and educational needs. *General Hospital Psychiatry, 20*(6), 360–367.

U.S. Public Health Service. (2000). *Report of the surgeon general's conference on children's mental health: A national action agenda.* Washington, DC: National Institute of Mental Health.

Wilens, T. E., Spencer, T., Biederman, J., Wozniak, J., & Connor, D. (1995). Combined pharmacotherapy: An emerging trend in pediatric psychopharmacology. *Journal of the American Academy of Child and Adolescent Psychiatry, 34*(1), 110–112.

Woodruff, D. W., Osher, D., Hoffman, C. C., Gruner, A., King, M. A., Snow, S. T., & McIntire, J. C. (1999). The role of education in a system of care: Effectively serving children with emotional or behavioral disorders. In *Systems of care: Promising practices in children's mental health* (1998 Series, Vol. 3). Washington, DC: Center for Effective Collaboration and Practice, American Institutes for Research.

The Role of Families in Supporting Children With Emotional and Behavioral Concerns

10

Karla Anhalt, Richard Simpson, and Laura Zionts

There is no question that children are influenced by their parents and families. In fact, no other single experience so profoundly affects children's subsequent reactions to the world and its people. Values, attitudes, and unique ways of behaving are often a direct result of parent and family influence. This is not to suggest that children and adolescents will not develop behaviors that are uniquely their own; that they will not rebel against or reject certain family traditions and values; or that they will not be influenced by others, such as peers. Still, parents and families can play a pivotal role in addressing concerns of children with emotional and behavioral problems. In fact, parent and family support is necessary for children's optimal growth and development. In this regard, the role of parents and families may include acting as referral agents, advocates for their children, and support agents. We discuss these roles throughout the chapter. In addition, we offer school personnel techniques and tips to enhance collaborative efforts with families.

PARENTS AS REFERRAL AGENTS

Contact With Medical Personnel

Before children enter their years of schooling, parents may feel alone if they are confronted with questions about developmental and behavioral

175

issues. Parents may then discuss these questions with pediatricians or family physicians. Such conversations may result in referrals to professionals who can formally evaluate their concerns (e.g., psychologists, early intervention services). However, parental concerns sometimes may not be validated by professionals they trust.

> Recently, the American Pediatrics Association has recognized the need to better prepare physicians to detect delayed development, refer families earlier for more specific assessment, and adequately provide ongoing care and services to families of children with disabilities through the establishment of the Medical Home for Children with Disabilities program. (American Academy of Pediatrics, 2001)

Contact With Teachers

As in dealings with medical personnel, teacher contacts are most productive when concerns are specific and documented. The child's teacher should be informed of concerns the parent may have about the child, how frequently the problem of concern occurs, and its duration. Public schools are required to provide assessment and educational services for children and youth with special needs, including those with behavioral and emotional problems. Thus, an evaluation can be secured at no cost to the parent or legal guardian. If it is agreed that the child has a problem that should be investigated, parents can ask the teacher to initiate a referral for evaluation.

As we've mentioned, this process of evaluating children who are suspected of having delays or disabilities is termed *child find*. Schools are required to advertise these services, even to families with very young children who are not yet enrolled in school. A common barrier to the effectiveness of these ads has been the use of jargon (such as *child find*) or overly broad solicitations, such as "Do you have a child you are concerned about? Call this number for help." Parents have no real indicators as to what the ad is talking about or what would be considered a reasonable concern or even a good sense of what categories of concerns would apply (i.e., any concerns at all, behavioral, cognitive, physical, etc.). They typically provide little information about who or what types of help may be offered if they call the number. It is clear why many parents would dismiss these ads without recognizing that their own child may be well served by a phone call. One of the most helpful things that can be done for parents is for schools and pediatricians to make lots of information available about typical development (including emotional and behavioral guidelines covering more than the first year of life). It is helpful to make this content accessible using pictures and varying levels of information.

Sometimes, parents are reluctant to talk about problems and concerns regarding a child's development because they are concerned that professionals will interpret the problems as failings on the parents' behalf. Two ways that educators and other school personnel can help families feel more comfortable is to occasionally share their own anecdotes about raising their own children, including their own struggles or feelings of occasional uncertainty. Parents need to recognize that professionals are people too, and often are parents themselves. Professionals need to realize that allowing parents to see that aspect of themselves can strengthen their professional impact. The other recommendation is that professionals *listen* when parents come to them without immediately jumping in to solve the problem or asking the parent to change their family life without taking time to really hear the parents' explanation, family living situation, and other important factors that can affect what is realistic for a family to do at a certain point in time. By listening and by conveying a sense of empathy for the difficulty of assessing developmental stages and typical versus atypical development in children, the teacher can provide support and begin a partnership with parents. Each of these suggestions can help school professionals make families feel more comfortable asking for advice and assistance.

Parents or legal guardians should be informed that concerns such as depression, anxiety, and eating disorders might be less apparent than conduct problems and are less likely to be recognized and targeted for treatment by school staff. Conduct problems often disrupt school and family activities in a manner that requires immediate intervention, whereas internalizing problems (e.g., anxiety and depression) may not be seen as critical unless or until they precipitate a crisis (Albano, Chorpita, & Barlow, 1996). Middle and high schools should attend to helping parents understand typical physical, behavioral, and emotional development in youth, just as is done in early childhood programs. Often, parents of preteens and older adolescents are unaware of the range of levels of sleep, activity, privacy, seclusion, independence, and so on, that are proposed as acceptable for these age groups. As an example, it may be easy for parents to accept unusually high levels of seclusion without recognizing that a problem such as depression may exist (see the American Academy of Pediatrics [www.aap.org] for resources currently available in these areas).

If a teacher does not agree that a problem exists, parents may still request an evaluation. Such a request should be made if parents have reason to believe that the child has a serious problem. To request an evaluation, parents should write the director of special education in their local school district. This individual's name and address can be accessed by contacting the board of education or school administration office in the child's school district. The letter should specify the basis for parental concern, request a district evaluation, and be accompanied by copies of relevant background documents (e.g., evaluation reports, developmental charts). School districts are required by state and federal mandate to consider parental requests for evaluation (Lowe & Reynolds, 2000).

TEACHERS AS REFERRAL AGENTS

Sometimes, teachers recommend evaluations for children who exhibit negative or concerning behaviors in the classroom. Parents may be eager to give permission for such evaluations. However, it may be difficult for some caregivers to understand the need for an assessment, especially if the problematic behaviors are only observed in the school setting.

We believe that caregivers may be more willing to agree to evaluations if they are given concrete examples of concerning behaviors. For example, if the teacher believes a student is having difficulty finishing assignments, he or she could show parents work samples completed by the referred student and compare them to those of an average student in the classroom. It is important that the student be compared to the average student as opposed to the A+ student. The evaluation process also may be less threatening if caregivers are aware that its conclusions can span from determining that a child is behaving in a developmentally appropriate manner to suggesting that special services may be needed. Another strategy that many parents find reassuring is the teacher talking about the child's personality and likes and dislikes within the conference on abilities and challenges. When parents feel comfortable that teachers really *know* their child, they tend to trust the teacher's observations and opinions about their child more willingly. Last, it will be helpful for families to know that if the child qualifies for special services, the goal of interventions will be to improve the child's academic and social performance at school.

PARENTS AS ADVOCATES FOR THEIR CHILDREN WITH EMOTIONAL AND BEHAVIORAL CONCERNS

The dictionary (Mish et al., 1994) defines *advocate* as "one who pleads the cause of another." In the case of parents of children who have emotional disturbance or behavioral disorders, advocacy means that children's interests receive priority status. Although this may lead parents to view their situations differently than professionals do, it does not mean that parents should necessarily disagree with or distrust professionals.

Conversely, parents should not unthinkingly accept all recommendations and suggestions without considering child and family needs. Parents and professionals must strive for a partnership in which both parties have the right to voice their opinions and to disagree. Such a relationship, although at times uncomfortable, ultimately improves services to children.

One form of parental advocacy is well illustrated by the following example:

> The parents of a 16-year-old adolescent with a behavior disorder found themselves caught between loyalty to their local school district and their son's interests. The school district had historically been responsive to their child's needs, including starting an elementary program for children with behavior problems. When the boy outgrew the elementary program, however, the district did not have an available suitable alternative. Instead, school personnel recommended that the boy be placed in a high school learning disability program because that was the only service available. The parents found themselves in the uncomfortable position of wanting to support the school district, but knowing that the recommended service was not in their son's best interest. Open discussion of concerns between school staff and parents led the district to contract for appropriate services from a neighboring district. These parents were able to secure a suitable program only after advocating for their son and putting their child's interests first.

It is important for parents and legal guardians to know that they have certain rights under IDEA (1997). For example, parents have the opportunity to examine all of their child's educational records and to be an active participant in meetings to identify, evaluate, and place their child with emotional and behavioral problems. Also, parents or legal guardians have the opportunity to file complaints with the school district for situations pertaining to identification, evaluation, or placement of their child (Lowe & Reynolds, 2000). Two excellent resources are *A Guide to the Individualized Education Program* (Office of Special Education and Rehabilitative Services, 2000) and a user-friendly manual of parent rights under IDEA, titled *What a Good IDEA*, which is also available in Spanish, *Que Bueno IDEA* (ARC of Texas and Advocacy Incorporated, 1999). Another key source for legal information for parents is the National Clearinghouse for Children and Youth with Disabilities. These organizations can be accessed through the information provided in the resource section at the end of this book. Also, individual state departments of education often provide such information for parents.

Parents can support and advocate for their child by becoming as involved as possible with the special education program in which their child participates. There are many ways parents can be involved, from attending

IEP meetings, to frequently touching base with the child's teacher(s) so as to informally address progress and stumbling blocks, to carefully monitoring and sharing information with school staff regarding medication usage, and by becoming as educated as possible about community-based supports available to extend or enhance school-based interventions.

We encourage parents to assemble a file at home that contains important paperwork regarding their child and his or her educational program and any additional services related to EBD. School-based personnel should make sure parents are aware of the importance of keeping such records and should provide parents with a list of what is important to assemble, such as the example list shown in Box 10.1.

THE IMPORTANCE OF BEING A SUPPORT AGENT

Children with emotional and behavioral problems seldom make significant improvement unless the meaningful individuals in their lives work together. The parents' role in this regard will vary, but it can be expected to include support for agreed-on plans between them and school staff. Parents may be asked to collect certain types of information at home in support of the program for their child at school. When parents and families are accepted as equal decision-making partners, parents are more likely to accept and follow through on decisions made by the team. Once a decision has been reached involving home life, parents must be the ones to support it. Therefore, it is important that as plans are being made, they be considered by parents in terms of commitment of time or reorganization of home structure.

Some research has suggested that children's behavior at school may improve significantly when parents make efforts to resolve behavior problems at home through parent education programs (e.g., McNeil, Eyberg, Eisenstadt, Newcomb, & Funderburk, 1991). However, other studies have found that when conduct problems are treated in a clinic or home setting, challenging behaviors at school remain unchanged (e.g., Breiner & Forehand, 1981). Thus, it would seem that improvement in behavior across settings is more likely to be achieved when interventions are implemented in all relevant environmental contexts, including home and school (McMahon & Wells, 1998).

Parents can be involved in making changes at home *and* at school. There are many advantages to parents being involved in creating and monitoring plans to improve their child's behavior at school. For example, parents have information about their child that may not be available to school staff, such as strategies implemented at home that have worked to improve behavior and knowledge of activities and objects rewarding to

Box 10.1
What to Include in Your Child's Special Education File

- Each year, list your child's special education teacher, general education teacher(s), any related services personnel (such as speech-language therapists or counselors), the principal, and the director of special education for the school district.
- Keep a list of the names, addresses, and phone numbers of local (school building then district level) personnel in the channels of authority to whom support may be obtained or complaints filed, and continue to note the proper channels of authority up through the state department of education level. For example, find out who your school district ombudsman is (with whom one files formal complaints regarding special education services or suspected legal infractions).
- Have a copy of the Individuals with Disabilities Education Act (downloadable from the U.S. Department of Education's Office of Special Education Programs).
- Report cards and progress reports
- Copies of any independent evaluations
- All written letters and notes to and from school personnel (even those that are handwritten)
- Dated notes from parent-teacher conferences
- Dated notes on all telephone conversations with school personnel regarding your child
- All written communication with professionals outside of the school district regarding your child's needs and strengths
- Dated notes from conversations with your child's physician, psychologist, or other service provider
- A list of medications your child is taking at home and at school as authorized by your child's physician or psychiatrist. Include the kind of medication, time and dosage information. In addition, note the RX numbers, as well as any changes in dosage or reactions (side effects).
- The phone numbers for two or three other parents whose children are receiving special education services from your school who can serve as advocates and share information with you about the special education system

their child. Also, school staff appreciate parents' commitment to their child's success at school. Parental involvement may range from participating in a problem-solving meeting to receiving information from the child's teacher about the child's behavior every day to playing a role in implementing the behavior program. One strategy in particular, *school-home notes*, has been effective in improving children's performance at school (Carper & Kelley, 1990).

Children can participate in a school-home note program from the time they enter school until they become adolescents. The program has several elements, and a sample school-home note can be found in Table 10.1. First, teachers, parents, and children decide on a reasonable number of goals for the student and on the way they will be evaluated. These goals should be stated positively (e.g., "Maria kept her hands and feet to herself" instead of "Maria did not kick or hit"). A goal stated in this manner will inform the child what behavior is expected of him or her rather than what behaviors are not wanted. A problem with ruling out certain behaviors is that kids who do not have strong reasoning abilities may replace one inappropriate behavior with another. For example, a child who hits or kicks when frustrated may be told not to hit or kick. Instead, that child may become frustrated and pull someone else's hair. Technically speaking, the child was following the rule that was given. It is a clearer communication to simply focus on teaching the student what behavior you do want to see rather than what is not OK. The other important aspect of this positive-wording policy is that it provides its own setup for providing positive feedback and praising the child for doing the right thing. The second step in setting up a school-home note policy is that the teacher and parents (or the IEP team, as the case may be) agree on the positive consequences that will be given to the child for having a so-called good note and the negative consequences for an unsatisfactory note.

When the note program is first implemented, the student's interest is most likely to be achieved if the student can obtain rewards for meeting reasonable goals. Initially, for example, a note may be judged as good for receiving four out of eight "yes" marks for the day. Negative consequences (e.g., extra chores, loss of privileges) can be introduced once the student is motivated and understands his or her role in the program. When goals are set too high, kids will give up, so the plan may seem ineffective. When the goals are set too low, kids will exceed the goal daily, leaving little room for growth or incentive for diligence. The team of parents and teachers may find that they need to revisit the goals and incentives several times before they find the right fit for a given child.

Rewards do not need to be costly, and they do not need to be activities or tangibles that are usually reserved for special days (e.g., toys the child

Table 10.1   Sample School-Home Note

Jimmy's Daily School-Home Note		Date _____	
SUBJECT: _____			
Followed directions without arguing	Yes	No	N/A
Worked on materials assigned during class	Yes	No	N/A
SUBJECT: _____			
Followed directions without arguing	Yes	No	N/A
Worked on materials assigned during class	Yes	No	N/A
SUBJECT: _____			
Followed directions without arguing	Yes	No	N/A
Worked on materials assigned during class	Yes	No	N/A
SUBJECT: _____			
Followed directions without arguing	Yes	No	N/A
Worked on materials assigned during class	Yes	No	N/A
Number of "Yes" marks: _____			
Teacher comments: _____			
Parent comments, including consequences provided last night: _____			

wants, dinner at a restaurant). There are a variety of rewards that can be incorporated easily into the routine at home. Parents and families that are having trouble with this task may want to refer to the following Web site for hundreds of reward ideas for children from preschool through adolescence: http://ww.cdipage.cpm/behave/htm. Parents should also keep in mind that activities children usually access may be conceptualized as privileges under a school-home note. For example, once the note program is implemented, playing computer games may be a privilege that has to be earned.

A school-home note typically improves parent-teacher, teacher-child, and parent-child communication about school behavior. It also has the potential to change the focus of feedback. Specifically, the discussion of child behavior can change from reporting about negative behavior to praise for positive behavior. In fact, in addition to the rewards obtained at home, it is hoped that the child can receive positive feedback throughout the day from his or her teacher. A comment about using this approach with older youth: When available, e-mail may be more effective than a physical note sent home—there is a lower likelihood of "loss."

Caregivers that are working with a mental health professional to address behavioral concerns at home may want to ask them to help set up a school-home note. Furthermore, this professional can help parents monitor the program's progress. Also, the school psychologist assigned to the child's school can be enlisted to help. More information about setting up a school-home note can be found in the books by Russell Barkley (e.g., 1997), which are listed at the end of this chapter.

Carefully selected interventions for children with emotional and behavioral disorders can be quite effective in reducing or eliminating problems. However, even with positive outcomes, behavioral or emotional problems may resurface. And some children may not resolve a particular problem before the end of their school life. For example, a child with social phobia who has received an intervention may not have that concern again in the future, but most children with EBD will need continuous, individually tailored interventions to succeed academically.

IMPLEMENTING CHANGES AT HOME

In this section, we present specific strategies that may assist caregivers at home in decreasing behavior problems. After reading our suggestions, this task may appear a bit daunting. Well, it most likely will be! Still, families do not need to do this work on their own. In fact, there are a number of mental health professionals who are trained to work with parents of children with emotional and behavioral problems. We suggest that as consumers of mental health services, parents seek professionals that are familiar with treatments proven to be helpful with different populations. For example, ideal professionals to address the problems of children with behavioral disorders are therapists who can implement parent-child inter-action programs to improve the twosome's relationship and the discipline strategies used at home. Typically, these are therapists who have a sound understanding of behavior principles. Examples of these programs include *Helping the Noncompliant Child* (Forehand & McMahon, 1981), *Parent-Child Interaction Therapy* (Hembree-Kigin & McNeil, 1995), *SOS! Help for Parents* (Clark, 1996), and *Defiant Children* (Barkley, 1997). At the end of this chapter, we have listed self-help books for parents of children with emotional and behavioral problems in case they are interested in reading more about the topics we have addressed.

Potential strategies to implement at home are presented in two sections. First, we introduce ideas to improve the parent-child or parent-adolescent relationship. This is an important component of interventions at home for children with emotional and behavioral problems. In fact, many therapy programs that have been evaluated have found that it is essential to enhance parent-child relationships to improve the behavioral of children who have difficulties with authority and peers (e.g., Hembree-Kigin & McNeil, 1995; McMahon & Forehand, 1984; Robin & Foster, 1989). The second component found to be helpful in improving behavior at home includes strategies to change discipline procedures (e.g., Hembree-Kigin & McNeil, 1995; McMahon & Forehand, 1984).

Suggestions to Provide to Parents That Are Designed to Improve the Parent-Child Relationship

Listen to Your Child

Listening, especially *effective listening*, is not as easy as one might think. Children and adolescents have often observed that their parents do not listen to what they have to say. For example, the following comments are typical:

> "My parents get angry and yell at me whenever I try to honestly tell them how I feel."

> "My mother never has time to listen to me. Whenever I try to talk to her, she tells me, 'Hold that thought—I'll get back to you.'"

> "My dad never really listens to me. After a few minutes, he interrupts me and says every kid has the same thoughts and feelings. He just tells me to 'hang in there' and everything will be all right."

On the other side of the communication barrier, parents have observed that their children fail to talk to them. Some typical parent observations follow:

> "My kid never tells me anything—At the dinner table, I ask him what he did at school, and he says 'nothing.'"

> "My son resists my becoming a part of his life. Whenever I take an interest in what he's doing or ask questions about school, he tells me to mind my own business."

> "Every time I try to talk to my daughter about something important, she says, 'Oh, Mother!' and walks away."

The foregoing comments all reveal a desire to communicate. People have a strong need to be heard and understood. Yet children and their parents are not always able to satisfy this need for each other, particularly when children and youth with problems are involved.

Children and adults must feel accepted and valued. People often go to great lengths to satisfy this need, including acting in ways that appear the opposite of how they feel. For example, a child may tell his parents that he does not want to be a part of the family or that he does not care whether they are interested in his well-being. Thus, children may say the opposite of what they feel as a way of protecting themselves from rejection (e.g., "You don't care about me—just leave me alone, I don't need you."). In spite of what they may say, children and adolescents will strive to satisfy their need for acceptance and love, both at home and away from home.

Suggestions to Provide to Parents for Improving Communication Skills

Communication skills can have a tremendous impact on improving the parent-child relationship. If parents and children improve in this area, the effects will be seen in their ability to discuss problems, negotiate solutions, and express feelings and thoughts about each other. In the following paragraphs, several suggestions for improving communication skills are presented. These include setting aside time to talk, using active listening, and making eye contact. School professionals may elect to share this information directly, or they may send the information home through parent education seminars or in newsletters.

Parents Can Set Aside Time to Talk to Their Children

Developing a relationship that fosters communication takes time and effort. Thus, parents must not expect their children to talk with them only during problem periods or when parents consider it necessary. Good relationships must develop first. To improve communication with their child or adolescent, parents should arrange a time to interact in a positive manner—perhaps before or after dinner, during a daily commute to school and work, or whenever both parties have at least 15 minutes available. Parents should not push their children to talk about their problems. Begin by talking about simple topics for the child, like areas of interest to him or her. Without investing time to build rapport and trust that you will listen and accept their opinions about less consequential matters, kids will not trust you with issues that are important to them.

Adults should concentrate on spending quality time with their children. Most children will find it easier to talk to their parents if they are involved in activities chosen by the child. This may include playing video games or playing basketball outside. The trust developed through such activities often increases children's willingness to discuss issues with their parents.

Parents Can Listen Without Lecturing or Making Suggestions

Adults often forget that the problems their children deal with are the same ones they dealt with years earlier. It is very easy, for example, for parents to predict that friendships will endure the crisis of wearing the same color of dress to the prom; or that being rejected by a friend is not the biggest problem one will encounter. Similarly, it is tempting for parents to tell their children how they should feel, what they should do, or that their problems are relatively insignificant. Thus, if the goal is to improve communication, parents should try to understand children's feelings and problems instead of giving advice or suggestions. When children want advice and are ready to accept it, they will ask!

Parents Can Use Eye Contact, a Basic Feature of Good Listening

Poets and writers have reminded us that the eyes are pathways to understanding. In a less formal manner, children have made the same observations (e.g., "My dad says he's listening to me while he's reading the paper. I can't believe he's listening, though, when he hides behind the paper."). The message is simple: Listening requires the use of both the ears and the eyes.

Parents Can Be "Real" People in the Presence of their Children

Few parental responsibilities are formally taught. Thus, parents make mistakes and engage, at times, in less-than-perfect child-rearing practices. One teenage girl described her need to discuss "boys and sex" but noted that she was unable to do so with her mother. This reluctance stemmed from the impression that her mother did not show much interest in the topic and that "Mom and I have never been able to talk about such things." Yet other women often sought out her mother as a confidante, particularly on interpersonal and sexual issues. This parent was able to discuss sensitive matters with others but not with her daughter. Although it is not always easy, parents should show the same sensitivity and willingness to discuss matters with their children as they do with others.

Parents may also, from time to time, consider admitting when they do not know all of the answers or share situations when they have erred in judgment or opinion. This should be done not only when sharing during a discussion of the child's problems but at unrelated times as well ("Gosh, I guess I am a little stressed out tonight because I made a big mistake at work, and I am trying to figure out how to correct it."). Children need to see that their parents make mistakes, and not to be underappreciated is the importance of having role models of appropriate problem solving and taking responsibility when a mistake has been made.

An Example of Supportive Communication From Parent to Child

The following discussion between an 11-year-old and his mother illustrates a style of communication that is likely to increase the child's willingness to talk:

Child: I'm not doing so hot in school this year. The teacher doesn't like me—she's always yelling—and my grades . . . Boy, my grades.

Parent: Things are not exactly going the way you wanted, are they?

Child: Yeah . . . I really wanted to do better this year . . . to make things different . . . I don't know what's going to happen.

Parent: Your intentions were good—but things are not working out.

Child: Maybe you and Dad can help me with math. I still don't think that teacher is ever going to like me, no matter what I do.

Parent: Sounds like you may have some ideas for improving things.

In the foregoing example, the parent used three basic effective communication procedures:

1. A willingness to listen: The mother allowed her son to talk without interruption. She tried to understand her son without immediately offering solutions, becoming upset, or moralizing.

2. A willingness to accept the child's views and feelings: One way for parents to establish a good relationship with their child is to attempt to understand and accept his or her views, opinions, and feelings. Through such acceptance, parents can show that they are listening, help the child hear and understand his or her own feelings and thoughts, and communicate that it is acceptable to display one's feelings. Such acceptance does not necessarily mean that the parents agree with the child's ideas (e.g., "School is stupid"; "Nobody likes me"). Rather, it shows that they are trying to understand what their child is saying. This process is the basis for future problem solving.

3. A willingness to make empathic responses: *Empathy* is a Greek word that literally means "suffering in." While empathizing, an individual attempts to identify with somebody else's thoughts, feelings, and emotions. In the current context, this type of response serves to acknowledge the child's feelings and demonstrates the parent's willingness to understand and accept.

EXERCISES FOR IMPROVING COMMUNICATION

Parents may find the techniques presented in this section for improving communication to be new to them. These techniques may not come naturally. Caregivers will need to practice, and their children may not respond. With time and effort, however, parents can improve their relationship with their child. School personnel may want to conduct a series of parent meetings to address communication skills or offer refresher courses throughout the school year. Self-help books on communication skills for parents and children should be an essential piece of any lending library or resource lists maintained by the school.

We recommend that parents complete the following exercise by themselves before trying out the techniques with their child.

Exercise 1. Choose the Best Response

Child (on entering the house after school): If that stupid teacher calls, you can tell her I'm not ever going back!

Parent: (a) Sounds like you had a tough day.

(b) What happened? Why is the teacher going to call me?

(c) This is not a good day for you to have screwed up in school. I've got my own problems today.

In this example, the first response, (a), was most appropriate. The parent sent the message that he or she was interested and willing to listen. In addition, an attempt was made to communicate that he or she was aware and accepting of the child's feelings. Response (b) was accusatory. Hence, little or no productive interaction could be expected as a result. Response (c) revealed parental disinterest and an unwillingness to listen. Responses of this type routinely lead to resentment and anger.

Exercise 2. Choose the Best Response

Parent (at the dinner table): What did you do today?

Child: Same as always—nothing! Nobody around here will play with me.

Parent: (a) Maybe if you weren't such a bully, kids would want to play with you.

(b) When I was a kid, I had more friends than you could shake a stick at.

(c) Sounds kind of lonely.

Response (c) is the preferred parental response. It communicates interest and an understanding of the child's feelings. It should open the door to further discussion and, eventually, solutions. Response (a) is accusatory and will probably provoke a defensive explanation (e.g., "I only fight to protect myself"), anger, or withdrawal. Response (b) communicates disinterest. The parent is more interested in talking about his or her own childhood than in hearing about the child's perceptions and feelings.

IDEAS TO IMPROVE DISCIPLINE STRATEGIES AT HOME

The Importance of Rules

Children and adolescents may claim they do not need rules. Yet the structure that comes from knowing limits and expectations is both necessary and beneficial. Setting and implementing rules involves several steps, which are discussed in the following paragraphs.

Rules Should Be Purposeful

For instance, a rule may state that a child will not play in the street because it is dangerous or that loud music can be played in the house until 7:00 p.m. on school nights because playing it later would interfere with doing homework. Thus, each rule should be designed to accomplish a specific goal, usually to protect a child or to maintain order. Such clarity requires that both a *specific* target behavior (e.g., failing to take the trash out, as opposed to "not minding") and a *specific* consequence (e.g., loss of bicycle privileges for 24 hours, as opposed to "something you will regret") be identified.

Rules should not be designed simply to demonstrate control. It is unacceptable for parents or school personnel to tell a child that he or she cannot do certain things merely to show that they are in charge and can control the child's behavior. In addition, children must not be expected to do things they cannot understand or perform. For example, it is unrealistic to expect an academically deficient high school student to make straight As (as opposed to *improving* grades). Likewise, it is unrealistic to expect a child who has an emotional or behavioral disorder to "get along with others and stop fighting" (as opposed to initiating a positive comment to a peer once each day or each class period, or to reduce the number of fights in a week).

The Number of Rules Should Be Limited

"The fewer the better" is a good rule on rules. Children and adults not only have difficulty remembering long lists of rules, they tend to consider them meaningless and take them less seriously.

Fair and Appropriate Consequences Should Be Established

Particularly with children who have behavioral and emotional problems, it is important to pay attention to rule compliance and noncompliance. First, children must understand precisely what will happen if they comply or fail to comply with rules (e.g., "If you study from 7:00 to 8:30 p.m.

Monday through Thursday, you may use the car Friday and Saturday nights"; "If you hit your sister, you must sit quietly in the corner for 3 minutes"). In addition, parents must make sure that consequences are reasonable and enforceable. Consequences must not be too light or too severe. Similarly, impulsive and unenforceable consequences must be avoided (e.g., "You are grounded for a year"; "You'll never use the car again"). Parents must be able to enforce established rules. For example, parents should avoid telling an adolescent that he or she cannot use the car unless specified rules are followed, when they have no means of enforcing such rules.

Consistency Is Necessary

A consequence must occur every time a rule condition is not met. This requires that adults be willing to apply the consequence any time the target behavior occurs, even if it happens at a highly inopportune time. In applying consequences, parents should attempt to adhere to the following guidelines: (a) When a rule infraction occurs, apply the stated consequence with a minimum of explanation and without allowing an argument to develop. (b) Avoid emotional displays when applying the consequence. In other words, parents should follow through with what they said they would do in a straightforward, businesslike manner; demonstrating to their child that they are hurt or upset usually has little positive effect. (c) Apply the consequence only after rule conditions have been met or not met. Telling a child, for example, that he or she has earned a trip prior to the conditions for the trip having been met will have a negative effect on the overall behavior management program.

An important element to consider when working with parents is whether it's a dual-household family. When children or adolescents are living in shared-custody situations, sometimes teachers or school psychologists can act as important mediators to involve both parents in developing rules, consequences, and consistency between homes. When children move from one home to the other, it is important that both parents have been involved in developing the intervention plans and contingencies. At times, the neutrality of school personnel can help to reduce interpersonal difficulties the two parents may have with each other by focusing the attention of all adults on what is good for the child.

Methods of Addressing Individual Behavioral Problems

Several steps are involved in setting up and carrying out an effective program:

Step 1: A Specific (Physically Observable) Behavior Should Be Identified to Be Increased or Decreased

Behavior management programs work best when applied to well-defined behaviors. For example, attempting to change a behavior such as "hyperactivity" or "bad attitude" is difficult because the target behavior may be seen differently in the eyes of various people, including the child. One parent might define "bad attitude" as failing to follow parental directions, whereas another may view it as kicking family members. As a result, parents wishing to change a behavior must specifically define it.

Definitions should include *what* the behavior is and *where* the behavior will be observed. The *what* requires that parents precisely define a behavior. For example, *hitting* might be defined as a child making contact with another person with his fist, hand, or arm. In this definition, no attempt is made to differentiate between soft and hard contacts or purposeful or accidental hitting. A hit is a hit! The *where* identifies settings and times when the behavior is more likely to occur and where the intervention will be implemented. For example, a program for hitting might be applied at home or at the baby-sitter's but not at the store, particularly if it is impossible to carry out the consequence in a store setting.

It is important for parents to make sure that the behavior they wish to change is under the child's control; otherwise, it cannot be changed through this management system. Slamming a door, saying "thank you," and throwing rocks at the family cat are under a child's control. In contrast, sweating and tics are examples of behaviors generally not under an individual's control and thus not usually subject to change using these techniques.

It is also important to consider that when an inappropriate behavior serves a meaningful purpose for a child, and it is eliminated, the child needs to be taught a more acceptable behavior to meet that same need. For example, if slamming the door serves the function of releasing frustration or anger for a youngster, adults must attend to teaching the child a more acceptable way to express frustration. If the sole focus is on eliminating a behavior that is interpreted as negative by adults, but the child felt it was a solution that worked, the child is likely to come up with another behavior that is equally unacceptable to the adults around him or her. It is fine to eliminate or reduce behaviors that interfere with the child's relationships or the ability to be successful, but it is wise to attend also to the child's needs to express his or her emotions or meet his or her own needs in acceptable ways.

The purpose behind a maladaptive behavior is sometimes difficult to determine, but through functional assessment, school personnel can assist families to figure out these issues. The Web site for the Center for

Effective Collaboration and Practice, listed in the Resource sections at the end of the chapter, and the end of the book, has several resources for conducting functional assessments to determine the purpose(s) maladaptive behaviors may serve for an individual child. The book, *100 Problems, 500 Solutions*, by Sprick & Howard (1999), is an excellent resource for schools and parents, providing different interventions depending on the adult's hypothesis of the reason the child is using the behavior.

Step 2: The Settings and Situations Surrounding the Problem Should Be Determined

This simply means that parents should examine the conditions associated with the problem. Does the behavior only occur around certain people (e.g., mother, baby-sitter) or at certain times (e.g., dinner, bedtime)? Identifying these factors is helpful. If it can be determined that a child has a certain problem only with the father, the solution may involve changing the parent's and child's social interactions or the ways in which the father implements consequences.

Step 3: The Response to the Behavior Should Be Evaluated

In dealing with their children's behavior, parents and families resort to a number of methods, some of which are more successful than others. Knowing what option has worked in the past is a basic step in planning for the future. In addition, parents should attempt to understand their own and other family members' reactions to a given problem. For instance, one mother, who was extremely concerned about her daughter's reluctance to play with other children, realized that her response to this problem might be maintaining it. She observed that when her child came home from school, she immediately began nagging her to go outside and play with neighborhood children. *Although the attention the child received from her mother was negative, it became apparent that the child enjoyed her mother's attention because the child began playing with other children when the mother ceased nagging.* This mother was able to maintain her daughter's prosocial behavior by attending to her *after* she had played with peers.

Step 4: If Appropriate, Changes in the Environment Should Be Made

Challenging behaviors often occur in particular situations that can be changed. For example, one child threw severe tantrums whenever he was forced to eat hominy. Because this was the only food that provoked this behavior and because hominy was not considered essential to the child's survival, the problem was dealt with by eliminating hominy from his diet. A mother solved her toddler's habit of throwing objects from the top of coffee tables and other furniture by moving the material out of the child's reach. In another situation, it was determined that the child was most apt to be destructive when she did not have something to do. As a result, her parents developed a list of activities she could do to stay engaged at home.

As suggested in the foregoing examples, simple changes in the environment can often have a great impact on behavior. Thus, we believe it is worthwhile to examine factors in the environment that can be changed to prevent problem behavior from occurring. These situations can include making instructions easier to follow (e.g., writing all steps on index cards), making an activity more interesting for the child (e.g., bringing crayons and paper to a restaurant so the child can be entertained), and reminding the child of rules and consequences applicable to different times of the day.

Step 5: Suitable Consequences Should Be Selected and Applied

After understanding why a behavior may be occurring (e.g., to obtain parental attention, to escape a demand), parents and families will be able to change the situation. For example, if parents realize that they become visibly upset when their child talks to them in a disrespectful way, they may conclude that their child may be exhibiting this behavior to obtain that reaction from them, even if it is negative. To change it, parents may decide to ignore their child's disrespectful behavior and display neutral facial expressions.

Caregivers that use ignoring as a technique to change behavior should consider the following: (a) This consequence is likely to work only if the child receives attention from their parents for the negative behavior; (b) ignoring works only if everyone involved is able to ignore in a consistent manner (the system will fail in instances where children are ignored only some of the time and only by some people); and (c) ignoring may initially increase the frequency of the behavior. Children will realize that it is harder to obtain parental attention because their behavior is being ignored. Thus, they may initially try harder to gain attention by increasing the frequency and intensity of problem behavior. Ignoring will be an ineffective or unadvisable solution when the behavior involves the safety of the child or others and when the behavior is being performed to get attention from people other than the ignorers (such as peers or siblings).

Eliminating or decreasing the chosen challenging behaviors will be difficult without a contrast effect. The child will learn to exhibit appropriate behaviors more quickly if he or she can see a contrast in parental reaction to his or her inappropriate and appropriate behaviors. Thus, consequences for prosocial behavior are just as important as reactions to negative behavior. Continuing the example mentioned in the previous paragraphs, caregivers would need to provide an intense reward when their child speaks to them with a decent tone of voice or talks to them respectfully. Parents may feel that their child never exhibits good social skills. However, in our experience, there are many missed opportunities to provide positive feedback for appropriate behavior to children with behavioral and emotional problems. Because negative behaviors can be so disruptive, peers and adults may not notice the positive behaviors that these children exhibit every day.

Parents and families that are having trouble thinking of rewards should remember that social reinforcers can be the most powerful of consequences. Social consequences include praise (e.g., "I am so proud of you for talking to me in a respectful way"; "Hey, thanks for talking to me that way—it's nice to hear"; "I like it when you use your big-girl voice"), parental attention, smiles, and hugs for desired behavior. When used consistently, these forms of human contact and appreciation are powerful motivators. If they do function as such, the child will be more likely to behave appropriately in the future.

Negative consequences or punishment refers to undesirable events that may follow specific behaviors. For example, children may lose certain privileges (e.g., leaving the yard, riding their bicycle) for exhibiting the targeted challenging behavior. For a detailed description of negative consequences, please refer to Chapter 7.

Step 6: The Effectiveness of Management Methods Should Be Evaluated

It is essential to evaluate a behavior management program. Without such evaluation, parents may be using strategies that could be increasing the frequency or intensity of negative behaviors. Evaluation ordinarily requires daily or otherwise regular monitoring of the target behavior. Sometimes, with particularly challenging behaviors, an intervention may be steadily decreasing the behavior but at a slow pace. Without having a record to look back at over time, parents (and teachers) can perceive that the behavior is not abating because of the level of concern or frustration it causes the adults who observe it. Parents are advised to seek the help of a psychologist or another qualified mental health professional or educator when developing evaluation methods. In fact, *we strongly recommend that parents and families seek professional guidance when setting up a behavior management program.* Once a program has been decided on, it is important that the plan is followed and potential changes are discussed with the professional providing assistance.

FINDING WAYS TO RELIEVE STRESS

Last but not least, it will be difficult for caregivers to play the roles described in this chapter if they feel unsupported in this process, or if they feel overwhelmed. It is important for parents to know that many people are willing to help make their lives more balanced and manageable. At the end of this chapter, we have listed a variety of organizations that can be accessed for information about family support. If the Internet cannot be accessed at home, most public libraries are now equipped with that service, and individuals can browse through the Internet for free. It can be helpful for local and national resources to be provided to parents at IEP meetings or when the child is initially labeled, in addition to times when a particular need or issue arises for a family.

Family support Web sites have information about services, such as respite care, which literally give parents a break (e.g., for an afternoon and evening) from caring for their child with emotional or behavioral problems. Also, caregivers can find information about parent support groups throughout the country. There are support groups for parents of children with ADHD (search the CHADD Web site) and family education programs for caregivers of people with mental illness (search the NAMI Web site), among others.

Some school districts have recognized the need for parents to understand the special education system and their child's area of disability by establishing a system of parent support by other parents within the district whose children have similar disabilities. "Veteran" parents, who have learned about EBD and special education services as well as community-based services and other supports available to families in a particular district, receive training by the school district and receive a stipend to reach out as a district parent liaison to newer families to the system. These parent liaisons act as sounding boards, acronym decoders, advocates, referral sources, and educators about both special education and EBD. Parents who have participated in such programs are grateful for the support from another parent who understands the system, and they are often relieved to have someone who is not a professional to call when they are confused or concerned about their child or the process of participating in special education. We encourage school personnel to consider this type of program within their districts. It is worth its weight in gold!

Tips for Professionals Working With Parents of Children Who Have EBD

Last, here are some tips for working with families on a practical level that may help both professionals and parents feel more collaborative. They have been assembled from firsthand feedback by parents who have children who have EBD.

- When attending meetings, name tags with formal titles are very helpful to parents.
- If you call the parents by their first names, please call the professionals by their first names, also. As a caveat to that tip, it would be atypical to refer to the principal as "Principal" during the meeting and to the special education teacher as "special education teacher," so avoid referring to the parents as "Mom" and "Dad" when speaking directly to or about them in their presence.
- Written reports and verbal comments should build on strengths of families, not weaknesses. No parent or family is perfect, not even the families of the professionals on the team.
- Providing parents with encouragement and praise will create a situation in which they will feel more supportive of school recommendations. This is as true for adults as it is for the students we work with. *Everyone* performs better when they feel encouraged.
- A phone call home from a school-based person that the parent knows (perhaps the teacher) to explain any paperwork or procedural issues will help parents feel more comfortable completing paperwork and understand what is taking place and what the purposes are for the activities that will occur.
- Initiate contact in a *proactive* way to inform parents when services, supports, or other agreed-on arrangements change or must be altered, *even if only temporarily*. Parents who discover such changes by accident feel deceived and frustrated. It sometimes appears that the school is hiding information from them, when the situation may simply be that the adults working in the building all knew the details of the situation by their proximity, and quite honestly, no one thought to call the parent. Although a cliché, it is true that an ounce of prevention is worth a pound of cure.

SUMMARY

Parents and other family members play prominent roles in the growth and development of their children. They serve as referral agents and advocates, behavior managers, and supporters of home and school programs. Adequately fulfilling these roles is essential to the progress of children with behavioral and emotional problems. We hope this has been a helpful introduction to the roles that parents and families can play in helping children. School personnel can employ a number of proactive strategies to facilitate the abilities of families to fulfill each of these roles successfully. Last, we encourage parents and families to access the resources listed at the end of this chapter, and we encourage schools to make these resources available to families.

REFERENCES

Albano, M. A., Chorpita, B. F., & Barlow, D. H. (1996). Childhood anxiety disorders. In E. J. Mash & R. A. Barkley (Eds.), *Child psychopathology* (pp. 196–241). New York: Guilford.

American Academy of Pediatrics. (2001). [On-line]) Available: [October 21, 2001].

ARC of Texas and Advocacy Incorporated. (1999). *What a good IDEA: The manual for parents and students about special education services in Texas.* Austin, TX: Authors.

Barkley, R. A. (1997). *Defiant children: A clinician's manual for assessment and parent training* (2nd ed.). New York: Guilford.

Breiner, J. L., & Forehand, R. (1981). An assessment of the effects of parent training on clinic-referred children's school behavior. *Behavioral Assessment, 3,* 31–42.

Carper, L., & Kelley, M. L. (1990). Literature review: The efficacy of school-home notes. In M. L. Kelley (Ed.), *School-home notes: Promoting children's classroom success.* New York: Guilford.

Clark, L. (1996). *SOS! Help for parents: A practical guide for handling common everyday problems* (2nd ed.). Bowling Green, KY: Parents Press.

Forehand, R. L., & McMahon, R. J. (1981). *Helping the noncompliant child: A clinician's guide to parent training.* New York: Guilford.

Hembree-Kigin, T. L., & McNeil, C. B. (1995). *Parent-child interaction therapy.* New York: Plenum.

Lowe, P. A., & Reynolds, C. R. (2000). Individuals with Disabilities Education Act (IDEA), Pub. L. No. 105–17. In C. R. Reynolds & E. Fletcher-Janzen (Eds.), *Encyclopedia of special education* (2nd ed., pp. 940–948). New York: John Wiley.

McMahon, R. J., & Forehand, R. (1984). Parent training for the noncompliant child: Treatment outcome, generalization, and adjunctive therapy procedures. In R. F. Dangel & R. A. Polster (Eds.), *Parent training: Foundations of research and practice* (pp. 298–328). New York: Guilford.

McMahon, R. J., & Wells, K. C. (1998). Conduct problems. In E. J. Mash & R. A. Barkley (Eds.), *Treatment of childhood disorders* (2nd ed.). New York: Guilford.

McNeil, C. B., Eyberg, S., Eisenstadt, T. H., Newcomb, K., & Funderburk, B. (1991). Parent-child interaction therapy with behavior problem children: Generalization of treatment effects to the school setting. *Journal of Clinical Child Psychology, 20,* 140–151.

Mish, F. C., et al. (1994). *Merriam-Webster's collegiate dictionary* (10th ed.). Springfield, MA: Merriam-Webster.

Office of Special Education and Rehabilitative Services. (2000). *A guide to the individualized education program.* Washington, DC: Author.

Robin, A. L., & Foster, S. L. (1989). *Negotiating parent-adolescent conflict: A behavioral-family systems approach.* New York: Guilford.

SUGGESTIONS FOR FURTHER READING

Information on Parenting Children
With Behavioral or Emotional Problems

Barkley, R. A. (2000). *Taking charge of ADHD: The complete, authoritative guide for parents* (2nd ed.). New York: Guilford.

Barkley, R. A., & Benton, C. M. (1998). *Your defiant child: Eight steps to better behavior*. New York: Guilford.

Christophersen, E. R. (1988). *Little people: Guidelines for commonsense child rearing* (3rd ed.). Kansas City, MO: Westport.

Forehand, R., & Long, N. (1996). *Parenting the strong-willed child*. Lincolnwood, IL: Contemporary Books.

Individuals with Disabilities Education Act. (1997). 20 CFR Part 33 et seq., 1999.

McIntire, R. W. (2000). *Teenagers and parents: 10 steps for a better relationship* (5th ed.). Berkeley Springs, WV: Summit Crossroads.

Rapee, R. M., Spence, S. H., Cobham, V., & Wignall, A. (2000). *Helping your anxious child: A step-by-step guide for parents*. Oakland, CA: New Harbinger.

Sprick, R., & Howard, L. (1997). *The teacher's encyclopedia of behavior management: 100 problems, 500 solutions*. Longmont, CO: Sopris West.

Parental Support and Information Resources

American Academy of Child and Adolescent Psychiatry: http://www. aacap.org/web/aacap/. When you have reached their Web site, you may want to look at their "Facts for Families" pages.

American Psychological Association (APA): http://www.apa.org. You may want to look at the APA resources for the public.

Center for Effective Collaboration and Practice: http://www.air-dc. org/cecep/.

CHADD (Children and Adults with Attention Deficit/Hyperactivity Disorder): http://chadd.u.servers.com/index.html.

Council for Children with Behavior Disorders: http://www.cebd.net.

Council for Exceptional Children: http://www.cec.sped.org/index.html.

Federation of Families for Children's Mental Health: http://www. ffcmh.org/enghome.htm. This Web site has a helpful list of links for parents at this address: http://www.ffcmh/org/info.htm.

NAMI (National Alliance for the Mentally Ill): http://www.naml. org/index.html.

Research and training center on family support and children's mental health: http://www.rtc.polx.edu/index.htm.

Web site for hundreds of reward ideas for children from preschool through adolescence: http://www.cdipage.com/behave.htm.

What Lies Ahead   **11**

Postschool Transition

The purpose of this chapter is to review some of the critical issues of this book and explain postschool planning issues for children and youth who have emotional and behavioral disorders. We look at assumptions that were developed through previous chapters and then discuss transition issues that need to be examined if individuals who have EBD hope to reach their potential as members of our adult community.

CRITICAL CONCEPTS ABOUT EBD

EBD Is a Disability

An emotional or behavioral disorder is a disability. It is analogous to any other type of disability. It is important to understand the ramifications of this concept. People with visual impairments are not expected to see, those with hearing impairments to hear, or those without legs to walk. No one expects to provide them with an education that will restore their senses or replace missing appendages. The goal is to teach these individuals to manage their disabilities in as many environments as possible. It is important to bear in mind this goal. It is also important to remember that teaching them to manage their disabilities is a goal, not an expectation. There will be certain environments and circumstances in which students' disabilities will be more handicapping than in others, regardless of the quality of support and services they receive. To expect to "cure" an individual with a disability can only give rise to frustration, for everyone involved.

Least Restrictive Environment Versus Inclusion

EBD is a disability that can evoke negative responses in almost any setting. One can conclude that if full inclusion in school or community is going to be successful, then one of two things must occur: (a) The environment has to be accepting of these individuals. This would include being tolerant during the times when they cannot manage their feelings or behaviors and, hopefully, providing the continual support needed to teach them how to manage their disabilities. Or (b) individuals must not behave in ways that demonstrate their disability. It seems that neither of these possibilities is very likely to occur all of the time nor in every type of setting.

Consequently, we propose that the inclusion of these individuals be in the most normal environments that will allow them to manage (or learn to manage) their behavior. The characteristics of both the environment and their abilities and disabilities must be taken into account. The least restrictive environment for an individual may not always be in the full-inclusion setting.

When determining a particular youth's least restrictive environment, opportunities for growth must be assessed. Occasions for learning can be nurtured through individually designed instruction. For some youth who have EBD, the demands of the general education classroom can be overwhelming. Although accommodation and supports can be placed in the environment to maximize the time spent there, consideration of the student's feelings about the demands of the general education setting should also be considered. As children who have EBD grow older, some supports are often perceived as embarrassing (for example, a full-time aide), and some behavioral demands can create intense feelings of pressure or anxiety that can set up the likelihood of an outburst (such as assignments that are confusing or kids who tease or taunt).

Knowing the individual characteristics of a youth who has EBD can allow adults to respond in an informed and prescriptive manner. It shows a level of respect for the individual's disability, in much the same way that a person who uses a wheelchair would consider the environments he or she will enter and what preparations will be needed to accomplish the goal(s) for being there.

Since the enactment of the Americans with Disabilities Act (1990) was mandated, the Architectural Compliance Committee of the U.S. government has enabled many people who use wheelchairs to freely access environments that were troubling in the past. However, for people who have emotional and behavioral support needs, no such federal or other agency exists to ensure preparation of the environment to receive the individual. Therefore, careful and sensitive planning are still vital issues when determining which environments are truly most handi-capping for youth who have the disability of EBD.

Behavior Is a Shared Responsibility

For individuals with EBD to experience success, it is important to understand the impact of their behavior on both themselves and their audience. In the classroom, students' behavior may evoke potentially inflammatory reactions by teachers and peers. These reactions can serve to exacerbate the problems of the youth. We have discussed that there are aspects of classroom management that can, when followed, minimize disruptive behavior. Interesting, well-planned lessons and teachers who react in a prescriptive manner to inappropriate behaviors (examining for purpose) can prevent some problems from escalating.

It is unreasonable to believe that students need to be cured in order to fit in, and in fact, that mindset can set the stage for failure. Careful examination and planning for the environments must occur in tandem with consideration of the individual's strengths and limitations. The issues examined in this chapter pertain equally to the communities in school as they do to home, work, and neighborhood—those outside the schoolhouse doors.

POSTSCHOOL SUCCESS

One of the central purposes of public school is to prepare youth to be functioning members of society. For students who have EBD, this may include anything from working in a very controlled (sheltered) environment to attending higher education. High school programming must reflect the possibilities that can occur for each student. Of all students who have disabilities, approximately 25.5% earn high school diplomas, including 22.3% of the students who have EBD (U.S. Department of Education, 2000). These numbers represent a gradual 4-year increase due to the increased emphasis on transition services and postschool planning. But these numbers do not give rise to optimism when one considers the job opportunities for the 3 out of 4 students with EBD who do *not* earn diplomas.

It should be remembered that all students who drop out of school tend to represent those with the most dismal outcomes. And teenagers with EBD are the most likely of our youth to drop out. To make matters worse, within 3 to 5 years after dropping out of high school, most have been arrested at least once. Everything possible must be done during junior high and high school to create effective programming that will enable our students to remain in school and to have supervised work experiences that will create a competitive edge with their nondisabled peers.

Still, according to the 22nd Annual Report to Congress (U.S. Department of Education, 2000), the gap between those with and those without disabilities who are working has narrowed (57% and 60%, respectively). Several key pieces of legislation have played a role in creating the current situation.

- The School-to-Work Opportunities Act of 1994 supports all youth, including those who have disabilities, in more fully understanding career options through community-based training and classroom curricula.
- IDEA (1997) requires that students who have disabilities begin exploring and planning for their postschool options as early as 14 years of age.
- The Ticket to Work and Work Incentives Improvement Act of 1999 allows people who receive Social Security disability benefits (SSI or SSDI) to select their own employment support provider and have that agency paid only after employment has been secured that earns more than the Social Security benefits. Schools can serve as this employment facilitator if they choose to be paid for these services.
- The Rehabilitation Act of 1973 (Sections 503 and 504) ensures equal access to employment and other civil rights in any program that receives federal assistance.
- The Developmental Disabilities Assistance and Bill of Rights Act of 1994, reauthorized in 2000, supports a comprehensive system of care, services, and supports to assist people in achieving independence, productivity, and inclusion.
- The Americans with Disabilities Act of 1990 has provided equal access to employment opportunities for people with disabilities by attempting to prohibit discrimination based on disability.

When examined together, these pieces of federal legislation have created a support network for youth with disabilities that opens doors and opportunities that have not existed in the past. Just how valuable that is can be evidenced in the gradual narrowing of the gap in the numbers of employed youth with and without disabilities on completion of high school.

Unfortunately, there is still much work to be done. Schools are not incorporating the many resources that are available to them in transition plan development. As supported by the most recent report to Congress on the implementation of IDEA (U.S. Department of Education, 2000), the notion of wraparound services is still underused. Most schools have not yet achieved formal, written responsibility-sharing agreements with other organizations and agencies that will need to provide services to the youth after high school (such as the state department of rehabilitation; social services; mental health service organizations; employers; representatives from technical, trade, or higher education programs). The annual report to Congress places responsibility for inviting collaboration on the local education agencies. Unfortunately, they also document the lack of transition knowledge or expertise of many school personnel.

Furthermore, parents still need to have increased meaningful participation in transition planning. One barrier to parental participation in transition goal setting has been that when initial planning occurs, parents are not well informed about its purpose and possibilities. They need to have time to reflect and consider their child's needs and abilities. When transition planning begins (often at age 14), parents are caught relatively unaware of the need for or rationale behind transition planning. They haven't yet begun to think seriously about the future for their children nor have teachers spent sufficient time over the student's school career discussing the various options and community supports that may be possible for consideration.

Parents are often unaware of the flexibility of the employment and postschool options that may be considered during transition planning. Parents need to understand that the school and other agencies will offer support as the youth transitions out of school and into the community. Parents sometimes share a concern that by participating in transition planning, they may inadvertently limit the options available to their son or daughter. There are multiple purposes to transition planning, but none of those are designed to lock children into particular paths. As they learn more about their options and abilities, career or postschool outcomes may change. They should be made aware that well-designed and collaborative transition services allow students to be more in charge of their future, with the other agencies to support them in that path. When a vision for the future changes, so will the path and supports needed. Transition serves are intended to broaden possibilities, not limit them.

Last, we need to improve the individualizing of our transition efforts. If there are students who need to have their transition programs carefully related to their abilities and disabilities, it is those with EBD. For example, one issue we should contemplate is that many of these students need to be employed in *non-people-focused* jobs. Working in positions in which success is contingent on interfacing well with customers or with other employees seems unlikely to be successful. Students who have EBD can maintain employment in many settings, depending on their strengths—just like the rest of us.

Luecking (2000) conducted a large study of youth transition issues. In his findings, youth with EBD had postschool work outcomes that were poorer than other youth with other disabilities. Furthermore, individuals who were educated in segregated educational settings also had poor work outcomes. One might hypothesize that it is the necessity for extensive support that leads to a more restrictive placement and, consequently, to difficulty maintaining competitive employment. Regardless, Luecking's overall findings support the notion that youth with disabilities can be successful in the workplace (as evaluated by their employers). Sustaining successful work performance after high school completion, however, remains problematic.

TRANSITION PLANNING

Transition: Law or Concept?

For transition from school to adulthood to be successful, a whole-life rather than solely work-related focus must occur. Success in the workplace is critical. But so is the ability to learn many facets of independent living, health maintenance, participation in and as a family, leisure activities, and community participation. Varying types and styles of supports, whether they are intermittent, limited, intensive, or pervasive, may need to be present for a lifetime. A false perception is that students with so-called mild disabilities will not need ongoing assistance and supports. Individuals with disabilities need to know how to recognize when they do and do not need help and where to access it when they need it.

In a sense, transition can be compared to the least restrictive environment in that it is both a framework and a legal requirement. Both terms are legal mandates and as such have certain documentation and required processes that must be maintained. At the same time, both are also broader concepts than their legal components. The *concept* of transition planning and services encompasses self-determination, self-advocacy, self-management, futures planning, interagency collaboration, and ongoing support beyond the public education system. Transition as a framework honors the fact that the ways in which disabilities manifest themselves have as much impact in a person's life after school as during school years. Simply put, disabling conditions do not cease to affect a person's activities simply because one stops attending IEP meetings.

Curriculum Considerations for School

For transitions to work well, the following components should be included (Halpern, 1998; Hanley-Maxwell & Collet-Klingenberg, 1998; National Council on Disability, 2000):

- Ongoing and multifaceted assessment
- Interagency linkages
- Person-centered planning
- Use of effective, research-based instructional practices (such as general case programming to teach problem solving, classroom and community-based instruction, use of natural supports, and reinforcement systems)
- Integration of self-advocacy and self-determination skills throughout K–12 curriculum
- Gradual, progressive educational programming linked between all grades K–12
- Job skills and interpersonal skills training
- Paid work experiences (with on-site training, supervision, or monitoring)

The components just described are broad and encompassing criteria. The specifics of a quality transition program must be tailored to the community in which most of the students will live. There are many transition and employment skills curricula available commercially. An important difference between this type of program and many other school-related curricula is that it will only work as well as the content has been sculpted to fit the context of the community in which the students will likely live and work. The process of tailoring a packaged curriculum to meet the needs of a community will require that teachers and administrators spend time in the likely workplaces—with employers, in businesses, with local community and religious leaders, and with families. Skills taught and plans laid must reflect the needs and priorities of the family, the community, and the individuals who will be consumers of the program.

Individualized Transition Plans

Since 1990, the legal requirements of IDEA have mandated individualized transition plans (ITPs), beginning as early as age 14 but no later than 16, for youth who have disabilities. One problem in implementing this practice has been the limited expertise of school personnel on the issues involved in transition planning. In much the way that other educational laws have been enacted, our officials expect compliance before sufficient and effective training has been conducted. However, even now, 10-plus years after the requirement for transition services was introduced, Congress has reported the persistence of a lack of transition knowledge among special educators and administrators who design and implement ITPs. The support offered through wraparound services may be one way to pool expertise and provide the best services for families.

Planning Programs Around People, Not Schools

It is difficult at all levels of so-called individual education planning to truly obtain individualized results. In a school that has a multitude of issues, many unrelated to special education, the demands facing IEP teams to meet the specialized needs of many students can become challenging at best. At worst, they can begin to make collective or district-level policy decisions that result in what's called standardized individualized planning. For example, some districts plan goals for U.S. History classes in such a way that ninth-grade students receive standard wording of goals and objectives (e.g., all students attending U.S. History receive the same three goals). Or all ninth-grade students receive a statement that consists of the same wording about their career exploration goals for that year.

Families and schools who are interested in avoiding these problems can take heart that there are several solutions to this dilemma. For example, person-centered planning is an approach to transition planning that allows for individualization. It is based in the truest sense of individualization. There are several variations on the theme (see Falvey, Forest, Pearpoint, & Rosenberg, 1995; Miner & Bates, 1997; Morningstar, 1995; Mount, Ducharme, & Beeman, 1991). The main concept, however, is that planning is developed from the ideas and goals expressed by the individual student for his or her future. A big picture is created of where the person envisions himself or herself at the end of high school or beyond. Goals and objectives are planned in reverse, from the end point backward to the present. By thinking in reverse, the person and his or her supporters can determine what needs to be accomplished by which points in time if the goal is to be realized by graduation (or whatever determination date is established).

Here is an example of person-centered planning:

A 15-year-old student who has EBD had determined that he wanted to work for his father's construction company after completing high school. He wanted to live in an apartment with a roommate who could assist him with minor complications from his epilepsy. He wanted to have a girlfriend. He wanted to have a mode of transportation that would allow him greater independence (he was not allowed to ride the public bus system in his city due to his frequent epileptic seizures).

In planning for Jake's future, his father and his IEP team worked backward from Jake's goals to determine the following plans. In Jake's sophomore year in high school, he began working for half pay for his father in a variety of positions. This allowed Jake to learn the responsibility of employment and the many jobs that were part of the family business. During his junior year, he was employed in one position for 15 hours per week at full pay. During his senior year, Jake decided that he would need additional training to be able to work in the position in his father's company that he most wanted to pursue. Consequently, his IEP team assisted Jake by enrolling him in a technical school for two classes, one in the fall semester and one in the spring.

Jake's father and IEP team also helped him identify what skills he would need in order to live independently with a roommate. They tailored his class schedule to meet the academic requirements for graduation while still allowing him to complete courses that would provide him with independent living skills. They invited members of two community agencies to join Jake's team during his junior and senior years: One assisted him in transportation issues and the other in obtaining an apartment and roommate. They initiated SSI paperwork with Jake's father. They assisted Jake in reflecting on what he would need to do to have a girlfriend. Jake determined, after some social skills training and group counseling, that he would need to attend private counseling sessions at the local mental health organization to work on anger management. He also attended weekly group counseling sessions on healthy relationships through his father's HMO.

By Jake's graduation, he was ready to work, comfortable in his experience and skills. He had begun receiving services through two community agencies that would continue to work with him on independent living and transportation issues. Last, he had dated two or three young women, although he had decided that he was not ready to enter a relationship. He decided instead to focus on building friendships with men and women and to continue anger management counseling.

A few commercially available models employ person-centered planning. One of the better known combines three programs: Making Action PlanS (MAPS), the Planning Alternative Tomorrows with Hope (PATH), and the complementary Circle of Friends, all created by Falvey et al. (1995). These programs can be used independently or in conjunction with each other. The Circle of Friends program is designed to assist children and youth who have disabilities to establish social support networks and friends in the school and community. The novel approach to building this network is in the advance preparation of others. Teachers are able to demonstrate the importance of such a network in all of our lives by working with general education students to develop a visual representation of their own circles of friends and social supports before enlisting their assistance to help a child who lacks such a network. Others volunteer, not to "be friends with Maria," but to support Maria's development of a network of varying levels of involvement by others that more closely approximates how many others live (i.e., fewer individuals who are paid to be involved in the person's life and greater opportunities for social involvement with people who have common interests).

In the MAPS program, a facilitator works with students and those they have invited to be part of their future planning process. Through a series of eight guided questions, they determine their future plans. Those people who have been invited to assist in planning are able to creatively plan how those goals can be accomplished. Through a facilitator (preferably someone who doesn't yet know the individual well and can be without an agenda for him or her), the student envisions life in the future, including companions. An interesting angle of this approach is that the facilitator also gathers information about what the student perceives as the worst nightmares regarding the future. This information is used to plan specific safety nets into the future goals and objectives to provide assurance that collectively, steps will be taken to protect against the possibility of those outcomes (i.e., being alone in life, being unable to maintain a job, living in an institution, etc.).

The PATH program was developed to help people using MAPS make the more detailed plan necessary to achieve their goals. Similar to the MAPS approach, PATH is an eight-step process that works from the desired results backward to the present. A facilitator assists during the planning meetings. The PATH process uses the students as the key plan makers. They have the responsibility for deciding who attends the meeting and who does not. (For example, people who have not been a source of support for a student may not be invited. These people may include teachers or parents in the initial stages of planning.)

The person-centered planning approaches, such as MAPS and PATH, are not intended to replace the IEP. They are intended to strengthen and add individualized value to the IEP and ITP. Although the PATH program can serve as an ITP, the goals and objectives of the IEP would remain school focused. In fact, that is one aspect of person-centered planning that can be particularly attractive to families and schools alike. Person-centered planning allows the family and the youth to feel as if they are receiving more of the "good stuff" they need to prepare teenagers for living as community members after their school days are over. At the same time, with the life focus accounted for through the person-centered planning process, schools and teachers may feel comfortable that the IEP can consist of academic goals that are of equal import in meeting graduation or completion requirements.

Self-Advocacy, Self-Responsibility, Self-Direction, and Self-Awareness: The Essential Transition Elements

Crucial to the development of an effective and individualized transition plan is attention to self-direction, self-advocacy, and self-responsibility. These three dimensions of self are only achieved in conjunction with attention to self-awareness. Without knowledge of self, none of the others will be possible. It is difficult to teach someone these qualities. These dimensions require the teacher, case manager, and parent to work closely with the student, investing significant time and attention that are not always related to subject area or other instruction. These skills can begin with simple goal-setting and self-reinforcement assignments specific to postschool activities as late as ninth grade but preferably, much earlier.

By elementary school levels, children should be learning the basics of self-advocacy. A quality considered a strength in a parent or teacher is the ability to know a student's learning and behavior needs well enough to anticipate potential problems and to prepare the student, peers, and activity to avoid creating a handicapping situation due to the disability. An even greater strength, however, would be one in the adult who is able to call the student's attention to exactly what was adapted or modified in the environment, activity, or participants to create success.

By prompting students about simple considerations and informing them of the importance of expressing these considerations to other adults (i.e., next year's teachers), the teacher then empowers students to create their success in other settings. For example, a teacher puts Jethro (a student who has EBD and ADHD) on the left end of the reading table because she knows he has nervous energy and bounces his leg, a habit that annoys others. By using this seating arrangement, all students can successfully concentrate and complete the lesson without arguing or fighting. The teacher deserves praise for having configured the seating arrangements in this way. How much stronger still would this teacher's talent be if she explained to Jethro why she had made these arrangements and prompted him to remember to let his teacher the next year know how much it helped him. This extra step, teaching self-advocacy, would be a gift to the student, his peers, and to the future teachers who may not be as savvy in devising as effective a remedy.

Initially, students who have EBD are not likely to be strong in self-awareness, self-advocacy, or self-responsibility. It is unlikely that these students receive many opportunities to practice such skills. Typically, interventions designed to provide structure and support for students who have EBD limit the levels of these three components that are possible. It requires a significant time investment and the expectation of mixed results to truly enable a student to apply these qualities. It will be a learning process—for both of you. Just as few of us were born "responsible," still fewer individuals who have EBD are born that way, and far fewer have been given genuine opportunities and instruction in how to become so. Unfortunately, the primary practice employed in the name of taking responsibility for one's action is punishment.

We strongly believe that one way to enable adolescents who have EBD to begin taking responsibility for their directions in life is through direct involvement in transition planning. Again, self-determination and self-advocacy can be taught through person-centered planning, through an employment program (allowing classroom instruction, active job support at the level needed, and paid employment opportunities), and through first attending and then leading their IEP meetings during middle and high school. When EBD programs at the secondary level rely primarily on adult-imposed structure and behavior intervention plans to control student behavior, two outcomes are predictable: (a) Extensive postschool support *must* be anticipated and planned for in the transition process, and (b) students whose support needs do not require this level of structure will be set up to fail in society. The rest of our society does not operate on the same ground rules (with the obvious exceptions of prison and the military).

In addition, structured opportunities at regular intervals (once or twice a semester) must allow a student to take a personal inventory of current goals and plans to evaluate if they are meaningful or if a different path is needed. This is an essential part of transition planning. Students can be taught to reflect on their paths to see if they are going where they want to go. They can be given support to revise their plans when they find that their direction has changed or that their plans are not working as intended. The following are a sample of questions that might guide this transition plan examination strategy:

- Am I learning to be independent? How?
- Am I learning to live and work with people in the community?
- Am I working where I want to?
- Am I living where I want to?
- Do I get to spend time with my friends?
- What could be better about my life?

Learning self-reflection is a skill that many adults could benefit from having. By teaching students to develop this set of "self" skills (self-advocacy, self-awareness, self-responsibility), they can be given tools for their future.

Transition-Related Programming
Specific to Youth Who Have EBD

There are three critical areas of instructional programming for youth who have EBD. None are adequately addressed by existing curriculum (Hanley-Maxwell & Collet-Klingenberg, 1998). The first is comprehensive teaching of civic rights and responsibilities. In addition to understanding information from a typical civics course, students who have EBD need intensive instruction in the complex realities of our civic system (i.e., *why* it is important to contribute positively to society, or *why* it is important to obey the law). These ideas are not always taught, for two reasons: First, they challenge teachers' own understandings (e.g., "because you *should*" may be the extent of some people's personal understanding), and second, in terms of Piagetian moral development (the ability to think and rationalize), some of our EBD students are greatly challenged by these questions because they do not have the ability to understand the nature of those rules beyond their consequences.

Still, it is important for youth who have EBD to be as responsible for their futures as possible. They must understand how to avoid victimization. They are more frequently the victims of social and legal infractions as they are the perpetrators of such violations. Often youth who have EBD become victims of other youth, of businesses, or of the criminal justice system. They need to learn about their rights and the laws. They also need instruction in how to help themselves if they feel they have experienced such a problem (e.g., who to contact for assistance: perhaps counselors, perhaps lawyers).

The second important area to be addressed in curriculum for students who have EBD is that of sexual relationships, marriage, and family. Although these topics are still somewhat unconventional to the standard high school curriculum, they are areas of central concern and, unfortunately, of failure for many youth who have EBD. These teenagers frequently do not understand nor have appropriate judgment regarding rape, abuse, prostitution, and appropriate everyday sexual relationships. Youth in juvenile detention centers are frequently fathers or mothers and may have been incarcerated for charges related to abuse of a partner, a child, or other family member.

It is more often the adults, not the youth, who resist these opportunities to teach and learn. Many students are willing to learn when provided opportunities. Without having skills and coping techniques, they cannot be expected to master these complex and perplexing interactions and responsibilities that occur within the realm of their area of disability. Nor can we continue to throw up our hands in despair when our students' own underdeveloped problem-solving skills end in unintended pregnancies, rape, or abuse. Youth who have EBD frequently aspire to maintain friendships, romantic relationships, and family affiliations. Due to the nature of their disability, though, goals of this nature must be carefully planned for and supported through counseling, instruction, and varying forms of ongoing support. Youth who have EBD will do no better at self-instruction in these matters than would youth who have mental retardation fare in self-teaching algebra.

A final curriculum concern specific to students who have EBD is that they must be provided a structured, well-documented mental health curriculum in their everyday settings (such as life-space intervention or rational-emotive behavior therapy). These interventions teach students that they can take a more active role in managing their feelings and behaviors. Responsibility is a massive undertaking for most teens (and some adults). For youth who have EBD, it requires additional investment in time and energy. Think for a moment about the alternatives to investing the time and to some extent the financial resources: Statistics suggest that most youth with EBD will not have successful futures without deliberate, focused instruction in the critical areas mentioned in this book. To deny a youth who has EBD the access to daily emotional and behavioral therapy is equal to failing to provide a student who is blind with mobility training. And in the case of these students, it will be a costly error because of the expenses needed to care for them during their adult lives. More important, it is unethical to not provide psychological services to the students who have this potentially debilitating disability.

Mental Health for All

Inclusion of individuals who have EBD in general education classrooms is contingent on many variables. A critical one is that the schools and communities they enter be tolerant of their feelings and behaviors. Schools, school boards, and politicians need to do a better job in developing an informed awareness about EBD and other disabilities. Mental illness has maintained a powerful stigma. We cannot continue to punish people because of their disabilities. We must make a concerted, ongoing effort to understand the myths and realities of what it means for students to have EBD.

Equal commitment must be made to educating classmates, teachers, policymakers, and others about this disability. Tolerance for emotional and behavioral disabilities will take some time to achieve. By educating children and youth through information, modeling, and at times specific training, we can hope to ready future business owners, community members, and politicians to accept this group of individuals who will live and work among us all.

A final issue in the importance of mental health education for all: Public school curricula must be bolder in order to meet the pressures and needs of all students in these early years of this millennium. Teaching social competence must be integral to curricula for all students. (Clearly, not only students who have EBD need help in this area.) Current estimates indicate that there are many kids who experience EBD who are never formally identified and served by our special education system. Still others may only experience emotional or behavioral problems for a short time, due perhaps to unfortunate life circumstances and events. And how many other youth are there who experience no identifiable emotional problems, who survive milder depression, anxiety, suicidal issues, or anger management challenges, but continue to struggle with these unidentified issues throughout their lives (often, through abuse of others or of substances)?

Civic lessons should include locating and using community resources (e.g., wraparound services) that are accessible to all individuals. All human beings have physical and psychological passages. Transitions between life events (school to work, significant relationships, home to independent living) can be quite unsettling for many people, let alone those who have EBD. It is critical that these students learn how to identify their psychological and personal needs. This would include learning how to use resources, such as psychologist, counselor, and physician.

SUMMARY

What lies ahead? Youth who receive wraparound or integrated services will fare better than youth who do not have these during-school and postschool supports available to them. When students have learned to identify their own needs, plan for their future, and act to meet their goals, they are more apt to be successful and more independent. There is no better opportunity to build these skills and capabilities in youth than through the person-centered transition process. Through this process, they are provided opportunities to learn while they still have the safety net of the other team members to support their development.

By exploring their goals and desires during and after high school, students can gradually take over the preparation and action necessary to fulfill their plans. They are not expected to achieve these goals independently; whole teams, composed of parents, teachers, and appropriate agencies, will support them. Youth who have even mild EBD will need transition services for an extended period. Given that fact, it can be a powerful tool to educate youth as to what supports are available to them in the community, how to set realistic goals, and how to self-advocate to accomplish their goals. Not only is the self-advocacy and knowledge of available supports critical, but equally important is the knowledge of self that comes through this process. It is a difficult challenge that must be met.

REFERENCES

Americans with Disabilities Act of 1990, Pub. L. No. 101–336, §2, 104 Stat. 328 (1991).

Developmental Disabilities Assistance and Bill of Rights Act of 2000, Pub. L. No. 106–402, 42 U.S.C. 6022–6029 and 42 U.S.C. 6042–6045 (2001).

Falvey, M., Forest, M., Pearpoint, J., & Rosenberg, R. (1995). *All my life's a circle using the tools: Circles, MAPS and PATH.* Toronto, Ontario, Canada: Inclusion.

Halpern, A. S. (1998). *An instructional approach to facilitate the transition of high school students with disabilities into adult life* (National Center to Improve the Tools of Educators, funded by the U.S. Office of Special Education Programs). [Online] Available: http://idea.uoregon.edu/~nciteldocuments/techrep/tech24.html [October 25, 2001].

Hanley-Maxwell, C., & Collet-Klingenberg, L. (1998). *Research synthesis on design of effective curricular practices in transition from school to the community* (National Center to Improve the Tools of Educators). [Online] Available: [October 25, 2001].

Individuals with Disabilities Education Act of 1997, Pub. L. No. 105-17, 20 U.S.C., Ch. 33, §§1400–1491.

Luecking, R. G. (2000). Paid internships and employment success for youth in transition. *Career Development for Exceptional Individuals, 23*(2), 205–221.

Miner, C. A., & Bates, P. E. (1997). Person-centered transition planning. *Teaching Exceptional Children, 30*(1), 66–69.

Morningstar, M. E. (1995). *Planning for the future.* Lawrence: University of Kansas, Department of Special Education.

Mount, B., Ducharme, G., & Beeman, P. (1991). *Person-centered development: A journey in learning to listen to people with disabilities.* Manchester, CT: Communitas.

National Council on Disability. (2000). *Transition and post-school outcomes for youth with disabilities: Closing the gaps to post-secondary education and employment.* Washington, DC: Social Security Administration.

Rehabilitation Act of 1973, 29 U.S.C. §794, Sec. 504.

School-to-Work Opportunities Act of 1994, Pub. L. No. 103–239, 108 §568 (1994).

Ticket to Work and Work Incentives Improvement Act of 1999. Self-Sufficient Program. 20 CFR Part 411, Dec. 2000.

U.S. Department of Education. (2000). *Twenty-second annual report to Congress on implementation of the Individuals with Disabilities Education Act.* Washington, DC: Author.

Resources
for Professionals
and Parents

Laura Zionts and Katherine deGeorge

RESOURCES IN PRINT

Benz, M. R., & Lindstrom, L. E. (1997). *Building school-to-work programs: Strategies for youth with special needs.* Austin, TX: PRO-ED.

Cipani, E. (1993). *Noncompliance: 4 strategies that work.* Arlington, VA: Council for Exceptional Children.

Coleman, M. C. (1996). *Emotional and behavioral disorders. Theory and practice* (3rd ed.). Needham Heights, MA: Allyn & Bacon.

Davis, M., & Clark, H. B. (Eds.). (2000). *Transition to adulthood: A resource for assisting young people with emotional or behavioral difficulties, skills for school success.* Baltimore: Brookes.

Dulcan, M. K., & Benton, T. (Eds.). (1998). *Helping parents, youth, and teachers understand medications for behavior and emotional problems: A resource book for medication information handouts.* Washington, DC: American Psychological Association Press.

Durand, V. M. (1990). *Severe behavior problems. A functional communication training approach.* New York: Guilford.

Garfinkel, L. F., Jordan, D., & Kragthorpe, C. (1997). *Unique challenges, hopeful responses: A handbook for professionals working with youth with disabilities in the juvenile justice system.* Minneapolis, MN: PACER Center.

Goldberg, D., & Goldberg, M. (1993). *The Americans with Disabilities Act. A guide for people with disabilities, their families, and advocates.* Minneapolis, MN: PACER Center.

Jordan, D., & Goldberg, P. (2000). *Honorable intentions: A parent's guide to educational planning for children with emotional or behavioral disorders* (2nd ed.). Minneapolis, MN: PACER Center.

Maag, J. (1996). *Parenting without punishment.* Philadelphia: Charles.

Maag, J. (1999). *Behavior management: From theoretical implications to practical applications*. San Diego, CA: Singular Press.

Morningstar, M. E. (1995). *Planning for the future.* Lawrence: The University of Kansas, Department of Special Education.

Pianta, R. C. (1999). *Enhancing relationships between children and teachers*. Washington, DC: American Psychological Association.

Rathvon, N. (1999). *Effective school interventions: Strategies for enhancing academic achievement and social competence*. New York: Guilford.

Rockwell, S. (1993). *Tough to reach, touch to teach.* Arlington, VA: Council for Exceptional Children.

Rockwell, S. (1995). *Back off, cool down, try again: Teaching students how to control aggressive behavior.* Arlington, VA: Council for Exceptional Children.

Smith Myles, B., Simpson, R. L., & Knoblock, J. (Eds.). (1998). *Asperger syndrome: A guide for educators and parents*. Austin, TX: PRO-ED.

Sprick, R. S., & Howard, L. M. (1995). *The teacher's encyclopedia of behavior management: 100 problems/500 plans*. Longmont, CO: Sopris West.

Walker, H. M. (1995). *The acting-out child: Coping with classroom disruption.* Longmont, CO: Sopris West.

Wehman, P. (2001). *Life beyond the classroom*. Baltimore: Brookes.

Zionts, P. (1996). *Teaching disturbed and disturbing students: An integrative approach* (2nd ed.). Austin, TX: PRO-ED.

INTERNET RESOURCES

Council for Exceptional Children
1110 N. Glebe Road, Suite 300
Arlington, VA 22201-5704
(703) 620-3660
(703) 264-9446 (TTY)
E-mail: cec@cec.sped.org
Web: Web:www.cec.sped.org

The Council for Exceptional Children is a parent and professional organization that provides a number of resources for educators and parents of students with disabilities.

Council for Children with Behavior Disorders (CCBD)
www.ccbd.net

This is a division of the Council for Exceptional Children. CCBD, whose members include educators, parents, mental health personnel, and a variety of other professionals, actively pursues quality educational services and program alternatives for persons with behavioral disorders, advocates for the needs of such children and youth, emphasizes research and professional growth as vehicles for better understanding behavioral disorders, and provides professional support for persons who are involved with and serve children and youth with behavioral disorders.

"Office of Special Education"
Curry School of Education at the University of Virginia
Web: http://curry.edschool.virginia.edu/curry/dept/ciselosel/homce.htm

This is an expansive Web site on special education, disabilities, and interventions maintained by Dr. John Wills Lloyd. It includes links and information about special education teacher training programs as well.

Emotional and Behavior Disorders Network
ISBE EBD/PBIS Network
Statewide Component
160 Ridgewood Avenue, #121
Riverside, IL 60546
(708) 447-3708
(708) 447-5682 (fax)
Web: www.EBD.network-IL.org

The Illinois Department of Education is a network that promotes increased school and community capacity to meet the needs of children with EBD. This organization focuses on systems-of-care approaches. It is sponsored by the Illinois Department of Education.

Office of Special Education in the Department of Education
U.S. Department of Education
Office of Special Education
400 Maryland Avenue, SW
Washington, DC 20202-0498
(800) USA-LEARN [(800) 872-5327]
Web: www.ed.gov/offices/OSERS/OSEP

The Office of Special Education Programs (OSEP) is a component of the Office of Special Education and Rehabilitative Services, which is one of the principal components of the U.S. Department of Education. OSEP's mission and organization focus on the free, appropriate public education of children and youth with disabilities, from birth through age 21.

Families and Advocates Partnership for Education
PACER Center
8161 Normandale Blvd.
Minneapolis, MN 55437-1044
(888) 248-0822
Web: www.fape.org

The Partnership is a new project, which aims to inform and educate families and advocates about the Individuals with Disabilities Education Act of 1997 and promising practices. The Partnership helps to ensure that families and advocates understand the changes made in IDEA and that the changes are put into practice at local and state levels.

MentalHealth.com
Internet Mental Health
601 West Broadway, Suite 902
Vancouver, BC
V5Z 4C2
CANADA

(604) 876-2254
(604) 876-4929 (fax)
Web: www.mentalhealth.com

This site provides information regarding definition of, identification of, and treatment of a number of mental illnesses, disorders, and disabilities. Their goal is to improve understanding, diagnosis, and treatment of mental illness throughout the world.

School Psychology Resources
School Psychology Resources for Psychologists, Parents, and Educators
Sandra Koser Steingart, Ph.D.
Office of Psychological Services
Baltimore County Public Schools,
Towson, MD 21204.
E-mail: Spromail@yahoo.com
Web: www.schoolpsychology.net

Information is available on learning disabilities, ADHD, functional behavioral assessment, autism, adolescence, parenting, psychological assessment, special education, mental retardation, mental health, and more.

The IDEA Partnerships
1110 North Glebe Road, Suite 300
Arlington, VA 22201-5704
(800) IDEAINFO
(877) CEC-IDEA (toll free)
(703) 264-9480 (TDD)
(703) 264-1637 (fax)
Web: www.ideapractices.org

The IDEA Partnerships are four national projects funded by the U.S. Department of Education's Office of Rehabilitative Services to deliver a common message about the landmark 1997 reauthorization of the Individuals with Disabilities Education Act. The Partners, working together for 5 years, inform professionals, families, and the public about IDEA '97 and strategies to improve educational results for children. Four linked projects work closely with a network of more than 105 organizations to realize the goals of IDEA '97:

- ASPIIRE: The Associations of Service Providers Implementing IDEA Reforms in Education at the Council for Exceptional Children brings together teachers and related services providers.
- ILIAD: The IDEA Local Implementation by Local Administrators Partnership, also at the Council for Exceptional Children, supports associations of educational leaders.
- FAPE: The Families and Advocates Partnership for Education at PACER Center links families, advocates, and self-advocates.
- PMP: The Policymaker Partnership at the National Association of State Directors of Special Education increases the capacity of policymakers.

Center for Effective Collaboration and Practice
1000 Thomas Jefferson St., NW, Suite 400
Washington, DC 20007
(202) 944-5300
(888) 457-1551 (toll free)
(202) 944-5454 (fax)
E-mail: center@air.org
Web: http://www.air.org/cep/

The goal of this group is improving services for children and youth with behavior disorders and helping communities create schools that promote emotional well-being, effective instruction, and safe learning. It is affiliated with the American Institutes for Research and is funded under a cooperative agreement with the Office of Special Education Programs and U.S. Department of Education, with supplemental funding from the Center for Mental Health Services, U.S. Department of Health and Human Services.

Technical Assistance Center on Positive Behavioral Interventions and Supports (PBIS)
PBIS Technical Assistance Center
Behavioral Research and Training
5262 University of Oregon
Eugene, OR 97403-5262
(541) 346-2505
(541) 346-5689 (fax)
Web: pbis@oregon.uoregon.edu
http://www.pbis.org/english/index.html

PBIS has been established by the Office of Special Education Programs, U.S. Department of Education, to give schools capacity-building information and technical assistance for identifying, adapting, and sustaining effective schoolwide disciplinary practices.

Family Section of the Beach Center
Beach Center on Families and Disability
The University of Kansas
Haworth Hall, Room 3136
1200 Sunnyside Avenue
Lawrence, KS 66045-7534
Web: beach@dole.lsi.ukans.edu

The Beach Center's primary purpose is to conduct research to enhance the quality of life of families who have a child with a disability. Most of their research relates to public policy and professional practice, especially family-parent partnerships. Addresses some of the questions that families commonly have and provides an overview of other sections of their Web site where families may find other information.

Mental Health Matters
Castelli Studios

211 Buckskill Rd.
East Hampton, NY
(631) 329-3813
Web: www.mental-health-matters.com

Mental Health Matters is a directory of mental health and mental illness resources for professionals, patients, and families. It contains selected listings of alternative treatments and mental health research for psychological disorders, mental health law, emotional support, mental health statistics, patients' rights, psychological help, support groups, and self-help.

National Mental Health and Education Center for Children and Families
Leslie Carter
Manager of Professional Resources
NASP
(301) 657-0270 x235
E-mail: lcarter@naspweb.org
Web: http://www.naspweb.org/center/

The National Mental Health and Education Center for Children and Families, a public service of the National Association of School Psychologists, is an information and action network to foster best practices in education and mental health for children and families—building on strengths, understanding diversity, and supporting families.

Pendulum Resources: Bipolar Disorders Portal
Web: www.pendulum.org

The information at this Web site is for consumers, family members, and mental health workers to make informed decisions about the care and treatment of bipolar disorder, also known as manic-depression.

National Alliance for the Mentally Ill
NAMI Office of Development
2107 Wilson Blvd., Suite 300
Arlington, VA 22201-3042
(703) 524-7600
Web: www.nami.org

The National Alliance for the Mentally Ill (NAMI) is a nonprofit, grassroots, self-help, support, and advocacy organization of consumers, families, and friends of people with severe mental illnesses, such as schizophrenia, major depression, bipolar disorder, obsessive-compulsive disorder, and anxiety disorders.

BP Kids
1187 Wilmette Ave., PM.B. #331
Wilmette, IL 60091
(847) 256-8525
(847) 920-9498 (fax)
Web: www.bpkids.org

Child & Adolescent Bipolar Foundation (CABF) provides education, support, and advocacy for children, adolescents, and families. It is a community of people who care about children and adolescents with bipolar disorders (manic-depressive illness).

National Coalition of Advocates for Students
100 Boylston Street, Suite 737
Boston, MA 02116
(617) 357-8507
Web: www.ncas1.org

The National Coalition of Advocates for Students (NCAS) is a national, non-profit, education advocacy organization with 20 member groups in 14 states. NCAS works to achieve equal access to a quality public education for students who are most vulnerable to school failure. NCAS's constituencies include low-income students; members of racial, ethnic, or language minority groups; recent immigrants; migrant farm workers; and those with disabilities. Focusing on kindergarten through grade 12, NCAS informs and mobilizes parents, concerned educators, and communities to help resolve critical education issues.

www.schizophrenia.com

This is a site that strives to quickly improve the lives of families suffering from schizophrenia by providing an Internet focal point for education, research, and discussions on the subject. It also offers a weekly e-mail update and volunteer opportunities to support this nonprofit site.

Brian Chiko
E-mail: briane@infomaniac.com

Children's Mental Health Education Campaign
Center for Mental Health Services
Bernard S. Arons, MD, Director
Camille Barry, PhD, Deputy Director
5600 Fishers Lane Room 17–99
Rockville, MD 20857
Web: http://www.mentalhealth.org/cmhs/ChildrensCampaign/index.htm

The Children's Mental Health Education Campaign is a 4-year national public education campaign to increase awareness about the emotional problems of America's children and adolescents and gain support for needed services. CMHS leads federal efforts to treat mental illnesses by promoting mental health and by preventing the development or worsening of mental illness when possible. CMHS promotes consumer participation in the design, financing, and delivery of mental health and related support services.

National Information Center for Children and Youth with Disabilities
NICHCY
P.O. Box 1492
Washington, DC 20013

(800) 695-0285
Web: www.nichcy.org

NICHCY is the national information and referral center that provides information on disabilities and disability-related issues for families, educators, and other professionals. Their special focus is children and youth (birth to age 22). NICHCY provides information and makes referrals in areas related to specific disabilities, early intervention, special education and related services, individualized education programs, family issues, disability organizations, professional associations, education rights, transition to adult life, and more.

Our-Kids
Randy, Our-Kids Administrator:
E-mail: irryan@pacbell.net
Our-Kids Outreach:
Anne, anne.maclellan@sympatico.ca
Ellen, ellen.forrest@primus.ca
Web: www.our-kids.org

A site devoted to raising children with special needs. Our-Kids is a "family" of parents, caregivers, and others who are working with children with physical and/or mental disabilities and delays. Our-Kids operates a listserv to provide support to parents of kids who have disabilities. The *Our-Kids* list consists of over 800 people representing children of varying diagnoses, everything from indefinite developmental delays and sensory integration problems, to cerebral palsy, to rare genetic disorders. Over 35 countries are represented on the list.

The Council of Parent Attorneys and Advocates (COPAA)
P.O. Box 81-7327
Hollywood, FL 33081-0327
(954) 966-4489
(954) 966-8561 (fax)
Web: www.copaa.net

COPAA is an independent, nonprofit, tax-exempt organization of attorneys, advocates, and parents established to improve the quality and quantity of legal assistance for parents of children with disabilities.

Wrightslaw
Pete and Pam Wright
c/o The Special Ed Advocate
P.O. Box 1008
Deltaville, VA 23043
(804) 257-0857
Web: www.wrightslaw.com

Parents, advocates, educators, and attorneys go to Wrightslaw for accurate, up-to-date information about advocacy for children with disabilities. This site offers a free online newsletter about special education law, advocacy, research, and other topics.

Adolescence Directory On-Line (ADOL)
Center for Adolescent Studies
School of Education
Indiana University
Bloomington, IN 47405
(812) 856-8113
Web: http://education.indiana.edu/cas/adol.html

Adolescence Directory On-Line (ADOL) is an electronic guide to information on adolescent issues. It is a service of the Center for Adolescent Studies at Indiana University. Educators, counselors, parents, researchers, health practitioners, and teens can use ADOL to find Web resources on violence, mental health, health, and health risk issues. It includes a teens-only section.

www.mhsource.com

This is a Web site devoted to mood disorders in children and adolescents. Check out the symptoms and signs of depression in children.

http://www.disabilityresources.org/

This is a guide to disability resources on the Internet, featuring thousands of the best Web sites conveniently arranged by subject or state.

CLEARINGHOUSES

Center on Positive Behavioral Interventions and Support
1761 Alder Street
1235 University of Oregon
Eugene, OR 97403-5262
(541) 346-2505
E-mail: pbis@oregon.uoregon.edu
Web: www.pbis.org

ERIC Clearinghouse on Disabilities and Gifted Education
Council for Exceptional Children (CEC)
1110 N. Glebe Road, Suite 300
Arlington, VA 22201-5704
(800) 328-0272 (voice/TTY)
E-mail: ericec@cec.sped.org
Web: http://ericec.org

The National Center on Education, Disability, and Juvenile Justice (EDJJ)
http://www.edji.org/about.html

EDJJ is a collaborative research, training, technical assistance, and dissemination program designed to develop more effective responses to the needs of youth with disabilities in the juvenile justice system or those at risk for involvement with the juvenile justice system. A core issue for this organization is that youth with disabilities are overrepresented within the juvenile justice system.

ORGANIZATIONS

Anxiety Disorders Association of America
11900 Parklawn Drive #100
Rockville, MD 20852-2624
(301) 231-9350
E-mail: AnxDis@adaa.org
Web: www.adaa.org

Center for Mental Health Services
Knowledge Exchange Network
P.O. Box 42490
Washington, DC 20015
(800) 789-2647; (301) 443-9006 (TTY)
E-mail: ken@mentalhealth.org
Web: www.mentalhealth.org

Publications available in Spanish

Children and Adults with Attention-Deficit/Hyperactivity Disorder (CHADD)
8181 Professional Place, Suite 201
Landover, MD 20785
(301) 306-7070
(800) 233-4050 (to request information packet)
E-mail: national@chadd.org
Web: www.chadd.org

Council for Exceptional Children (CEC)
1110 N. Glebe Road, Suite 300
Arlington, VA 22201-5704
(703) 620-3660
(703) 264-9446 (TTY)
E-mail: cec@cec.sped.org
Web: www.cec.sped.org/

Federation of Families for Children's Mental Health
1101 King Street, Suite 420
Alexandria, VA 22314
(703) 684-7710
E-mail: ffcmh@ffcmh.com
Web: www.ffcmh.org

Publications available in Spanish

National Alliance for the Mentally Ill (NAMI)
Colonial Place Three, 2107 Wilson Blvd., Suite 300
Arlington, VA 22201-3042
(800) 950-6264; (703) 524-7600
(703) 516-7991 (TTY)
E-mail: namiofc@aol.com
Web: www.nami.org

Publications available in Spanish; Spanish speaker on staff.
National Mental Health Association
1021 Prince Street
Alexandria, VA 22314-2971
(800) 969-6642; (703) 684-7722
(800) 433-5959 (TTY)
E-mail: nmhainfo@aol

Publications available in Spanish

National Parent Network on Disabilities
1130 17th Street NW, Suite 400
Washington, DC 20036
(202) 463-2299 (V/TTY)
E-Mail: npnd@cs.com
Web: www.npnd.org

National Parent to Parent Support and Information System, Inc.
P.O. Box 907
Blue Ridge, GA 30513
(800) 651-1151; (706) 374-3822
E-mail: nppsis@ellijay.com
Web: www.nppsis.org

Obsessive Compulsive Foundation, Inc.
337 Notch Hill Road
North Branford, CT 06471
(203) 315-2190
E-mail: info@ocfoundation.org
Web: www.ocfoundation.org

Parent-Directed Family Resource Center for Children with Special Needs
3041 Olcott St.
Santa Clara, CA 95054
(408) 727-5775
E-mail: info@php.com
Web: www.php.com

Publications available in Spanish; Spanish speaker on staff.

Pathways Awareness Foundation
123 North Wacker Drive
Chicago, IL 60606
(800) 955-2445; (312) 236-7411 (TTY)
Web: www.pathwaysawareness.org

Brochure and video available in Spanish

Prader-Willi Syndrome Association
5700 Midnight Pass Road, Suite 6

Sarasota, FL 34242
(800) 926-4797; (941) 312-0400
E-mail: pwsausa@aol.com
Web: www.pwsausa.org

Index

CORWIN
PRESS

The Corwin Press logo—a raven striding across an open book—represents the happy union of courage and learning. We are a professional-level publisher of books and journals for K-12 educators, and we are committed to creating and providing resources that embody these qualities. Corwin's motto is "Success for All Learners."